The Problem of Change

The north-eastern region of India has undergone radical change since Independence, more so than any other part of the country. 'Development' along with the introduction of modern political and administrative institutions, has had repercussions that have transformed the region into one of the most volatile territories in India. This book explores the processes of historical change in the light of recent history and the issues confronting the people in general and political and administrative institutions in particular after 1947. It also highlights the timelessness aspect of cultural forces operating in the region.

Balmiki Prasad Singh is currently Governor of Sikkim. A distinguished scholar, thinker, and public servant, he has been the recipient of several awards and fellowships, including the Jawaharlal Nehru Fellowship (1982–4) and Queen Elizabeth Fellowship (1989–90). Other important recognitions include Gulzari Lal Nanda Award for Outstanding Public Service (1998) and Man of Letters Award from His Holiness the Dalai Lama (2003).

Over the past four decades, he has held numerous important positions like Additional Secretary, Ministry of Environment & Forests (1993–5); Culture Secretary (1995–7); and Home Secretary (1997–9) in the Government of India. He was also the Executive Director and Ambassador at the World Bank (1999–2002).

B.P. Singh has authored five books including *India's Culture: The State, the Arts and Beyond* (1998) and *Bahudhā and the Post 9/11 World* (2008). He is also Chief Editor of the *The Milennium Book* on New Delhi (2001).

The Problem of Change
A Study of North-East India

Balmiki Prasad Singh

OXFORD
UNIVERSITY PRESS

OXFORD
UNIVERSITY PRESS

YMCA Library Building, Jai Singh Road, New Delhi 110001

Oxford University Press is a department of the University of Oxford. It furthers the
University's objective of excellence in research, scholarship, and education by
publishing worldwide in

Oxford New York

Auckland Cape Town Dar es Salaam Hong Kong Karachi
Kuala Lumpur Madrid Melbourne Mexico City Nairobi
New Delhi Shanghai Taipei Toronto

With offices in
Argentina Austria Brazil Chile Czech Republic France Greece
Guatemala Hungary Italy Japan Poland Portugal Singapore
South Korea Switzerland Thailand Turkey Ukraine Vietnam

Oxford is a registered trade mark of Oxford University Press
in the UK and in certain other countries

Published in India
by Oxford University Press, New Delhi

First published 1987
Oxford India Paperbacks 1996
Third impression 2008

ISBN-13: 978-0-19-563969-8
ISBN-10: 0-19-563969-3

Published by Oxford University Press
YMCA Library Building, Jai Singh Road, New Delhi 110 001

To my Mother,
Champa Devi

Acknowledgements

In the course of writing this book, I have benefited from the advice and support of a number of people and institutions. My thanks are in particular, due to the following: Professor Ralph Buultjens for sharing with me thought-processes of the wider academic world and for his manifold assistance; Mr L.P. Singh, the former Governor of the North-Eastern States, who went through the first draft and offered valuable suggestions; Professor V. Venkata Rao for arousing my interest in writing on Assam when I first assumed charge as Assistant Commissioner at Gauhati in 1965; Mr Alok Jain, a member of the Indian Administrative Service, who was closely associated with every stage of the formulation of the book; India International Centre, New Delhi and the Nehru Memorial Museum and Library, New Delhi for providing a suitable environment in which to pursue my work; and more importantly, the Jawaharlal Nehru Memorial Fund, New Delhi and its Chairman, Mrs Indira Gandhi, for awarding a two-year Nehru Fellowship that made it possible for me to read, think and reflect on North-East India free from the daily chores of administration.

Contents

Prologue

This work has grown out of a project, 'An inquiry into the adequacy of the administrative system in Assam: imperatives for change', sponsored by the Jawaharlal Nehru Memorial Fund, which awarded me a Nehru Fellowship in 1982. But in several ways the project has a longer history, spanning the years from 1965 to 1985.

I went to Assam as an I.A.S. probationer in July 1965, after a year's stint at Mussoorie, and for the next ten years was intimately associated with various sections of the society of the region. I was witness to tumultuous events like the India–Pakistan wars of 1965 and 1971; the Mizo uprising of 1966, ethnic conflicts between Assamese and Marwari traders in 1968, and between Assamese and Bengalis in 1972–3; the creation of the sub-State of Meghalaya in 1969 and the full-fledged State of Meghalaya in 1971; and the separation of Mizoram from Assam in 1971, etc. As a Returning Officer, I conducted general elections in 1967, 1971 and 1972, and several bye-elections. Again, when the agitation over the 'foreign nationals' issue reached its peak in the Brahmaputra Valley in April 1980, I was summoned to Gauhati to assist the administration, and later became Assam's Resident Commissioner in New Delhi in April 1981; subsequently, protracted negotiations took place in Delhi between the Assam movement's leaders and the Central Government. As the Observer of the Election Commission of India in 1985 I had the opportunity to oversee the whole process of the preparation of electoral rolls, including the disposal of claims and objections, polling and the declaration of results. More important than all these associations was perhaps the opportunity to learn from people of various walks of life, who offered me their perceptions on various aspects of their society, economics and politics. In retrospect, I am grateful that, in the course of my work and in earning my daily bread, I had the chance of making the absorbing mental journey which has found expression in this book.

I have had the special advantage of receiving reactions from my children, who shared with me their candid feelings of what they saw, and heard from companions, in Assam as well as Delhi. When the manuscript was ready each one of them—Sumita, Rajeev and Pritty—read it, and told me where they found the text unintelligible, and of the possible reactions of college students of their age as well.

Some of the terms used in the book possibly need explanation: expressions such as 'Aryans', 'Assamese caste Hindus', 'Valley conflicts', 'modernization', 'socialization' and 'change' in particular. 'Aryans' denotes all those who migrated to Assam from north India and Bengal and, in particular, from Kanauj, Mithila, and Nawadeep in north Bengal at different periods. In the beginning of the Christian era and even earlier, these were the people who brought with them stories from the Ramayana and Mahabharata to Assam. Their subsequent migrations strengthened the growth of Brahminism in north-east India. Hindu rituals, however, underwent a change in the region thanks to the influence of its tribal faiths and the interaction among various ways of life.

The terms 'Assamese caste Hindus' or 'Caste Hindus' in the region are not synonymous with the high-caste syndrome elsewhere in India. In fact, Assamese caste Hindus not only include Brahmins, Kayasthas and Kalitas but also several segments of the Scheduled Castes. The region is fortunately free of sharp cleavages between high and low caste that exist in Bihar, Uttar Pradesh or Maharashtra. This does not mean that there is a total absence of conflict between different castes or between high and low castes in the region; however, the base of caste in the region is broader than elsewhere, for it includes the Scheduled Castes as well. Various factors like language, ethnic divisions, and the tradition of the Vaishnavite reformation movement have helped this process of consolidation.

The 'conflict' between the Brahmaputra and Surma Valleys was essentially a language conflict between Assamese and Bengalis. This was accentuated with the incorporation of Sylhet into Assam in 1873. The opposing claims of the Assamese and Bengalis over the language of instruction in schools and colleges, and the question of the official language in Assam ever since the region's annexation by the British in 1826, plus the known British policy of divide and rule, kept the conflict boiling steadily. Even after 1947, when Sylhet became a part of East Pakistan, the inter-Valley conflict remained. In fact, only after 1947 have linguistic riots and conflicts over the distribution of development funds, employment opportunities, etc. occurred.

'Modernization' has a very wide meaning. It takes into consideration the advancement in education, the spread of scientific and technological knowledge and appliances, media coverage, dress and food habits, the establishment of new industries, progress in communications, etc.

The term 'socialization' has been used in discussing the process of relationships which occurs when people interact with each other. The process is essentially socio-psychological and its ambit includes such adjustments that a group induces in the language and dialect, religion and form of worship and ways of life of other groups of people.

In the widest sense, 'change' means the process through which a person or group become different from what they were before the process began. In our study, the word 'change' is used more in the sense of social change, which takes into consideration the entire range of inter-human relationships, including values and the institutions of society.

There are at least five major works on different periods of the history and politics of north-east India, which have added significantly to our knowledge of and insights into the region: Edward Gait's *A History of Assam*, first published in 1905; S. K. Bhuyan's *Anglo-Assamese Relations (1771–1826)*, first published in 1949; H. K. Barpujari's *Assam in the Days of the Company (1826–1858)*, first published in 1963; V. Venkata Rao's *A Century of Tribal Politics in North-East India (1874–1974)*, published in 1976; and Amalendu Guha's *Planter-Raj to Swaraj: The Freedom Struggle and Electoral Politics in Assam (1826–1947)*, published in 1977. But no single work on the region covers all the aspects of its social life. Our study attempts to share perceptions on the processes of historical change particularly in the light of recent history and the issues confronting the people in general and political and administrative institutions in particular after 1947. The main aim is to penetrate the wall of bewilderment which appears to inhibit outsiders from taking an active interest in the affairs of the region. This book also brings out what I, for want of a better phrase, call the timeless aspect of cultural forces operating in the region. The question of political unity is important, but a more significant and dynamic challenge is the

At the risk of stating what becomes obvious from a reading of this book, I should mention tha my approach towards the problems of change in north-east India is not that of a trained economist, a social anthropologist or historian. It is the perspective of an administrator who has worked in the area at various levels over the years. I have followed a traditional district officer's approach: before recording opinions one sees the ground, talks to the people concerned and consults the available records. In these pages I have only attempted to present the visible social, cultural and political factors that came to my notice during two decades of association with the people, geography and environment of the region, as well as through extensive reading about it. I have dealt with the present situation in the light of developments since 1947 and while, in the final analysis this work is my own, it represents the culmination of years of personal and intellectual exchange with scores of colleagues and friends in administration, in academia, in public life, and from contact with the life of the common people.

At every stage of development and discussion there will be a large number of people—politicians, civil servants, mediamen, artists, social scientists, social workers and students—who wish to understand the incredibly diverse problems caused by a plurality of ethnic elements and castes, languages and dialects, gods and rites, customs and behaviour—all existing at different levels of consciousness in north-east India, and trying to forge greater unity amongst themselves and with the rest of India and the world. If this study helps serve this wider purpose even in a small measure, I would feel rewarded.

To me the usefulness of a work lies in whether it speaks in times of crisis when consulted or becomes an ornament on a shelf. As the Hindi poet Ramdhari Singh Dinkar wrote:

> Creation is complete,
>   but does it have life?
> If I interrogate it,
>   will the idol reply?
> If one day fire erupts,
>   in the temple's heart
> Will the idol speak,
>   or remain still in strife?

I submit this book to such a test.

Balmiki Prasad Singh

Introduction

North-East India, which comprises the States of Assam, Nagaland, Meghalaya, Manipur, Tripura, Arunachal Pradesh and
Mizoram*, is a region that has witnessed particularly major
changes in the years after the Second World War. During this
period, north-east India watchers have always viewed the region
as 'troubled' and afflicted with one 'crisis' or the other. This crisis
syndrome has in fact, been caused by, or is central to, a number
of rapid and inter-related changes in demography, production
technology, political institutions, religious practices, attitudes
towards language, changes in the environment of national security as well as in consumption patterns and the responses of
people to these new realities.

The occupation of parts of Manipur by the Japanese and the
battle between the Allied and Axis powers at Kohima during the
Second World War stirred the people of north-east India and
gave them both a new spatial consciousness and an awareness of
modern technology. Hitherto, only a small section of the literati
and business elite of the region had travelled outside India,
acquired the habit of reading newspapers and hearing the radio
as part of a daily routine. Most people in the region had no perception of the world beyond the Brahmaputra Valley, or any
familiarity with modern technology and weapons of war. Within
north-east there existed several societies at different levels of
economic and political consciousness. There were glaring dis-
similarities in the hills between an Apatani of Arunachal Pradesh
bordering Tibet and a Khasi of Shillong, the seat of State
administration, in terms of educational attainments, language
and consumption patterns. None the less, a broad synthesis between the people of the hills and those of the plains was widely
assumed by scholars, politicians and administrators at the time of
Independence.

In the hills, the tribal political consciousness was confined to
the village, within the clan and contacts with other clans, or with
the markets in the plains. The technology used in the production
of food, weaving, dyeing and the construction of houses was

*On 20 February 1987 Mizoram and Arunachal Pradesh became the 23rd and 24th
States of the Indian Union.

primitive. The village iron-smith made tools like the *dao,* axe, hammer, chisel, tongs and arrows from iron procured from the plains. These instruments were used for myriad purposes in agricultural operations, hunting, and in the preparation of food. The cloth used was mostly made from hand-spun cotton yarn on simple looms, and indigenous vegetable dyes were used for colouring. Locally available forest materials were used in the construction of houses. The *jhumming,* or slash and burn method, was used in the preparation of fields, as well as to keep the land fertile. The land was essentially communally owned.

The situation was different in the plains. Here the economy was predominantly based around settled rice-cultivation, particularly in the Assam plains, Manipur Valley and Tripura. There was widespread permanent cultivation of *sali,* wet rice, the land was individually owned, and there were also arrangements for minor irrigation. Weaving and spinning were widely practiced and the plains' people produced exquisite silk and other handicrafts. Although in most crafts and agricultural operations simple bamboo and wooden implements were used alongside iron implements, the tea industry and limited oil exploration had made the plains' people familiar with industrial technology. Automobiles, railways and aircraft were also known. Brick houses were unique to urban centres. While barter was an important form of exchange in the hills as well as in the plains, in the latter, currency was in circulation and the villagers had acquired the habit of paying land revenue in currency notes and coins. The process of monetization of the economy had received a fillip with the introduction of railways, particularly those connecting tea-producing centres with the markets of Calcutta, the exploitation of jute crops for factories located in East Bengal and Calcutta and oil exploration works.

It also needs to be highlighted that the phenomenon of temporal change in north-east India is different from that in other parts of the country. The advent of the industrial revolution, the development of communications and the remarkable cultural renaissance that characterized the rest of India from the second half of the eighteenth century—all these did not make any significant impact on north-east India till the twentieth century. Although the Brahmaputra and Surma Valleys were the fiirst to receive modernization ideals, this new breeze did not reach the masses in the region. Nevertheless, a small but significant begin-

ning was made with the establishment of Cotton College at
Gauhati in 1901. It was only from the 1920s onwards, with the
arrival of Mahatma Gandhi on the scene, that a perceptible
change occurred: the freedom movement led to a cultural
resurgence. In this new task, the princely orders and the Christian
missionaries played conflicting roles. Manipur and Tripura,
which the British left to be administered by the princely orders,
and large tracts of the hill areas, which were more under the care
of Christian missionaries than of the British administrative system, could not become active participants in the new cultural,
nationalistic and scientific movements even as late as the beginning of the twentieth century. The princely states of Manipur and
Tripura helped in the propagation of new ideals of reform, like the
abolition of Sati, the removal of untouchability, etc., and in the
preservation of the cultural heritage of the Ramayana–
Mahabharata tradition. Similarly, Christian missionaries in the
hill areas of the region and elsewhere popularized modern education and health care. However, in so far as dissemination of the
ideals of freedom and equality and a sense of belonging to the
'great' Indian nation were concerned, the Christian missionaries
played a negative role. Similarly, the princely orders did not
believe in the democratic rights of the peasantry and worked for
continuation of age-old systems of inequality and the divine right
of kings. British administrative policy segregated the hills from
the plains and one result of this policy was that the hill areas
remained virtually uninvolved in the national freedom struggle
and its liberating social impact.

At the time of Independence, with the exception of the Surma
and Brahmaputra Valleys, north-east India was far behind the
rest of the country in education, political awareness and administration and the entire region was economically backward. Yet all
the political and administrative changes in the country which
were introduced in the 1950s found their application in north-east
India too.

The one-person-one-vote system for election to the Assembly
and the Lok Sabha, the setting up of district councils in tribal
areas and election of its members on similar principles had an
unprecedented impact. The introduction of community development schemes in the 1950s not only took the State apparatus to
every village, but the insistence on participation of the villagers in

development schemes brought in an unprecedented change in the political and economic consciousness of the people. This was in sharp contrast to the colonial master–servant relationship between the State and the people. In the hills, in particular, the concept of equality among the members of the clan was now extended to the entire gamut of economic and political activities, increasing manifold the capability of the population to interact with the economic, political and administrative organization of society. Hitherto dormant aspirations surfaced with great force, almost like the release of water from a dam, and flooded the State system with various demands. In the public eye, the State assumed the responsibility of being the chief agent of fulfilment of individual and group aspirations. In this new phenomenon the State appeared not only larger than the family or the clan, which in fact it was, but also demanded greater loyalty and the subordination of tribe and caste interests. It was difficult for people in certain areas to give their loyalties to a new State that was secular and primarily intangible, except that it found physical expression in the villages through a small presence of transferable civil servants and elected representatives with fixed tenures. The strengthening of police structure and the sizeable presence of security personnel, although justified on rational considerations, did not help improve matters.

Certain groups and, in fact, several tribes treated the new State as an intruder and the instrument of subjugation. The Nagas and, later, the Mizos revolted against the new order and claimed independence. It had long been realized that the only way India could be administered from New Delhi would be with the consent of the centres of power of small nationalities; but what was not realized was that the State apparatus of Assam, the centrally administered territories of Manipur and Tripura, and the district councils under these administrations were inadequate to cater to the aspirations of the people. These were a product of the new forces of modernization interacting with the old loyalties to language, tribe, clan, tradition and cultural diversity.

On the political side, the independence of India in 1947 was accompanied by vivisection both of its eastern and western territories. These developments were followed by the establishment of an independent State of Burma, with Tibet becoming part of a powerful State of China, and East Bengal of the new State of

Pakistan. Borders were marked by the presence of security forces of the respective States and the Sino-Indian hostilities of 1962 turned the area into a sensitive security zone.

In the east, the ceding of East Bengal to Pakistan disrupted traditional economic institutions in north-east India. It deprived the hill areas of the market for their agricultural products and handicrafts. It also meant an abnormal increase in the price of fish, a staple food, and a decline in the price of jute. River communications as well as road links were disrupted between one political unit and another in Tripura, Manipur, Cachar and Mizoram. Henceforth, the people of East Bengal needed passports to lawfully enter the Brahmaputra Valley and the tribals of the Chittagong hill tracts to enter the Mizo hills; the people of Arunachal Pradesh were confronted by security forces near the borders of Tibet; the Nagas found themselves living in India as well as in Burma; and the Mizos in India were separated from their kinsmen in Burma. All these groups had hitherto moved freely and resented international frontiers that restricted their 'natural' movements.

Both the Indian National Congress and the leftist parties of India popularized modernization ideals and the need for change in socio-economic structure. Thus, in the late 1940s there was more concern in India with education, health care, freedom, equality, land reforms, community development than ever before. After Independence, these ideals were officially recognized in the Preamble and Directive Principles of State Policy of the Constitution.

Several positive and negative factors operated in north-east India that were almost unique to the region. On the positive side, the region was not afflicted with the scourges of untouchability or the dowry system; the caste system was less rigid than elsewhere; Hindu–Muslim relations were closer; and socially and economically it was not marked by the widespread and deadening inequality of say, Bihar or Uttar Pradesh. On the negative side, Manipur and Tripura had princely orders which firmly believed in economic parasitism and gave respectability and sanction to Hindu obscurantist practices. The Congress and leftist parties, all of which had affiliations down to the village level in other parts of India, were absent or ineffectual in Arunachal Pradesh, Mizoram, Nagaland and the other hills of the region (with the

exception of the Shillong area). The activities of Christian missionaries in these areas for nearly a century had successfully prevented the people from viewing themselves as part of the sufferings and aspirations of the Indian people. Even some years after
Independence, the government's presence in parts of these areas
remained symbolic—Arunachal Pradesh and Mizoram had no
police system till the mid-1960s.

Against this backdrop, several tribes of north-east India were
simply not equipped, by inclination or experience, to deal with
the new phenomenon of democratic institutions. The impact of
change was, at places, bewildering because of the sudden gradua-
tion of some groups of people from a near-primitive situation to
modernity. While in the rest of India the slogans of land reform,
socialism, etc. were accepted on the surface, people knew, on
account of their being meaningful participants in politics, that
earlier traditions would continue to prevail. In most areas of
north-east India this duality was never understood.

The social landscape of north-east India has always presented
great ethnic variety. People have their origins in Aryan and
Dravidian stock as well as to the Indo-Burmese, Indo-Tibetan,
Kuki-Lushais, Meiteis, Chin-Kukis and Shán-Tais. Though
these people came to the region at different periods of history,
there was no major flow of population from the thirteenth to the
first half of nineteenth century. The population assessment that
followed Assam's annexation by the British in 1826 revealed
fewer than a million people in the region. The British encouraged
the migration of people from East Bengal, Orissa and Bihar into
the region to encourage the expansion of the newly established tea
industry and for the reclamation of land and agricultural operations. This process of migration from East Bengal, now
Bangladesh, in particular, has continued despite the Partition of
India in 1947. During the last century and a half (1826–1981),
the population of north-east India increased from less than one
million to a sizeable 26 million people. Unfortunately, while in
terms of geography it was possible to accommodate this massive
increase in population in terms of social engineering it posed
serious problems and continues to do so.

The management of change is as complex a phenomenon as the
process itself. On the one hand, it is widely advocated that social
change must be radical and encompass the entire gamut of a

social order; and on the other, and equally important, is the need to appreciate that in order to keep the social fabric intact, the forces of change must be properly articulated and prevented from disrupting the social setting to the extent that anarchy prevails. The powers of the State, although considerable, are limited in its ability to control or direct the development of a rapidly changing society. Institutions like political parties, religious organizations, social and ethnic groups, trade organizations, middle class and even government servants in their personal capacities have a greater role to play in giving direction to processes of change towards orderly progress. Changes brought about through discussion and consent are more enduring. There is no denying that the State-system has the duty to protect and also a responsibility to advise, but it must not arrogate to itself powers of omnipotence, however pious its objective may be. When innovations are called for, as at present in north-east India, to strengthen economic institutions, to make democratic organizations fully participatory, to secularize the polity, to regulate migration of population, and to resolve cultural and linguistic conflicts, the State-system must be sensitive enough to respond to the opinions of various groups of people. Otherwise, the State-system will alienate large sections of the people it was planning to serve.

CHAPTER I

Setting and Argument

On 26 January, 1950, north-east India consisted of the State of Assam and the Union Territories of Manipur and Tripura. With the passage of the North-Eastern Areas (Reorganization) Act, 1971, the region emerged as a significant administrative concept with a North-Eastern Council (N.E.C.) as its regional planning and security organization, replacing the hitherto more familiar unit of public imagination: Assam. Administratively, the area consists of seven States: the States of Assam, Nagaland, Meghalaya, Manipur, Tripura, Arunachal Pradesh and Mizoram. The region accounts for 8 per cent of the total land surface of India and has a population of over 26 million. Some basic statistics are shown in Table 1 below:

TABLE 1

State/U.T.	Area (sq. kms.)	Population (million)	Growth rate of population (per cent)	Density of population (per sq. km)	% of region	Literacy rate (per cent)
Assam	87,523	19.90	36.09	254	74.48	36
Nagaland	16,527	07.73	49.73	47	2.94	41.99
Meghalaya	22,487	1.32	31.25	59	5.36	33.22
Manipur	22,356	1.43	33.65	64	5.39	41.99
Tripura	19,447	2.00	32.37	196	7.64	41.58
Mizoram	21,087	04.87	46.75	23	1.83	59.50
Arunachal Pradesh	83,578	06.28	46.75	7	2.36	20.09
India	32,87,782	683.8	34.75	221	Not applicable .	36.17

(*Source:* Census of India: 1981)

Social Order

The foremost feature of the social order of north-east India is its plural character. It consists of the hills as well as the plains and is inhabited by three distinct groups of people—the hill tribes, the plains' tribes, and the non-tribal population of the plains. All three groups are very heterogenous. The hill areas alone have more than a hundred tribes of Mongoloid origin. There are ethnic groups with their origins in the Indo-Burmese, Indo-Tibetan, Kuki-Lushais, Meiteis, Chin-Kukis, Shan-Tais and Indo-Aryan peoples. Each group of tribes has its own language and culture, and more than four hundred languages and dialects are spoken. All the tribes and sub-tribes have a profound distrust of and antipathy towards outsiders. The plains' tribals have ethnic links with the hill tribes, but these links have either been snapped or weakened over time; the plains' tribals have forged links with neighbours in the plains in terms of religion, language and economic activities. While a majority of those living in the plains are Hindus or Muslims, a very large percentage of the tribals in Mizoram, Nagaland and Meghalaya are Christians. In addition, there are Buddhists as well as Animists. In education, the Bengalis, the Assamese caste-Hindus, the Khasis and the Mizos are predominant, thanks to a variety of historical factors.

Geography

Geography has always played a specially important role in the economy, politics and administration of north-east India. The chief geographical features are: (1) the Hills; (2) the Brahmaputra Valley; and (3) the Barak or the Surma Valley. The hills and basins of the region are a mixture of high mountain ranges, plateaus and low hills covering an area of 90,160 sq. kms (roughly 60 per cent of the whole region) and the people living in these hills provide a variety which is a perennial source of interest and delight to sociologists, anthropologists and social or religious workers. The next geographic unit in size, but the most populous and developed, is the Brahmaputra Valley, which is spread over 65,339 sq. kms and constitutes a little over 25 per cent of the region. The Valley is 720 km long from Sadiya in upper Assam to Dhubri bordering Bangladesh and West Bengal, and its width, as if earmarked for nucleated human dwellings, varies between 50 to 120 kms. The Valley's only outlet is to the west and then on to the rest of India.

Economy

The economy of the States and Union Territories comprising
north-east India is more underdeveloped than in other parts of
India. There is little industry and agriculture is largely backward,
despite the great variety of resources and potential of the region.
In the field of hydro-potential, the north-east could provide 20
million KW of power from the Brahmaputra and Barak river systems. Its principal mineral resources are petroleum, natural gas,
coal, limestone-dolomite, and ceramic and refractory raw materials. Recent surveys have also located some deposits of metallic
minerals. Its forest resources are impressive and the region also
has the potential to develop new forests. All these natural
resources are yet to be fully harnessed, except perhaps in the field
of petroleum and tea cultivation, where sizeable achievements
have been made. While a large proportion of the region's educated manpower is unemployed, its agricultural scene is marked
by chronic underutilization of manpower and excessive dependence on it. The general economic scene is indicated by the following table.

TABLE 2

State	Per Capita (7th Finance Commission)	Road length per 100 sq. kms.	Per capita consumption of electricity (in kWT)	Agricultural workers to total workers	Per capita bank deposits	Per capita bank advances	Irrigated area to net cultivated area	Railways* (per 100)
Assam	791	72.59	31.59	76.68	150	62	21.4	16.40
Nagaland	820	35.06	39.61	79.43	196	50	33.3	13.82
Meghalaya	820	16.40	24.65	71.69	339	52	24.7	—
Manipur	870	39.47	4.88	72.28	81	29	46.4	—
Tripura	830	74.63	10.70	76.58	117	44	12.5	13.82
Mizoram	Not available	13.82	5.23	84.16	108	6	10.4	—
Arunachal	–do–	13.82	9.50	80.44	107	6	20.0	—
All India	1379	49.90	111.68	72.05	353	241	24.6	48.90

(*Source* : North-Eastern Council, Shillong, 1983)

* North-East India constitutes 8 per cent of the area of the country, but has only 3.2
per cent of its railway track kilometrage.

The industrial sector is undeveloped. While the natural resource endowments of the region are capable of supporting a large number of industries, the rate of industrialization is yet to be accelerated. Upto 1986, there were only 62 medium and large industrial units in the entire region, of which 48 were in Assam. As per the Guidelines, PT-1, 1982, 7 districts of Assam, 2 of Meghalaya, 3 of Nagaland, the entire area of Manipur, Tripura, Arunachal Pradesh and of Mizoram are backward. The limited expansion in the industrial sector and a near stagnant primary sector is having its consequential impact on the economy. The expansion in educational opportunities and modernization has led to phenomenal growth in the tertiary sector and north- east India has several times more of government servants, contractors and middlemen than industrialists, entrepreneurs and modern farmers. This level of under-development has in turn its own impact on operation and utilization of economic forces and opportunities in the region.

The reasons for the shortcomings in agriculture have been identified—mainly the prevalence of shifting cultivation, the lack of irrigation facilities, low consumption of fertilizer, the single-crop system, inadequate credit and marketing, land alienation and tardy land reforms. In industry, the lack of infrastructure, of local entrepreneurs, inadequate skilled manpower and, above all, the lack of capital, contribute to backwardness.

Ramayana–Mahabharata Tradition

The diverse ethnic origins of the people inhabiting north-east India in a territory of difficult and tortuous terrain naturally led to the growth of centrifugal forces directly stemming out of various ways of living, different forms of worship and separate dialects. None the less, over the years, there emerged a cultural communality which greatly contributed to social cohesion. The legends, myths, folklore and customs of the area were woven with those of the rest of India and originated from the same source: the Ramayana–Mahabharata tradition.

Both the Ramayana and the Mahabharata make distinct references to Pragjyotisha and Kamrup—the ancient and medieval names of Assam.[2] The *Kalika Purana* and the *Vishnu Purana* are replete with references to places in north-east India. The legendary king Bhagdatta, the founder of Pragjyotishpur (present Gauhati), figures in the Mahabharata war as heading a 'vast army of Kiratas and Chinas' on the side of the Kauravas. Sonitpur (present day Tezpur, where I served as Deputy Commissioner in the early 1970s) is still full of stories frequently related in schools and homes as being the land of Usha, who was enamoured of Anirudha the prince of Dwarka. Arunachal—'the land of the rising sun'—was the homeland of Rukmini, whose beauty enchanted Krishna. Manipur is associated with the abode of the Pandavas in distress. Nagaland is the place where Arjuna's Ulipi was born. The ancient ruler of Tripura had attended Yudhishtira's *Rajasuya Yagna* in Mahabharata days. The Ramayana tradition is reflected in Vasistha Ashram near Gauhati and Parsuramkunda in Arunachal Pradesh, bordering Dibrugarh district in Assam. The Shiva tradition has the shrine of Kamakhya, the centre of Tantrik worship in the Nilachal hills of Gauhati, and the remnants of near ten million idols of Shiva were supposedly deposited on the banks of the Brahmaputra at Bishwanathghat in the Sonitpur district of Assam by Ravana, the demon king of the Ramayana epic.

It is interesting to delve into the factors that led to the build-up of this tradition in north-east India. Recorded history is not much of a guide in such an exploration, but recorded legends are. Interpreting the latter, it appears that the link was established by the legendary king of Mongoloid origin, Bhagdatta, in about 1000 B.C. Bhagdatta accepted the composite religion and culture of Gangetic India and thus initiated the process of Aryanization or Sanskritization in Assam and the other territories of north-east India.

The earliest recorded history of the region is by the Chinese traveller and scholar, Hiuen Tsang, who visited India in the first half of the seventh century. Hiuen Tsang visited Kamrup. Bhaskaravarman, as Hiuen Tsang recorded, popularized the Ramayana–Mahabharata tradition in his kingdom with the help of Brahmins and forged close links with Harshavardhana, whose seat of power was at Kanauj. The early migration of Brahmin scholars from Kanauj to Assam began at about this time and was a crucial factor in the cultural and political relationship between Kamrup and Kanauj. The Kamrup empire at the time encompassed the whole of north-east India (except the Naga and Mizo hills and Manipur) and extended over the greater part of Bengal.[3] Despite the gradual decline of the Kamrup Kingdom, the process of building up the Ramayana–Mahabharata tradition was continued in the subsequent centuries.

This tradition received a set back in the first half of the thirteenth century, with the advent of Ahom rule[4] over upper Assam in 1228. But it was gradually overcome as interaction between the Ahoms and the indigenized Hindu population increased. Assam again started looking towards Mithila, Magadh and Kanauj and drew inspiration from these kingdoms in shaping its institutions. This was enhanced by the policy of the Ahom rulers of bringing Brahmin scholars to their courts to promote learning and culture, a process that continued over a long span of time. These Brahmin families settled permanently and integrated with local society. The respect accorded to the Brahmins and their close interaction with the rulers and other tribal autochthones helped accelerate the process of Sanskritization. Ramayana and Mahabharata tales—the latter in particular—spread to large segments of society and became essential ingredients of local culture, to find expression in such forms as folk-song and dance, and they were transmitted from generation to generation in the highest traditions of *sruti* and *smriti*.

The spread of education among the upper castes helped consolidate the Ramayana–Mahabharata tradition further. Schools were founded in Assam, and the abler students encouraged to visit the seats of learning elsewhere—Varanasi in northern India, and, later, Nawadweep in West Bengal attracted a large number of students seeking to develop their knowledge of Sanskrit, Indian philosophy and mathematics. On returning to the north-east they spread the ideas imbibed in these places among their people and, in particular, other students.

The Ramayana–Mahabharata tradition reached its zenith and received mass support in the Brahmaputra Valley and, to a lesser extent, in the neighbouring hills, with the neo-Vaishnav movement led by Sankardev (1449–1569) in the fifteenth and sixteenth centuries. The movement was part of the Bhakti cult and built

around the heroes of the Ramayana and the Mahabharata. Until
then, both the Ahom Koch kings who, between them, ruled over
most of the Brahmaputra Valley and beyond, were under the
baneful influence of self-seeking priests, astrologers and curious
beliefs. The Ahoms believed in Tai and Hindu rituals, while the
Koch kings were devotees of the Shakti cult, and human sacrifices
were common. Sankardev succeeded in ridding the local religions
of their magical rituals and beliefs and, instead, emphasized religion's role in individual salvation, political and social development. *Satras* (monasteries) were established and they became
centres of equality among castes and tribes. *Namghars* and *Kirtanghars* were set up in most villages and the *satradhikars* and senior
priests visited them regularly, even in the far-flung areas of the
Jaintia, Cachar and Arunachal hills. Krishna thus became the
key figure in the religious life of the region as well as in the entire
gamut of this thought processes of the people. The reformation
movement helped integrate the Brahmins, Kalitas and Keots into
a group of caste Hindus; it also created concord not only between
caste Hindus and Muslims but also between Hindus and the various tribes.

British Annexation and Policies

However, the fact remains that at the time of the British annexation of Assam (1826) and other areas of north-east India slightly
later, the spread and depth of the Ramayana–Mahabharata tradition as an integrating cultural force was far from complete. The
later half of the eighteenth century witnessed the first ever military clash between the *Satras* and the State in upper Assam; in this
the Moamarias of Mayamara *Satra* forcibly captured the seat of
Ahom power on 21 November 1769 and remained in authority till
their violent overthrow five months later. The challenge thrown
up by the consequent civil wars had a feeble political response and
the decline of the polity thereafter was sharp. A successful agricultural economy, which had helped in the development of a culture,
was shattered after these civil wars.[5] Sovereignty passed from
Ahom to Burmese hands in 1819, and the rule of the Burmese over
the Brahmaputra Valley, though brief, was a severe blow to earlier traditions of cultural unity. It led to an unprecedented flight
of population from the Brahmaputra Valley to Bengal, Arakan

and Tibet in the face of atrocities and the destruction of religious institutions. The British annexation of Assam and other hill areas thereafter led to a restoration of peace and order, but the new cultural policy did not encourage the Ramayana–Mahabharata tradition.

The policies pursued by the British had both positive and negative effects on the process of integration in north-east India. The restoration of peace and order, the stopping of head-hunting and raids by the tribals, and the abolition of slavery, balked the flight of population, restored agricultural operations and resurrected some of the earlier religious life. *Namghars, Kirtanghars, Satras* and schools in the Brahmaputra Valley were repaired. The political integration of the hills with Assam, as also the establishment of administrative headquarters at Shillong in 1874 helped in the socialization process between the plains and hill peoples, particularly of the Khasi, Jaintia and Garo Hills.[6] Similarly, the modernization that commenced with the construction of railway lines and roads, the setting-up of schools, colleges, printing presses, hospitals and dispensaries, and the beginnings of political institutions, with the advent of legislative councils, political parties and associations, encouraged the people of north-east India to view themselves as part of India and to know more about the country's cultural heritage, traditions and values. All these developments led to the growth of nationalism. It is another matter that, in many cases, certain ideals flourished in spite of them.

At the same time, British attitudes and institutions naturally did not result in a wholesale restoration of the past. British administration in 'greater' Assam, based on principles of Anglo-Saxon jurisprudence, the insistence upon recording evidence and the elaborate maintenance of land records, was far removed from the local traditional systems of oral evidence and community ownership of property. This led to the induction of a new class of administrators and clerks into Assam from Bengal. The Bengali *Bhadralok* knew English and established themselves as 'second class rulers' between the alien rulers and the local population. In their bid to establish supremacy, they prevailed upon the British to declare Bengali and English as the languages of administration. This policy had far-reaching, adverse consequences. It posed a serious strain on the Ramayana–Mahabharata tradition in north-east India, as the Assamese language had emerged as the chief agent of propagation of this tradition among large segments of the population, and was also slowly emerging as the lingua-franca of the region. The replacement of Bengali by Assamese in 1873 as the official language of administration and the medium of instruction in schools did not, unfortunately, lead to a restoration of the earlier patterns of relationship between the Assamese and Bengalis. It left a near permanent distrust between them and gave birth to linguistic chauvinism in the Brahmaputra Valley, which worsened with the increasing migration of people to Assam from various parts of Bengal, a process which persists even today.

The policy of encouraging Christian missionaries to play an active role in north-east India had a very significant impact on the culture and traditions of the indigenous as well as migrant peoples. Among the missionaries, the American Baptists were the first to come to Assam: they set up missions at Nowgong and Gauhati from 1837 onwards. In 1867, they started a mission in Goalpara for work among the Garos, a tribe of head-hunters. Missions were established in 1867 to work among the Ao Nagas, in 1879 to work among the Lhota Nagas and in 1880, among the Angami Nagas. The success of missionary activities led to the setting up of establishments among the Mikirs in 1895 and the Assamese Hindus at Dibrugarh in 1900. Besides American Baptist missions, various European missionary societies were also working in Assam. The Welsh Calvinistic missions became active in the Khasi and Jaintia Hills as well as the Lushai Hills during the second half of the nineteenth century. Among the Catholic missionaries, the Salvatorians or the 'German fathers' started their work in 1890, which continued up to 1915, when they were expelled in the wake of the First World War. During this period, they established a large number of missions at various places in the Brahmaputra and Surma Valleys and among the hill tribes.

During 1840–65 Christian missionaries demanded and received financial support in their philanthropic and educational work, and official protection and explicit recognition of their role were given by officials 'speaking in a personal and not official capacity', etc. In Assam, the tea planters prepared the way for the touring missionary. As the German missionary, C. Becker, records: 'Without their help it would have been unthinkable to undertake long and extensive tours, to cross the Assam Valley in all directions and to visit the Christian communities dispersed over such a vast area."[7] The Government of Assam afforded Catholic missionaries the privilege of staying free of charge in dak bungalows when on tour, a facility that is usually accorded only to state functionaries. Similarly, generous grants were made to Christian missionaries towards the construction and mainte- nance of schools and hospitals and, in times of natural calamities, they worked with the administration to provide relief and succour to the needy. As a result, the spread of Christianity, specially among the tribal and tea-garden populations, became very rapid.

The induction of Christianity was a new process and greatly contributed to the growth in literacy and better health care. For the tribals, it meant a stoppage of head-hunting. The Roman script was introduced in tribal languages. At the same time, these developments led to a loosening of intra-tribal bonds of unity and a decline in the authority of tribal chiefs. The tribals also dis- carded their traditional dress and forms of music in favour of Western dress and music. The process goes on. Christian mis- sionaries did not, however, succeed in propagating their religion among the Muslims or high caste Hindus.

The economic policies of the British rulers also had serious social and cultural repercussions. The modernization of tradi- tional agriculture demanded raising crops on all cultivable but fallow land, reclamation of marshy or swamp lands, and the intro- duction of new crops of vegetables, mustard and jute. These inno- vations required investment in irrigation, flood control measures, etc. But the government did not want to pay for such measures. They preferred to search for cheap and dependable human labour, which was not available locally. This led the British to induct into the region Bengali Muslim cultivators from East Ben- gal who were willing to move out of their homelands thanks to pressures in their area. The majority of Bengali Muslims mig- rated from Mymensingh district (all migrants from East Bengal are popularly described as Mymensinghias) occupied land in the vicinity of the Brahmaputra and its tributaries, and settled there.

The discovery of tea in Assam led to a further induction of tribal labour into Assam in large numbers, this time from Chotanagpur and Orissa. The British also adopted the policy of leasing land to their compatriots in Assam. By 1928, 1,629,529 acres of waste land were allocated to planters and nearly 1.2 million migrant labourers were working on their plantations. The 1921 census estimated that migrants to tea gardens and their descendants numbered 1.3 million, one-sixth of the total population of Assam.

The increased production of grains and newly found tea attracted the Marwaris—the celebrated business community of Rajasthan—to migrate to Assam, but the construction work on railway-tracks and roads induced Bihari labourers to frequently visit Assam as seasonal labourers. A large number of Nepalis who came to serve the British army did not return to their homeland and settled on forest and river islands as cattle-farmers, domestic servants, etc.

The question naturally arises as to what the British response was to this unprecedented stress on the social and cultural fabric of the Brahmaputra Valley and other regions of the area. Notwithstanding the notes recorded by some perceptive British administrators and demographers, the British attitude was largely one of benign neglect towards social and cultural issues. The British response concentrated on administrative reorganization and furthered the segregation of ethnic groups.

At higher policy-formulation levels in the British administration, the territorial and administrative reorganization of northeast India was considered the answer to its myriad problems. For a variety of reasons, the fundamental, economic and social issues were relegated to the background. Assam was reorganized in 1874, 1905, 1912, 1919 and 1947 in decisive ways. The territory of Assam after annexation in 1826 was included in Bengal Presidency, but became a separate Chief Commissoner's Province in 1874. It was next attached to East Bengal when Bengal was partitioned in 1905. After the annulment of this partition, Assam was reconstituted as a separate Chief Commissioner's Province in 1912. It became a Governor's Province under the Government of India Act 1919 and continued to be so under the Act of 1935. By the Radcliffe Award, the greater part of the district of Sylhet— under a referendum—was transferred from Assam to Pakistan in 1947. With Independence, too, this process was continued, but the objectives were different and the reorganization of Assam was done through years of dialogue and consultation, keeping in view both the facts of history and the wishes of its tribal population to manage their own affairs through democratic politics.

The pre-Independence reorganization demonstrated a lack of understanding of the social and cultural distinctiveness of the region. The compulsions of political expediency on the part of the British made them tag the north-east on to Bengal which added a new element of Bengali linguistic and cultural domination to the polyglot region. The comparative lack of education, non-involvement of the masses in public affairs and underdevelopment of a cadre of senior civil servants in the north-east prompted Lord Curzon in 1905 to reorganize the State. Curzon had strong imperial reasons to split up Bengal, but to link Assam and East Bengal was perhaps window-dressing, notwithstanding Curzon's argument that the reconstituted province of 'Eastern Bengal and Assam' would help Assam develop into a 'self-contained administration' capable of playing the same role in the north-east frontier of India that the Central Province fulfilled in the centre. The partition was annuled in 1912 and Assam returned to its previous position as a Chief Commissioner's Province.

British policy was, however, clear on two counts: first, the administration of the north-east was essential for the maintenance of the Empire of India, as it could be threatened from the north by Czarist Russia in collusion with Burma, China and Tibet; and secondly, the economic exploitation of Assam oil, tea and forest resources would augment the financial resources of the Empire and, towards that end, administrative efforts were to be reviewed at periodic intervals. Nevertheless, Assam's political linkage with Bengal did expose the people of the north-east to new situations, and many of its current problems are traceable to this association. Regardless of the advantages and disadvantages of Assam's linkage with Bengal, the fact remains that administrators and politicians during the nineteenth century thought that the reorganization of the north-east was comparatively simple and that it would solve problems of administrative management, apart from providing economic development and social harmony.

A policy of segregation emerged out of the British perception of the tribal situation.

The British did, in fact, once apply themselves to the question of opening up the frontier tribal population, but decided against doing so. This decision led to the adoption of an 'inner line' policy in areas like Arunachal Pradesh, Nagaland and Mizoram. The policy laid down a line beyond which no person could move without the explicit permission of the district authorities and the possession of land in these areas was forbidden to non-residents. The British also maintained a minimal administration in the region and encouraged Christian missionaries in their religious and philanthropic work. The 'inner line' policy discouraged Brahmins and Gosains from travelling to these areas, and thus contained the spread of the Ramayana–Mahabharata tradition and Hinduism. The policy was pursued with such rigidity that even the national independence movement could not penetrate into these regions. Jawaharlal Nehru summed up this position when he observed:

> For half a century or more, we have had a struggle for freedom in this country culminating in the achievement of independence. That struggle itself, apart from the result, had a liberating tendency. It raised us and improved us and hid for the moment some of our weaknesses and other qualities. We must remember that this experience of hundreds of millions of Indian people did not extend to the tribal area... we were not allowed to go by the old British authorities, so that our freedom movement did not reach these people. Rumours of it reached them. Sometimes they reacted rightly and sometimes wrongly, but whether they functioned rightly or wrongly is not the point. The essence of the struggle for freedom, which meant raising some kind of a liberating force in India, did not reach these areas, chiefly the frontier areas which are the most important tribal areas. The result is that we have been psychologically prepared for the last thirty, forty or fifty years for various changes in India, while those frontier areas were not so psychologically prepared. In fact, they were prepared the other way by British officers or sometimes the missionaries who were there. The missionaries did very good work there and I am full of praise for them, but politically speaking they did not particularly like changes in India. In fact, just when changes were coming in India, there was a movement in north-eastern India, supported by many foreigners there, to encourage those people of the north-east to form separate and independent States.[8]

Similarly, when tensions grew between the indigenous people and immigrant Muslims over land rights, the British administrative response was one of segregation rather than a solution through socialization or a process of adjustment. A 'line' was drawn in various territorial units to settle immigrants in segregated areas specified for their exclusive settlement. No thought was given to the long tradition of socialization between the Muslims and Hindus of the Brahmaputra Valley, and division was encouraged.

Post-Independence Policies

A debate on the policy framework for the administration of northeast India commenced as soon as the Constitutent Assembly started its deliberations in 1946. The political ethos was then dominated by: (1) the compulsions of universal adult franchise; (2) the genuine desire for economic development; (3) the secularization of the Indian political system through a policy of non-interference in religious faith on the part of the State and all its institutions; and (4) the need for integration of the hill areas as well as the princely States within the Indian Union.

The political system which was made applicable throughout the country with the inauguration of the Republic on 26 January 1950 had, for our purposes, four distinct features: (1) every adult citizen became a participant in the electoral process to elect a representative to the Assembly of a State and another to the House of the People of Parliament; (2) the Planning Commission, formulated, in conjunction with the States, five-year plans for economic development of the country; (3) Zonal Councils, consisting of States of a geographical area, were to act as a forum for deliberations in respect of inter-State projects of economic importance and problems of administration; and (4) the all-India Services—I.A.S. and the I.P.S.—were common to the Union and States and aimed at securing minimum standards of administration everywhere and to be agents of national integration. These all-India provisions, however, were not considered adequate either for the aspirations of the tribal people or in tune with their long traditions of autonomy and isolation. An additional political and administrative framework was considered necessary and provided for. These included: (1) the creation of autonomous District Councils under the Sixth Schedule of the Constitution to look after social, economic and even minor criminal and civil matters of the tribal people; (2) the imposition of restrictions on the right of Indian nationals to acquire landed property within District Council areas; and (3) the constitution of Tribal Belts and Blocks in the plains' areas to prevent alienation of land from plains' tribals to others.

There were, however, ominous signs from the day the District Councils were inaugurated in 1952. The District Council could not be constituted for the Naga Hills as the Nagas boycotted the election to the Council, while some Nagas demanded full statehood and several others clamoured for independence. There were other complicating factors, like the language policy of the Government of Assam, which created suspicion in tribal minds about Assamese intentions regarding their identity. The most important destabilization factor came from the tribal elite, who were highly proficient in English, accepted western dress and modes of living and were keen to become chief ministers and ministers of their own lands. The reorganization of Assam in 1971–2 enabled the principal tribes to have their own councils of ministers. The basic aims of democracy and secularism continued to guide all state policies.

Insurgency and Political Unrest

The political scene in north-east India from the Second World War period—when Kohima and Imphal became prominent battle scenes—has never been placid. Immediately after Independence, insurgency commenced in Nagaland and gradually spread to other areas. Even now the youth of the region are playing a major role in keeping mass movements outside the forum of electoral politics. The problems in each political unit are seemingly different, but are products of the rapid changes that the region has undergone on account of democratization and modernization processes.

On 22 March 1956, the Naga National Council (NNC) proclaimed the independent 'Naga Federal Government' under the leadership of Phizo—and insurgency commenced in an organized manner. Two decades later, with the signing of the Shillong Accord in November 1975, Nagland is a comparatively quiet state[9] and in elections held in November 1982, the Indian National Congress (I) has been returned to power. But the trouble is far from over as a group of Naga rebels is still in neighbouring Burma and has plans to start fresh incursions at an opportune time.

On 1 March 1966, it was the turn of the Mizo National Front (MNF), led by Laldenga, to raise the banner of revolt against the government and start a revolt almost on the Nagaland pattern. But peace has returned to Mizoram, elections have been held and a People's Conference government is in power. However, with the talks with Laldenga having failed and threats of 'Quit-Mizoram' notices hanging over outsiders, deft handling will be continuously needed to stem any fresh wave of insurgency in the area.

The trouble in Manipur was signalled by Meitei insurgents in June 1978, under the leadership of Biseswar and the People's Liberation Army (PLA) and, a little later, by the People's Revolutionary Party of Kangleipak (PREPAK)—a Marxist-Leninist organization under the leadership of Tulachandra. The Meiteis have been smarting from a sense of neglect and depriva-tion in the matter of employment vis-a-vis tribals. The frustration is so deep for the proud Meiteis that they want to renounce their Vaishnav heritage and revive old tribal loyalties.

The Tripura tribals revolted in June 1980 against the loss of political power caused by an influx of Bengalis from Bangladesh, which reduced them to a minority as well as subjecting them to Bengali economic domination which led to the alienation of their land, their being deprived of jobs and exploited in trade. The Tripura Upajati Juba Samiti (T.U.J.S.), formed in 1967, has been agitating for restoration of tribal land, the deportation of foreigners and the creation of an autonomous district council for tribals. The State is under Communist Party of India(Marxist) leadership, a party which is identified in the north-east with Ben-gali nationalism. The elections of January 1982 returned the Left Front under CPM leadership to power, although with slightly reduced strength. Tripura poses the most serious problem of ethnic harmony in the region.

Assam—the senior partner and a bastion of the Indian National Congress up to 1977—came under the grip of an agita-tion led by All-Assam Students' Union (AASU) and All-Assam Gana Sangram Parishad (AAGSP) over the 'foreign nationals' issue in 1979; an agitation which has caused serious damage to the national economy as well as national unity. The democratic pro-cess, which was virtually suspended, was restored with elections to the State Assembly in February 1983, but it has generated divi-sive forces in the State on a scale that surpasses even those at the

time of partition of Assam in 1947. In terms of election-time violence, Assam in 1983 saw the bloodiest election in India's electoral history.

The disenchantment of the plains' people with the political system in the Brahmaputra Valley can be seen in the break-up of the
Indian National Congress and the cessation of its historic role as
the umbrella for all ethnic conflicts and their solution, as an effective channel between the State and the Centre and between districts and the State. The process of the Congress break-up began
after the 1967 elections, culminating in a formal division in 1969.
B. P. Chaliha—the then Chief Minister and leader of Assam—
played an important but unsuccessful role in patching up differences between the 'Syndicate' leaders in control of party organization and Indira Gandhi, the head of the national government.
In a very rare conversation with the then Chief Secretary* and the
author, on the politics of those days, Chaliha mentioned that, on
principle, he was with the organization leaders, but the interests
of Assam demanded that there should be no division of the Congress in Assam—a strategic frontier state. He also underlined
that it was essential to have the same party ruling over Assam and
the Centre. While Chaliha's efforts failed at the national level and
the Congress split into the Congress (Organization) and Congress (Ruling), he succeeded in keeping the party united in
Assam, despite press reports that his colleague Mahendra Mohan
Choudhury—who later succeeded Chaliha for a brief while—
would go over to the Congress (Organization). The 1977 elections to Parliament brought the Janata Party to the seat of government at the Centre and Janata captured power in Assam as well
in the 1978 Lok Sabha elections. A new process of understanding
and adjustment had barely commenced at the political level, not
to mention the social and economic levels, when two fundamental
changes occurred. First, the Congress broke up in Assam for the
first time in 1978 as a result of a second division at the national
level, the dominant Congress group in Assam opting against that
led by Indira Gandhi. Secondly, the break-up of Janata in 1979
led to the downfall of the Janata government at the centre as well
as in Assam. For a short while political power in Assam was held
by a local variant of the Janata Party

During 1977–9, Assam's socio-political order was deprived of
the centre of adjustment—a role so effectively performed by the

*A.N. Kidwai, I.C.S.

Congress for over fifty years. During the years, electoral politics had struck an equilibrium between caste Hindus, immigrant Muslims, Bengali Hindus, the plains' tribals and others. Caste-Hindus always win a majority of seats as members of the Congress, with the solid backing of Muslim 'vote-banks' or 'tea-garden labour vote blocks'. In 1971 an attempt was made to develop the OBC (Other Backward Classes) vote banks, but this did not succeed. By 1979, however, there was a free for all, which led to a consolidation on ethnic lines amongst Muslims. In the Muhkama Parishad (a sub-divisional panchayat organization) elections held in Assam in 1979, out of nineteen posts of Chief Executive Councillors, Bengali Muslims captured six posts, three went to tribals, one to Bengali Hindus and nine to all the groups of Assamese Hindus, including Ahoms and the Other Backward Classes. This was a signal to the Assamese elite; the bye-elections to the Lok Sabha of Mangaldoi Constituency in 1979 ignited the agitation over the foreign nationals' issue and generated unprecedented fears amongst Hindu Assamese of cultural and political domination by outsiders. The basic apprehension was that once political power went to the Muslims and their supporters—which seemed very likely in the face of numbers and the ethnic consolidation among Muslims and others—everything that the caste Hindu have, including language and culture, would be gone.

The tribal state of Meghalaya also caught up with the agitation over 'foreign nationals' almost as a spread effect of developments in Assam and Arunachal Pradesh was soon stormed by fears of the mass conversion of tribals to Christianity.

The national response has been to give the people of north-east India a degree of autonomy within the Constitution, to develop according to their own genius, to highlight the factors of economic interdependence among the 'seven sisters' of the north-east and grant them generous financial assistance. During the 1970s, the policy of uniting the 'seven sisters' under the regional forum of the North-Eastern Council was laid down and has been pursued since then. Almost as an antithesis to this philosophy has been the approach of the 'disgruntled' elements to unite the 'insurgents' under the banner of the U.S.A. (the United States of Assam) or the NAMMAT (denoting Nagaland, Assam, Manipur, Mizoram, Arunachal Pradesh and Tripura). There are also revivalist movements aimed at uniting people with a common

Mongoloid heritage and para-military organizations, like the North-Eastern Region Defence Army (NERDA), apart from various 'liberation' armies in Assam, Manipur, Mizoram, Nagaland and Tripura.

While inability to meet basic needs in a changed economic environment is the principal cause of discontent, the problems of north-east India need to be viewed in the context of history, demographic change, the existing political system, security requirements and the aspirations of the people of the region. One also has to appreciate the role of modernization, which has sharpened encounters between the imperatives of the past—ethnicity, religions and geography—with the imperatives of the present and future—political, scientific and economic. The process of shaping a collective consciousness in north-east India, which was slow and obscure in the past has become rapid and strident in present circumstances.

CHAPTER II

Inheritance: Ethnicity, Religions and Polity Management

Every generation bequeaths to its successor certain attitudes, values and forms of organization. Although over the years these features undergo change, the essence underlying them remain and play important roles in social life. Any scholar of social history and politics has to take note of these enduring features of society as they acquire a kind of permanence in human affairs. Ethnicity, religions and values have played a considerable role in shaping the political attitudes of the people of north-east India, and continue to do so.

In analysing the significance of inheritance, I am deliberately leaving from discussion the impact of the geography of northeast India, which by itself is considerable. However, mention should be made of the Himalaya and the Brahmaputra, which together have profoundly influenced the economic, social and cultural life of the region. The Brahmaputra Valley was a colourful corridor between the two great civilizations of India and China. As Bridget and Raymond Allchin acutely observe:

> The eastern border regions, represented by the hills of Assam and Bengal, show many profound influences from Burma and South China, and it is not surprising that the Neolithic culture known from surface collections of stone implements and from the few excavations should reflect cultural traits deriving from the same direction. . . . It is noteworthy that their distribution in India is approximately limited to the areas in which today Tibeto-Burman or Munda languages are spoken. Here, culturally, one is on the frontiers of South-East Asia and China, just as in the far west one reaches the frontiers of Iran and central Asia. Perhaps, partly because of the difficulties of communication through the thickly forested mountains of Burma and South China, and partly because of other factors, these eastern influences do not seem to have played nearly so obvious a role as do the western in making up of Indian civilisation.[1]

The difference between the Brahmaputra and the other great river, the Ganga, is interesting. The Ganga has nucleated village and urban settlements, but the Brahmaputra has always frowned upon permanent settlements on its banks and its fury has repeatedly caused the eclipse of villages and farms. The character of socialization in the valleys of the two river systems has naturally adopted different courses. While the Ganga has been for generations of Hindus a sacred river, looked upon as a 'mother' with 'her' banks constituting innumerable pilgrim centres, the Brahmaputra, although not altogether devoid of sanctity, never attained the same status and is, indeed, the only main river in India that is given male attributes.

Things were changed in the Brahmaputra region with the emergence of nation-states and rigid national frontiers, as well as the operation of democratic and modernization forces among various groups of people has increased thanks to better transport and communications, electoral processes and the spurt in economic activity. All these have resulted in the stretching of psychological and cultural boundaries, and various cultural and ethnic groups in north-east India have felt both benefited as well as threatened.

Against this background, it is appropriate to analyse various ethnic and religious factors that have a bearing on present-day life in north-east India. These factors have made a powerful impact on the consciousness of the people and have influenced their ways of looking at democratic values.

ETHNICITY

Ethnicity and religion have provided enduring symbols of identity to various groups of people in the region. In the past, ethnic ties and religious affiliations helped individuals find their identity; organized kingdoms and clans used these identities to defeat their neighbours. To an outsider a person living in Assam is an Assamese, in Nagaland a Naga, in Mizoram a Mizo, in Manipur a Manipuri, and so on. But the real situation is baffling, and purely from the angle of ethnic variety the people of north-east India have a greater variety to offer than perhaps any other part of the globe.

There are as many as 217 Scheduled Tribes in north-east India and any number of erstwhile tribes are clamouring for Scheduled Tribe recognition. Today in Assam there are 20 tribes: 11 in the hills and 9 in the plains. The prominent tribes are: Bodos, Mishings, Karbis, Dimasas and Kacharis. In Nagaland, there are 39 tribes, including the Konyaks, Aos, Semas, Angamis, Lothas, Rengmas and Kukis. In Manipur, besides the Meiteis, there are two groups of tribals: the Nagas and Kukis. The Nagas have eight distinct tribes and a number of sub-tribes. The Kukis have seven major tribes, which are further sub-divided into a number of sub-tribes. In Tripura, there are 9 Scheduled Tribes: the Kukis alone in Tripura have 26 sub-tribes. In Tripura, the prominent tribes are the Tripuris, Reangs, Jamatias, Chakmas, Halams, Noatias and Moghs. Meghalaya is the homeland of three ancient hill communities: the Khasis, Jaintias and Garos, with their numerous divisions into clans. In Arunachal Pradesh, there are 110 Scheduled Tribes. The better known tribes are the Monpas, Apatanis, Adis, Kamptis, Singphos, Wanchos and Nishis. In Mizoram, the major tribes are the Lushai, Hamar, Fanais, Tlanglans, Pangs, Pakis and Lakhers. There are Reangs and Chakmas as well.

In the Assam plains, the Assamese and the Bengalis are two distinct linguistic communities. The Assamese are further divided into Ahoms, Koches, Kalitas, and others. There are Muslims with linguistic affinities to Assamese as well as Bengali. Bengalis dominate the demographic profile of Tripura and are also present in Meghalaya and Manipur. The trading community of Rajasthanis, and the working forces from Bihar, Uttar Pradesh, Tamil Nadu, Kerala, Andhra Pradesh and Bengal are found everywhere in north-east India.

It is thus not easy to determine the ethnic affinities of the population of north-east India. Broadly, the Scheduled Tribe population in the hills and plains have Mongoloid features. The Indo-European-speaking peoples in the plains have mainly Caucasian features. However, in the western part of the plains we find a blend of Caucasian with Dravidian and pre-Dravidian elements, while in the east there is a blend of Caucasian and Mongoloid features. From the anthropological angle, peoples of five groups entered north-east India at different periods of history

— the Austrics, Negroids, the Kiratas, Dravidians, and the Aryans.

The Austrics were perhaps the first group to inhabit the region. The Khasis and the Jaintias of Meghalaya and the Morans of Assam belong to this lineage. The Austrics are also found in China, Indonesia and Burma; they believe in the immortality of the soul, and worship stones and trees as they believe in one of the articles of their faith that the spirit of a person after his death takes shelter in a rock or a tree. The Austrics prefer women as managers of property, and also accept their leadership in family and property matters. This tradition helps explain the existence of matrilineal societies among the Khasis and the Jaintias. Almost in tune with this tradition, but driven by secular considerations, the women in these tribes participated in demonstrations and public meetings in the 1960s and thus worked for the attainment of separate statehood for Meghalaya in 1971–2.

The Negroids came from South and South-west China and today the closest to the Negroids in the region are the Nagas of Nagaland. The Nagas are not the 'naked' people, as is erroneously understood by the word 'Naga'. Except for the Angami sub-clan, the Nagas are a group who developed strong village institutions under the leadership of a chief and loved their freedom passionately. Stone worship is common among the Nagas as they believe that they are born of stone. The various tribes of Nagas, each speaking a dialect of its own, had one thing in common and that was their sense of valour. At different periods of history the Nagas have indulged in constant feuds and head- hunting. The Nagas' conflicts with Manipur, the British forces and the security forces in the post-Independence era are well-known. The feud between the Assamese plainsmen bordering Naga territory is almost a constant feature of known history. In their socio-political outlook, while the Nagas accord equal rights to men and women, the women are prevented from participating in politics, fighting and hunting. The political process in Nagaland, in tune with its past traditions, has not sent any significant number of womenfolk to their legislative assemblies. The traditional Naga attitude towards property was one of 'renunciation'. The Feasts of Merit, which bestowed distinction on their donors, was intended to show the virtues of distributing wealth over its possession. While the

Feasts of Merit are still in vogue, the attitude towards property has changed. Acquisitiveness is now dominant, and the traditional institution of communal ownership of property is cracking. The process seems irreversible.

'Kirata' is a term that refers to people of Mongolian origin. Ancient records call the people living on the Himalayan borders and in Assam Kiratas. Anthropologists have, however, identified the Kiratas with the Bodos, who have a large representation among the tribes living in Assam, Tripura, Meghalaya, north Bengal and Bangladesh. The Kiratas were the first group to introduce the cultivation of silk of different varieties in Assam and also contributed to agriculture. The Bodos have a developed language and are an important political force in northeast India.

Dravidians did not enter north-east India in significant numbers until the present century, when a sizeable population from south India migrated into north-east India. However, this migration is quite different from that in the early periods of history.

The Aryans were a well-organized and powerful people and by forcefully sweeping away every obstacle before them, soon established the dominance from Persia to the Punjab. The Aryans were late entrants to the north-eastern region. The Aryans of the Assam Valley were migrants from north Bihar and arrived from Magadha and Mithila perhaps in the fourth century B.C. It appears that north Bengal came under their control later than Kamrup. Asoka's empire extended over north Bengal, which continued to be a part of the Magadha kingdom. The Assamese historian, K. L. Barua, records:

> This area continued to be included in the Magadha empire, at least till the sixth century A.D. During the rule of the Imperial Guptas this stretch was known as Pundravardhana. To the east and north of Pundravardhana, Kamarupa continued as an independent kingdom ruled over by an indigenous line of kings who traced descent from Naraka, Bhagadatta and Vajradatta, heroes mentioned in the epics. From epigraphic records so far brought to light, it is possible to trace an almost unbroken genealogy of these kings from about the middle of the fourth century A.D. down to the twelfth century, or a period of nearly nine hundred years. Very few of the old Hindu kingdoms in India can present such unique genealogical records covering such long periods.[2]

The Aryans did not reach north-east India with the same direct thrust with which they spread over other parts of India. It is also a fact that they did not conquer north-east India as they did other parts of India. There was a significant tribalization of Aryan values and an Aryanization of tribal systems and, as a result of the blending, non-Aryan kings with Brahmins acting as their advisers and ministers were a common feature. The Mongoloid cultural values and ways of life greatly contributed towards a liberalization in the orthodoxy of Hinduism. The Tantric form of worship, which originated in north-east India, was a result of the fusion between Hinduism and tribal animism. The kingdom of Kamrup played an important role in the process of fusion of different races. Aryan culture, which was essentially an agrarian culture, spread in the Brahmaputra Valley while the hills remained the abode of earlier migrants who practised slash and burn cultivation.

In the process of socialization between the hills and the plains, a great part was played in the region by matrimonial relations and the market or bazars.

The *Buranjis*³ maintained by the Ahom kings firmly establish the fact of matrimonial relations between the people of the hills and the plains as well as among the tribes themselves. For instance, *Buranjis* reveal that several Ahom kings had wives from the hills, and Assamese women from the plains migrated to the hills as brides for the hillmen. Manipuri women were favourite queens of the Ahom and Tripura kings. In the writings of British administrators and anthropologists like J. P. Mills and W. Hunter one comes across comments on certain groups of the Nagas as having 'more admixture of actual Assamese blood'. It needs to be mentioned that, although matrimonial relations between the people of the plains and the hills were always on a limited scale, they nevertheless had far-reaching social implications.

Historical records from the days of Hiuen Tsang speak of the widespread existence of 'bazars' or *hats* in the region at fixed central places. These bazars were centres of trade and were visited by people in the neighbourhood, irrespective of their clan loyalties and the like. Trade operations, though at lower levels, encompassed several groups of people dealing in silk and cotton goods, salt, vegetables, oil, grain and gold. *Katha-guru-charita,* which contains biographies of Vaishnav saints of the sixteenth century, clearly establishes the role of bazars in the socialization process. The *Katha-guru-charita* also indicates that several enterprising Assamese merchants took their trading boats to Dacca or followed an overland route across the Jaintia Hills to Sylhet to trade with Bengal. A chain of weekly *hats* or bazars in the foothills, such as at Nagahat, Borhat, Kacharihat, Rahahat, Gobhahat, Ranihat and Phulaghrihat, facilitated regular trade between plainsmen and the people of the hills of the region. In these markets, there was an exchange of raw cotton and iron from the hills for rice, fried fish and cotton and silk fabrics from the plains.⁴ The bazars on the extreme south had facilitated contact with the people of Burma and on the north with Tibet, and on the west with those of Bangladesh. Over the centuries, in the ethnic cauldron of northeast India a process of assimilation and efforts to maintain ethnic identities have been a notable feature of the social history of the region.

The political impact of the recognition of each tribe for the conferment of certain administrative and electoral privileges that was set in motion in 1935 has been strengthened with reservations of jobs for Scheduled Castes and Tribes under the Constitution of India. The economic aspirations and, above all, politicization of ethnic identity in electoral processes, and demands for development programmes among the areas of a particular tribe, have all continued to further politicize ethnic bonds. There is a far greater awareness of ethnic labels after Independence than at any earlier time.

The way in which the different tribes have acquired their present identity as well as nomenclatures is an interesting phenomenon in itself. In pre-British days, most tribes were not conscious of their ethnic heritage and their spatial consciousness was limited to their family, clan and village. Sociologists have established that the present, somewhat emotive nomenclatures like Naga, Kuki, Lushai, Garo and Abor were names that the plains' people gave to various tribes. As a belated reaction to this, we now have the Miris of the Brahmaputra Valley wanting to be called Mishings, and the Abors and Daflas of Arunachal Pradesh to be called Adis and Nishis respectively, and so on. Each group dwelling in the hills or in the plains, indigenous or migrants, Hindus, Christians, Muslims or animists, wants to retain its customs and traditions, actuated by a strong desire to improve its status in

economic and political terms. All these aspirations involve competition, conflict and power struggles between members of different ethnic groups.

The electoral process in which universal franchise was firmly
established was considered to be the answer to every conflict. But,
unfortunately, for a variety of historical factors, this instrument of
confict resolution was not acceptable to certain groups for many
years. The following remarks by B. K. Nehru a former governor
of the area, hold good and echo the sentiments of visitors and temporary settlers in many parts of north-east India:

> My coming here as Governor of Assam gave me a cultural shock......
> For I discovered in North-Eastern India an universal insistence on
> maintaining the cultural identity of one's own particular social unit,
> no matter how small that unit might be. The desire to emphasize one's
> separateness from one's neighbour, which this quest for identity
> created, was something which I was at first unable to comprehend and
> am not quite able to accept.[5]

Against historical background of limited socialization and
scarce job opportunities, the attitudes of one ethnic group
towards another in north-east India are likely to be governed by
mutual suspicion, despite grant of separate statehood for the
major tribes. The membership of an ethnic group will continue to
provide comfort and identity to its members. Rapid industrialization may provide the ultimate answer, but the fear of being
swamped by members of other communities will sustain the culture of isolation. Each ethnic group will want to remain 'foreign'
to the other as far as practicable. The ethnic realities will also prevent the growth of class structure. The presence of Christianity
among the tribals, in particular, has further prevented the growth
of socialist ideas. Similarly, the spread of communist ideology
amongst Bengalis dissuades those who decry Bengali domination
from embracing Marxism. But ethnic 'romanticism' in north-east
India will ultimately yield to the consumer aspirations of the
people and pave the way for the growth and expansion of a middle
class—an aspect which is discussed in Chapter III.

RELIGIONS

An analysis of religion and religious values and precepts is important in understanding most societies. In north-east India where,

until recently, mobility was greatly restricted, life expectancy was brief for want of medical care, and scientific developments were comparatively unknown, religious beliefs and traditional faiths have played a predominant role and placed their stamp on a wide range of human activities and social institutions. However, while talking about religious attitudes and beliefs, we are more concerned with religion as a cultural system and as a civilizational factor, than as a system of faith. Despite the spread of secularization after Independence, religions continue to play an important role in India, and we shall here examine the significance of the major systems in north-east India.[6]

Animism

The number of believers in tribal animistic faiths is declining, particularly since the beginning of the twentieth century. The adherents of animistic faiths have embraced the more 'developed' religions on Hinduism and Christianity. Aspects of animistic faiths are, however, still important, for on embracing a new faith a person does not overnight shed the traditional beliefs passed on to him from his forefathers. What are the root concepts in animistic beliefs and practices?

The tribals of north-east India treat the 'soul' as the first article of their beliefs. But ideas of the soul's size and shape differ in different parts of north-east India. Among the Lakhers of Mizoram, the soul is held to resemble the body in appearance and size. The Thadou Kukis of Manipur, on the other hand, conceive the soul as a minute replica of the individual. This idea is also prevalent among the Nagas of Manipur and Nagaland. The Sema Nagas, however, believe the soul to be the shadow or reflection of the body. Some tribes believe in a multiplicity of souls. The Ao Nagas hold that for every individual in this world there is a spiritual counterpart in the sky, called *tiya* or fate, and that for every person there are three souls on the earth and three in the sky. One of the three souls is in possession of fate, another accompanies the individual whenever he leaves his home, while the third remains within the hut. Similar beliefs are entertained by other tribes as well. After the death of a person the soul goes to 'the land of the dead' in the sky. The nature of life in the 'land of the dead' is not different from that on the earth. The Rengma Nagas and the

Sema Nagas entertain the belief that the same men marry the same women and the same children are born to them, and so on. The deeds of an individual on earth is far less important in determining the type of existence in after-life than the nature of his death or the manner of disposal of his dead body: death by accident or murder are considered inauspicious. A better life in the other world is also influenced by personal prowess in war, success in love and the performance of sacrifices.

The worship of spirits consists of the worship of the supreme deity, ancestor-spirits and deities of the village. The tribes of Mizoram generally believe that the destinies of the universe are in the hands of one god, called Khazangpa. He lives in the sky punishes evil-doers and gives handsome rewards for good deeds. Several Naga tribes, however, do not believe in a supreme deity. In the Naga tribes ancestor worship is not much in evidence, but ancestor-worship is a prominent feature of tribal society in north-east India. The Lushais, Lakhers, Manipuris, Khasis, and Jaintias worship their ancestors and make periodic offerings to them. The worship of *gram devta* or village god is found among the Khasis as well as the Kacharis. Traces of it are also evident among the Meiteis, Lakhers, and Sema Nagas. The other Naga tribes and most of the Kuki tribes do not believe in village deities.

'Nature' has always been a source of awe to human beings. The ancient tribes started worshipping various objects of nature and propitiating them from early times. The whims of supernatural beings, the tribals believe, can cause disease and death, destruction of crops and other natural calamities. The Ao Nagas believe in animal sacrifices to propitiate evil spirits. In every tribe we find worship of totems like stones, trees, snakes, rivers, mountains, plants, and so on, in one form or another.

From the middle of the nineteenth century, believers in animistic faiths in various parts of north-east India had extensive encounters with Christianity. The tribal peoples, who had marginal contacts with Hinduism and Buddhism, were converted to Christianity in large numbers from the beginning of the twentieth century. This has created its own problems. In Arunachal Pradesh the process of conversion to Christianity was resented and legislation had to be passed to forbid conversion by force, fraud, inducement and allurement. In Manipur the Meiteis, who embraced Hinduism centuries ago, are demanding severance of these cultural links and the revival of the animistic faiths that their ancestors practised more than five centuries ago. Various Hindu festivals are no longer performed. In 1979 a former Minister presided over the burning of Hindu scriptures at a site where over two and half centuries earlier the Brahmins had burnt tribal scriptures. All these developments are not solely guided by religious or spiritual concerns but have economic motivations. One has to appreciate that beliefs and practices which have given spiritual solace and are historically important values cannot be abruptly denied without causing feelings of hurt and deprivation.

Buddhism

Buddhism did not come to north-east India from Bihar, as was the case with Brahminism, but from across the borders of the country; from Tibet via Arunachal Pradesh and from Burma via Mizoram and then to other parts of north-east India. The Buddhists in north-east India are mostly Mahayanists.

Buddhism made little impact in Manipur despite its geographical contiguity with Burma and frequent contacts between Manipur and Burma. In the Brahmaputra Valley, Huien Tsang found that Buddhism was known but was not very popular and did not make much impact even during the reign of Bhaskaravarman. However, several ncted Buddhist scholars as well as opponents of Buddhism flourished in Kamrup between the eighth and the tenth centuries. Buddhism also provided a channel of interaction between the two kingdoms of Kamrup and Tibet.

Buddhism was a civilizing force in the hills of Arunachal Pradesh, and gave the tribes a feeling of universal charity and tenderness to all living things. The tolerant spirit of Buddhism spread the doctrine of metempsychosis and the potency of acquired merit by good deeds and, consequently, altered local habits. The adherents of Buddhism are mild in behaviour although, like other tribes, they have rough exteriors.

The various tribes in Arunachal Pradesh established links with the plains' people and lived in harmony with them. Buddhist vihars were set up in Tezpur, Narayanpur, Dibrugarh, Sadiya and other places in the Brahmaputra Valley and the tribals of Arunachal Pradesh regularly visited them. In fact, Buddhism greatly facilitated harmonious relationships between the various tribes of Arunachal Pradesh and the indigenous population of the Brahmaputra Valley.

Hinduism

When the British entered north-east India in 1826, Hinduism was widely known in the region, but it was not the accepted religion of the entire population. The hill areas still practised animistic faiths and beliefs, although both Buddhism and the Ramayana–Mahabharata tradition were appreciated. It was mostly through an evolutionary process that the plains' areas like the Brahmaputra, Manipur and Surma Valleys and Tripura began professing the Hinduism of Shakta or Vaishnavism or a combination of the two. For clarity, it is proposed to discuss Hinduism in a three-fold perspective: first, the nature and content of the Ramayana–Mahabharata tradition, second, the spread of Hinduism in the Brahmaputra Valley and in the predominantly tribal area of the Manipur Valley, and finally, we should have some appreciation of the factors leading to the rejection of Hinduism in the hills.

Ramayana–Mahabharata Tradition

The Ramayana and Mahabharata, along with the *Puranas* constitute the epic literature of India comprising the *Itihasa* and the *Purana*. Both the Ramayana and Mahabharata are secular in their origins and have had a profound impact on the life and thought of the Indian people, including those of the north-east. The *Bhagvata*, one of the *Puranas*, found particularly wide acceptability in the north-east.

In north-east India the Brahmaputra Valley became the centre of the Ramayana and Mahabharata tradition. It was in Assam that the interaction between tribal animism and Hinduism led to the birth of the Tantric form of Hinduism. Tantric rituals centering around the temple of Kamakhya became famous for magic as well as sacrifice and attracted not only all the groups inhabiting north-east India but also from the rest of the country. The Manipuris or the Meiteis were Hinduized in the fifteenth century and initially cam to have faith in Shiva and Kamakhya—only in the eighteenth century did Vaishnavism come to be accepted by the people of Manipur. Similarly, the Kalais and Rupinis of Tripura first came under the spell of the Ramayana–Mahabharata tradition and later accepted Vaishnavism. The former tradition was no doubt known in the hills, but it was only in the sixteenth century that we come across characters like Narottam Atta — a Naga, Govinda Ata — a Garo, Bolai Ata — a Mikir, and several others, who carried the message of Sankardev to their respective hills.

Spread of Hinduism: The Brahmaputra Valley

There is no part of India which is more interesting in some respects to the student of Hinduism and Hindu polity than the Brahmaputra Valley. Here we are on the borderland of the Hindu faith and see the significant interaction between Hinduism and tribal practices.

The process of Hinduization in the Brahmaputra Valley commenced prior to Aryanization of this land. However, this is not to suggest any major conflict between Hinduism and Aryanization, but only to emphasize that the roots of Hinduism in north-east India are prehistoric and not, as is popularly held, that Hinduism was a much later transplant on animist society. One could approvingly mention in this connection the name of Assam's legendary king, Bhagdatta, who fought on the side of the Kauravas in the battle of Kurukshetra. Writing about Bhagdatta, S. K. Chatterji records: He is symbolical of a Kirata or Mongoloid chief who came within the fold of the Brahminical world as it was developing in the mayadesh or Midland round about 1000 B.C.

The excavations in Ambari near Gauhati suggest a civilized settlement dating back to the fourth century A.D. The most significant period, however, was the reign of Bhaskaravarman. He was a contemporary of Harshavardhana, who had made Kanauj the centre of government of the most powerful Kingdom of north India[8]. During the rule of Bhaskaravarman, Hinduism gave a sense of identity to rulers of Kamrup and, to some extent, a large number of officials and leading members of his kingdom. During this period the boundaries of Kamrup were extended up to the eastern part of the present district of Purnea (Bihar); abutting the territories of Mithila. This contact facilitated the migration of

Brahmins and Kayasthas from Mithila to several parts of Kam-
rup and also Sylhet (now a district of Bangladesh). The ancient
Assamese dialect was greatly influenced by Maithili and
Magadhi, and Huien Tsang found that the spoken dialect of
Kamrup differed only a little from that in Mithila and Magadha.

The Varna system, which emerged in northern India as a
sound system and stratified order, had a shaky start in Assam. For
one, Kshatriyas were not to be found in Assam for, the kings and
chiefs were tribals. There is speculation even about the caste of
Bhaskaravarman: while some scholars conclude he was a Kshat-
riya, others believe he was a Kayastha. While the protagonists of
the Varna system contrived to treat the Koches as Kshatriyas, the
Kalitas were universally considered to be Aryan settlers and
accorded a high place in the social order. The inability of the
Brahmins to give a neat Varna system to Assam could be ascribed
to the diverse ethnic origins of the rulers in Assam, as also to the
indigenous system of governance. The task was complicated by
the presence of people of Austric and Mongoloid origin—who
believed in and practised equality among the members of their
tribes, subject, of course, to the authority of their chiefs. The land
belonged to the community, with the tribal chiefs in overall
charge and functioning as protectors, unlike in northern India
where land belonged to the king. The entire community worked
on the land, in contrast to northern India, where the lower castes
usually worked the land and soiled their hands. The Brahmins,
however, succeeded in getting land grants in exchange for working in temples, interpreting the Sastras and performing religious
rites. When Huien Tsang visited Kamrup he noticed a large
number of Brahmins and thousands of Hindu temples. The
impact of the 'weak' beginnings of the Varna system in Assam
could still be seen in a caste system that seemed fairly flexible in
comparison to that in Bihar whose people helped in the Hinduization of Assam. None the less, the Varna system brought into the
Hindu fold new castes which had no precedents in the Hindu
social heirarchy elsewere.

There is no doubt that Hinduism was the dominant force in the
process of integration and the fusion between Aryan and non-
Aryan cultures. It also had economic and political implications.
Economically, to the tribal system of *Jhum* (shifting) cultivation
was added permanent or fixed cultivation in the plains and the

introduction of ploughs from neighbouring Mithila and Magadha, and all these brought in a great improvement in the technology of production. Politically, during the ancient period and up to A.D. 1200 Assam, despite geographical isolation and the overwhelming Austric-Mongoloid composition of its population, looked towards Mithila, Magadha and Kanauj and drew inspiration from the system of governance prevailing in those kingdoms in shaping her institutions. This in turn was possible because of the policy of its tribal rulers to import Brahmin scholars for their courts. Since the migration of Brahmins was a recurring phenomenon, it was possible for more Brahmins to come from north-India with fresh ideas and experience. The process of social consolidation progressed rapidly in as much as Brahmin families who migrated to Assam never returned to their original home states. The respect accorded to them and their close interaction with the rulers and other tribal chiefs helped the Brahmins to accelerate the process of Sanskritization. The tales of the Ramayana and Mahabharata soon spread to all sections of society and became living parts of local folk-song and were carried from generation to generation in the highest tradition of Sruti. The lack of contact that the Austric and Mongol rulers had with the areas of their origin helped the process of socialization.

The Mongoloids influenced Hinduism by participating and, later accepting its ways and beliefs and by acting as its transmitters to Burma, Tibet and other countries. Despite the Sanskritization or detribalization, the Mongoloids retained their special characteristics, which were of considerable relevance to their socio-political attitudes. They never fully accepted the creed of *ahimsa* and, sometimes, they appeared 'to be rather credulous, and at times they can be very cruel to both men and beasts'.[9] Some of these qualities have persisted to this day: the Brahmins and Kayasthas who migrated from northern India to Assam not only influenced the Mongoloids, but were themselves influenced and imbibed some of the local traits. The development of a common Assamese dialect and non-emergence of a rigid Varna system helped in the growth of socialization, but problems of terrain, the polyglot nature of the population and prevailing socio-political attitudes, stated earlier, acted as severe constraints. None the less, an Assamese way of life was distinguishable from the rest.

The break-up of the Kamrup kingdoms by the end of the

twelfth century led to the entry of the Ahoms—a branch of the Tai
or Shan race, into the Brahmaputra Valley. The Ahoms ruled
over Assam for six hundred years, from 1228. They gradually
accepted Hinduism and greatly contributed to the spread of the
Ramayana–Mahabharata tradition in the region. The most significant period for our purpose is the Vaishnavite movement led
by Sankardev (1449–1569) in the Brahmaputra Valley.

The Bhakti movement was an all-India phenomenon and also
touched north-east India. The movement, in north-east was not a
reaction to Islamic ideas, as in some other instances elsewhere in
the country, and it did not reach the people in the hills. Thus,
while Bhakti did not integrate the entire population, it did not
create cleavages between Hindus and Muslims. The Bhakti
movement in north-east India fully integrated Muslims into the
social mainstream, together with the tribal population in the
plains and in the foothills. The most important developments in
this direction took place in the Brahmaputra Valley.

The culture of the Brahmaputra Valley and, indeed, of the
entire eastern Himalayan region underwent a radical change with
the emergence of the neo-Vaishnavite movement led by Sankardev. It brought in an era of touchability and socialization among
Hindus and the tribes. Both the Ahom and Koch kings who, between them, ruled over most of the Brahmaputra Valley and
areas beyond, had so far been in the grip of priests and astrologers
and believed in Tai and Hindu rituals. Sankardev succeeded in
great measure in ridding the Hinduism of the region of its magical
rituals and beliefs, and substituting them with pragmatic thinking about religion's role in the spiritual development of an individual in a cohesive social order.

Sankardev found the community life, congregational gather-
ings, art forms, music and dances of the tribals particularly
attractive and encouraged their adoption by the plains' people. A
composite culture thus developed, which suited the genius of an
Assamese people composed of diverse ethnic elements. In his personal life, Sankardev selected his close friends and disciples from
different communities: for example, Chand Sai was a Muslim,
Govinda a Garo, Jayant Hari a Bhutia, Sriram a Kavivarta, and
Madhav a potter.

Sankardev viewed Assam as part of India. Through his plays,
poems and songs he widened the consciousness of the people of

the Brahmaputra Valley and enabled them to view themselves as inheritors of a pan-Indian culture. The Assamese language was so developed by Sankardev that it took the best from Sanskrit, Magadhi and Maithili and has close affinities with Oriya and Bengali. His religion was a reformed one, free of obscurantism and tantric practices, and was a part of the Ramayana-Mahabharata tradition that had bound the people of Assam with the rest of India through the ages. His *Ek Sarna Namdharma* enabled the various tribes and castes of the Brahmaputra Valley to enrich village and social life collectively; the institution of the *Namghar* (prayer hall) became a platform for collective action for social development. Sankardev had an all-India perception and always considered 'Bharatvarsa' as his country: he proclaimed that 'Gods even covet to be born as mortals in "Bharatvarsa"'; this feeling, however, did not permeate to the masses and remained confined to the elite of the neo-Vaishnavite movement. But the forging of an abiding sense of unity among the various communities of the Assamese people, whether in lower or upper Assam, was most significantly achieved, leading to the growth of an Assamese cultural personality. In historical perspective, the reform movement, assimilated a vast majority of the tribals into the Hindu fold and ingrained in them a national cultural consciousness.

The Bhakti movement almost unconsciously became an ideological weapon in the hands of the masses. Like Nanak and Kabir, Sankardev gave a social philosophy of equality and brotherhood to his ideals of reform. His movement was taken forward by Madhavdev, Haridev and others. As a result, the Ahoms and the Koches were completely Hinduized and a relationship of tolerance and trust developed not only between them and Hinduism, but also between Hindus and Muslims in the Brahmaputra Valley.

Spread of Hinduism: The Manipur Valley

The spread of the Ramayana–Mahabharata tradition in the predominantly tribal Manipur Valley has an interesting history. The early history of Manipur is shrouded in mystery, although there is some scanty evidence to show that the Valley, like the Brahmaputra Valley, had links with the rest of India in the seventh century; the Meitei king Naothing Khong (who ascended the throne in A.D. 633) married a Hindu princess from north India. Regular Brahmin settlements were made in the fifteenth century and the process of migration of Brahmins to Manipur continued thereafter. The Brahmins came single and married Meitei women. It is reasonable to assume that the impact of the Ramayana–Mahabharata tradition became more vigorous thereafter, influencing the religious and spiritual world of the indigenous Manipuris.

The reigns of two Meitei kings, Charai Rongba and Garib Niwas, are particularly important when considering the spread of Hinduism in Manipur. During the region of Charai Rongba (1697–1706) Vaishnav Hinduism became a dominant force. In 1704, the first emissaries of Vaishnavism (the Nimbarka school) came to Manipur and the king and his family were initiated into this sect. Although the king himself formally took the sacred thread he did not attempt to establish Hinduism as the state religion or neglect the worship of the traditional *lai*, and the observance of other Meitei beliefs. Garib Niwas (1708–48) made Vaishnavism the official religion of the state. The principal influence in him was Santidas, a Brahmin who came to Manipur from Sylhet and introduced the worship of Ram and Hanuman. He became the Guru of Garib Niwas, and the Ramanandi school replaced the Nimbarka. The Krishna theme came to Manipur as a result of Chaitanya influence, again via Sylhet, and it became particularly popular in the second half of the eighteenth century.

With these developments, the earlier religion of the Meiteis (popularly known as *lais*, which included forest gods, snake-worship, stone-worship and human sacrifice) began to change. The Meitei pantheon was pruned and only the clan of household gods remained: however, in a peculiar synthesis, the new Hindu gods came to be identified with traditional deities. Panthoibi gradually became Durga, and Nongpok Ningthou came to be identified with Shiva. Krishna, in his cowherd aspect as Sri-Govinda, became the dominant deity. The reading of the *Bhagvat Purana* along with the Mahabharata became common. This also led to the growth of several customs, usages, ceremonies and songs in which the worship of Radha and Krishna became essential features. One of the more significant results of this fusion is Manipuri dance, which has become an accepted major Indian dance form:

its origins are attributed to the efforts of Bhagya Chandra Maharaj (1763–98) and Chandra Kriti (1850–68).

The Manipuris, however, never completely discarded their traditional beliefs. The ancient faiths and festivals continue to play an important role in their life, together with Vaishnavism. The result is an amalgam, in which the peculiar cultural and religious genius of the Meiteis has helped to shape the kind of Vaishnavism that is now dominant. Despite attempts by certain Meiteis today to denounce Hinduism in the Manipur Valley, it is safe to hold that the Manipuri brand of Hinduism cannot be easily discarded, for it has become a part of the psyche of the region.[10]

Hinduism in the Hills

Why did Hinduism fail to establish itself in the hills? It is often argued that there were certain inherent weaknesses in Hinduism which made it less attractive to the hill people. It is true that conversion is not accepted in Hinduism in as much as birth determines whether a person is Hindu or not. It is also true that the rigid caste structure, with its various divisions and subdivisions, was too complex for a straightforward tribal mind. Yet the main cause was a lack of effort on the part of Hindus. The Brahmins merely followed kings and did not move independently of them. Thus Hinduism did not prosper in the hills of Jowai, Shillong, Kohima, Aizawl and elsewhere in the north-east. Hindu kings of the region did not extend their sway to these areas.

The Brahmins were also ignorant of tribal dialects and made little effort to learn them or give them a script, a job that was successfully done by the Christian missionaries. In contrast, at all the important points of contact between Brahmins and the tribals, whether in the plains or in the hills, the tribals had to learn the Indo-European language, to the eventual cost of their own. Thus, the Hinduization of the Ahoms, far from making the Brahmins learn the well-developed Thai language, ultimately meant that even the Ahoms forgot the mother-tongue of their ancestors.

During the British period, the impact of the Bengal renaissance reached north-east India at a fairly late stage. The great reformers like Raja Ram Mohan Roy, Devendranath Tagore and Keshab Chandra Sen did not visit north-east India, and even the ideals of reform propounded by them came decades later to a small group of literati in the Brahmaputra Valley. Similarly, north-east India failed to produce any spiritual figure of the status of Sri Ramakrishna Paramhansa, Swami Vivekananda, Sri Aurobindo or Ramana Maharishi.

Islam

Historically, the impact of Islam in north-east India began in 1205–6 with the unsuccessful endeavours of the Turko-Afghan ruler of Bengal, Bukhtiar Khilji to conquer Assam. Although the Kamrup kings frustrated attempts by Muslim armies to invade Assam in 1227, 1254–5, 1321–2, 1357 and 1473–4, both the gospel of Islam and a number of Muslims stayed back in the Brahmaputra Valley each time. In Tripura, similar efforts led to a significant Muslim presence in the area. The subjugation of neighbouring East Bengal and the conversion of a large number of low-caste Hindus and tribals to the Islamic faith had its influence on north-east India as well. But more significant contact commenced during the reign of Jahangir (1605–27), when Koch-Hajo in lower Assam was subjugated and Muslim rule was installed. The process was furthered during the period of Shahjahan (1627–58). The Rajas of Jaintia, Cachar, and Tripura accepted vassal status under the Governor of Bengal. The accession of Aurangzeb (1658–1707) to the Mughal throne at Delhi ushered in a new era of relations between Delhi and north-east India. The imperial policy was furthered by Mir Jumla, the ablest army commander of Aurangzeb, who led an expedition into Cooch Behar and Assam. He occupied Cooch Behar on 18 December 1661 without any opposition and, later, the territory was restored to its former Raja against payment of annual tribute and his acceptance of allegiance to the imperial government. Mir Jumla forced his way to Garhgaon, the Ahom capital, and the Ahoms signed a peace treaty accepting Mughal suzerainty and undertaking to pay a war indemnity, tribute and hostage. Subsequently, the Ahoms under Chakradhiraj Singh (1663–9) and Udayaditya Singh (1669–73), raised the banner of revolt and defeated the Mughal army led by Raja Ram Singh in the famous battle at Saraighat near Gauhati. The Mughals ultimately left Assam in 1682. These developments made Islam the religion of a significant even if not ruling group of people in Assam, Cachar, Jaintia, Tripura and Manipur.

A process of natural influence had begun between the Muslim and Hindu populations in the thirteenth century and the Muslims had been accepted as part of the local population, racially and linguistically. This was the result of the secular policies of the local rulers. The Ahom rulers patronized Muslim saints with sizeable land grants and exemption from forced labour. Azan Fakir, the Muslim preacher who came to Assam towards the end of the seventeenth century, was given generous land grants by the Ahom king Gadhadhar Singh (1681–96), which helped him settle in the state permanently. Muslim religious preachers were attached to Ahom courts. The tolerant social outlook of the Ahoms and the teaching of Hindu reformers like Sankardev and Madhavdev in the sixteenth century brought Hindus and Muslims in Assam closer to one another. Based on Sufi religious songs, Zikir and Zari songs began to find a place in Assamese literature.

A more or less similar policy was followed in Jaintia, Cachar, Tripura and Manipur. The ruling elites of these areas did not discriminate against the Muslims on religious grounds and appointed them to government office, including service in the army. In Cachar, lands were granted to the Hindus and the Muslims in adjacent plots at various places. Jai Narayan (1698–1731), the Raja of Jaintia, invited a Muslim scholar from Hardwar to help in the education of the Muslim population of his state. In Manipur, the imaginative policies of Garib Niwas greatly helped in socialization among the Hindus and the Muslims. In Tripura, the Hindus held the dargah in great reverence and Muslims, in their turn, participated in the religious festivals of Hindus. In the entire region the impact of Islam gave rise to several new sects that preached against idolatory, polytheism and caste. The camaraderie in masjids and mosques and Islamic education through Madrasas helped the further spread of equality among the people.

In the Brahmaputra Valley we come across similarities amongst Hindus and Muslims in agricultural operations, food habits, and hospitality. Both Hindus and Muslims in the Brahmaputra valley refrain from ploughing on the death anniversary of their religious leaders and parents. Both Hindus and Muslims relish rice and fish, although fish preparations in Muslim households use more spice. Both the communities receive their guests by offering *pan* and *supari*; the honoured guests are served

these in *Bastas* or *Sarais* — two varieties of brass trays which, on
occasion, have a *Saphura* or a dome-shaped cover.[11]

The harmonious relationship between Hindus and the Muslims, which was inspired by the secular policies of different rulers
in north-east India, came under great stress after the annexation
of these areas by the British. Communal representation in the new
legislatures ultimately led to the division of the country, which
seriously affected north-east India. Today, thanks to the increasing importance of politics and *en-bloc* voting patterns among the
immigrant Muslims, Islam has become a significant political factor in north-east India. With the growth in communications and
the spread of education among immigrant Muslims, present-day
en-bloc voting at the behest of village bosses and leaders is slowly
yielding place to the exercise of franchise rights on less parochial
considerations. The cordial existence of mosques, temples and
churches in several villages of north-east India should help in
socialization, for exclusive settlements of Muslims, which were
resorted to during the British period, would be a major obstacle to
modernization and familiarization between people of different
religious faiths.

Sikhism

Sikhism made its entry into north-east India in a peculiar fashion.
During his Assam campaign in 1669, Raja Ram Singh, the commander of the Mughal army, brought with him the ninth Sikh
Guru, Teg Bahadur, and some of his followers. Although the
Mughal army was defeated and Guru Teg Bahadur also left
Assam, his followers stayed behind and introduced Sikhism in
Assam. The Sikh community in Nowgong claims descent from the
followers of Teg Bahadur. Like the migrant Muslims, the Sikhs
too were assimilated in the Brahmaputra Valley. The migration
of Sikhs to different parts of north-east India after Independence
is solely guided by economic motives, but, in the process, the Sikh
gurdwaras dot different parts of the region. The Sikhs do not pose
any threat to the maintenance of peace and harmony among the
people and the discords which have begun to characterize relations between the Sikhs and Hindus elsewhere are absent in
north-east India.

Christianity

We have already mentioned the gradual spread of Christianity in north-east India from 1837 onwards.

The impact of Christianity on north-east India was different in nature and content from that in other parts of the country. While the rest of ninetenth-century India was re-awakening under the impact (and threat) of the West, Assam and other parts of northeast India witnessed the decay of indigenous and free institutions of governance — a process that started with the conflict between the State and *Satras* (monastries) in Upper Assam in the last quarter of the eighteenth century, leading to the transfer of sovereignty from the Ahoms to the Burmese and then to the British. Further, the flight of population to Bengal, Tibet and the Arakan hills and the total absence of intellectual or spiritual pursuits contributed to an all round decline. Only in the 1850s and later did the Calcutta-educated Assamese bring about some sort of revival in the Brahmaputra Valley, and even this was on a very limited scale. The effort and example of Haliram Dhekial Phukan (1802–32) and Juggoram Dhekial Phukan (1805–38) and, immediately thereafter, of Anandaram Dhekial Phukan (1821–59), and Maniram Dewan (1806–58), need special mention. All of them championed in different ways the cause of modern education, equality before law, health care and economic development; and Maniram Dewan, in particular, fought for freedom. The need for a new approach towards spiritual and religious problems was also advocated.

The new spirit was furthered by Dinanath Bezbaruah (1818–95), a businessman and the initiator of the Brahmo movement in Assam, Gunabhiram Barua (1835–96) a social reformer and journalist, Madhavchandra Bordoloi (1847–1907), a teacher and lawyer, Anundoram Barua (1850–89) who joined the ICS in 1872 and was a distinguished scholar, Zalnur Ali Ahmad (1848–1921), who joined the Indian Medical Service in 1872; Haribilas Agarwalla (1842–1916), a publisher and businessman; Jagannath Barooah (1851–1907), the politician and reformer, Manik Chandra Baruah (1851–1915), a businessman and politician, Kamalakanta Bhattacharya (1853–1936) a poet, editor and leader of the Brahmo movement in Assam, and several others.

Some of them went to England and America for higher education. The new Assamese elite, which in economic terms constituted the nascent middle class, was actuated by the desire to improve Assamese social conditions in the light of developments in Bengal. However, thanks to the narrow educational base and the small size of the Assamese middle class, their achievements were on a minor scale when compared to those of their counterparts in Bengal. However, it needs to be mentioned that the new spirit did not spring from an interaction between the Assamese and Christian missionaries in Assam, but was imbibed in Calcutta.

The spread of new ideas by Christian missionaries began in the Brahmaputra Valley and in the neighbouring hills with the publication in 1846 of *Arunodoya*, a Baptist monthly in Assamese, the translation of the Bible into Assamese, which reduced the tribal languages into the Roman script, and the setting up of schools and colleges for boys and girls, culminating in the establishment of Cotton College at Gauhati in 1901. All these measures led to some, but still very limited, interaction between the missionary and indigenous culture, and to a new socialization process.

Urbanization was also slow in the nineteenth century. In 1861, Colonel Hopkinson, the Commissioner of Assam, while opposing the move of the Bengal Government to set up a municipality at Gauhati, had clearly mentioned: 'It appears to me that the social condition of Assam is not sufficiently advanced for the introduction of municipal government fully or partially, in any shape, on any terms.' He further observed that such places as Gauhati, Dibrugarh or Tezpur were 'merely villages used as centres for the policing of the surrounding country' and in Gauhati there was 'not a carpenter's shop nor a boat-builder nor a mason nor a tanner nor a shoe-maker'. He continued: 'the bulk of the population of Gauhati are out in the field cutting and bringing in their rice'. The conditions in Shillong were no better, although they started improving after the headquarters of the administration were shifted there from Cherapunjee in 1874.[12] Only in the present century did Gauhati and Shillong become small urban centres.

In the Brahmaputra Valley, the Hindus kept their age-old faith intact, but the impact of the Christian missionaries on the tribal population was spectacular. The conversion of animists or Hindu tribals to Christianity was phenomenal. Today the Christians comprise 80 per cent of Meghalaya's tribal population; 85 per cent of Nagland's, 96 per cent of Mizoram's, and 26.03 per cent of Manipur's. Four Chief Ministers out of the seven political units in Nagaland, Manipur, Mizoram and Meghalaya were Christian at one stage. In Nagaland, all but one member of the 60 member legislative assembly are Christian.

The Nagas, Mizos and Khasis in particular have undergone profound changes as a result of the spread of Christian ideals among them. Christianity taught these tribes the value of peace, tolerance and co-existence. The age-old practice of head-hunting and internecine feuds became a thing of the past. Christian ideals of universal brotherhood and modern education, as well as the availability of the Bible in local languages brought the tribal unit out of seclusion and isolation. The familiarization of these tribes with new ideals, coupled with the subsequent independence and democratization of the polity, have taken them into the modern world, with all its strengths and dangers.

ROLE OF RELIGION IN NORTH-EAST INDIA

It has been argued that Christianity has served as a 'defence mechanism' for tribal interests and identity, against the greater threat of dominance and absorption into the large Hindu society of the plains. The separatist tendencies amongst some hill tribes have been viewed by some as 'natural attempts on their part to define their socio-cultural identity vis-à-vis the others in the new circumstances of independence'. Others believe that all the tribal groups which have remained aloof from post-Independence political agitations have been non-Christian and more receptive towards the Centre. They hold insurgency in Nagaland and Mizoram to be 'Christianity-influenced'. There are others who consider violence in Assam, Manipur and Tripura as products of Hindu extremism.

It is not my task to either establish or deny any nexus between the Christian missionaries and insurrectionary movements in Nagaland, Mizoram and Manipur or between Hinduism and mass agitations in Assam, Manipur and Tripura. What needs to be highlighted in any analysis of the phenomenon of change, which these three views do not take into consideration, is the fundamental fact that religion has yielded to economics and politics as motivating social forces in north-east India. Besides, such

generalizations also ignore divergent views and conflicting
interests between the protagonists of the same religion, between
hillmen and plainsmen, and among the hillmen themselves on the
basic question of employment, the management of land in the face
of new realities of fragmentation and individual ownership, and
the fulfilment of consumer aspirations.

In any study of the role of religion in present-day north-east
India, religious conversions occupy an important place. It is
increasingly being appreciated that religious conversion creates
serious problems for the structure of a secular democracy, particularly when it is a product of fraud or inducement. Besides,
even in a normal case of change of faith, a person accepting a new
religion has his own problems in making the transitional emotional and mental adjustments. Historically, the Brahmins who
initiated tribal groups to the Hindu fold conceded the entry of several tribal gods and goddesses into the Hindu pantheon or facilitated the process of shaping tribal deities in the image of Hindu
gods and goddesses. The Christian approach was primarily
through education and health care. If we look at the spread of
Christianity among the Khasis of Meghalaya, we find that, prior
to the arrival of Christian missionaries in the 1840s, the Khasis
had no script of their own. The missionaries used the Roman
script for publishing pamphlets and newspapers in Khasi to pro-
pagate Christianity. They set up schools and hospitals. As a result
of these efforts, there was widespread conversion to Christianity.
By 1920s, the numbers of Christians amongst the Khasis rose to
30 per cent of their population At present, nearly 60 per cent of
the Khasi population is Christian, in a total of nearly 4 lakhs.

The acceptance of the Christian faith by an animist society had
its own impact on the inner functioning of the modern Khasi mind
in respect of religion. An interesting and highly relevant disclo-
sure comes from a member of the Khasi community, B.M. Pugh,
who writes:

> I have already stated that the conversion of my father to Christianity,
> to a very large extent, explains why I am a Christian. As I ponder over
> the faith of my forebears, the earlier Khasis, I feel ashamed that my
> faith in God and my belief in prayers are not as strong as theirs. A
> Khasi tribal has always believed in God the Creator and in the efficacy
> of prayer which is also considered as a means of communication with
> God. There are, of course, spirits and demons in the Khasi belief which

are responsible for evils, sufferings and disease in the world and have to be appeased, but they are lesser deities; and there are many of them, very often associated with peaks or valleys and even with trees. My faith and my belief have now become very much diluted. If there is a heaven I am sure that my non-Christian grandfather will be sitting in the higher heavens, while I, a professed Christian, may not even find a place in the lower heavens.[13]

B. M. Pugh is not the only person of his kind. Very many tribals converted either to Christianity, Islam or Hinduism are asking questions about their heritage and early beliefs.

If we look at the religious scene in north-east India, we find that, although from the angle of Hindu-Muslim amity, the situation is more placid here than in Bihar or U.P., the religious scene in itself is far more complicated. There are a number of situations which might lead to flashpoints. First, the efforts of Christian missionaries towards conversion are disliked by a number of Hindu organizations in north-east India. In December 1978, a private member of the Lok Sabha introduced 'The Freedom of Religion Bill, 1978' seeking to prohibit conversion from one religion to another by the use of 'force or inducement, or by fraudulent means'. On the face of it the Bill appeared well-intentioned, but the Christians organized massive demonstrations all over the country and particularly in north-east India, as they suspected the omnibus character assigned to 'force', 'fraud' and 'inducement', by which all conversions, even genuine changes of faith, could be banned by law. Such measures could well result in future communal clashes between Hindus and Christians in north-east India. Second, the plains' tribals and a large section of Hindus have lost their land to immigrant Muslims. During the election-related violence in Assam in February 1983, in a sleepy, rural area of Nellie in Nowgong district, the tribals indulged in ghastly massacres of immigrant Muslims and the two communities exhibited a frenzied hatred towards each other. Third, the Meitei reaction against Hindu temples and deities and the burning of scriptures in 1979 might be an internal revolt within the Hindu order, but it could also escalate into violence involving the tribals and the Hindus. Finally, it is deeply regrettable that, while publicly proclaiming that religion is a private matter and should not influence those in public life, various parties and groups are misusing religious issues on a scale never witnessed before in north-east India. All these factors need to be taken note of in the polity-management of the region, for with the decline of popular faith in political leaders, religious fanatics are drawing increasingly large crowds and believers in ethnicity are on the ascendant.

INHERITANCE AND POLITY MANAGEMENT

There is no denying that the internal visions, values and beliefs of all those who hold, or, at different periods of history held, political power in north-east India did influence the ethical or moral choices that were made in public policy. Examined within this focus, we find that, when the Brahmins migrated into the Brahmaputra Valley from Magadh and Mithila, they brought with them defined concepts of polity management as well as paths of salvation and strove hard to convert the indigenous population to these faiths and succeeded in doing so to a substantial extent. Hindu kingdoms were set up and ideals of polity management as enunciated in the Ramayana–Mahabharata tradition were popularized. Its spread was not only confined to the Brahmaputra Valley but its acceptance in Tripura, Manipur and Cachar and even Jaintia hills are well established.

When the Ahoms invaded Assam in the beginning of the thirteenth century, under the leadership of Sukapha, a new set of values and beliefs was imported. The Ahoms, however, did not impose their religion on the people of the Brahmaputra Valley when they began their rule. On the contrary, the rulers accepted the religion of those over whom they ruled. The explanation could be found in various facts of medieval tribal life but certainly not in the fact that the Ahoms did not have a religion. The Ahoms, like their kinsmen of Burma and ancestors in South China had a well-developed religious system and had been influenced by Buddhism. It is, another matter that the Ahom religion may not have been as developed as Hinduism, Buddhism or Islam. The main point is that their religious beliefs were less dominant than their political attitudes. The Ahoms were gradually Hinduized, and yet they retained several of their earlier beliefs and shaped their administrative system in Assam in the light of their inheritance.

The various efforts of the Muslim rulers to annex north-east India from the beginning of the thirteenth century onwards and their limited success in Assam, Tripura, Cachar, Jaintia and

Manipur no doubt led to the induction of Muslims into the area and to conversion of the indigenous plains' tribal and low-caste Hindu populations to Islam. But it was only with the complete annexation of north-east India by the British that conversions attained a major dimension. Christian missionaries found no field for propaganda amongst the Muslims and their main influence was exerted on the tribal and Hindu mind.

If we look at the freedom struggle, we find that the Congress was more concerned with reform of the social order than with divine dispensations. There was no bid to disown any religion and the emphasis was on how to accord equal respect to all religions. The inadequacy of religion as a cementing force and its role as a divisive factor were well-perceived, as demonstrated by the vivisection of India in 1947 on religious grounds and the break-up of Pakistan in 1971. Thus, in deciding secular issues on communal considerations and preaching hatred against others should have no place in reconstructive schemes of social order. This was strongly emphasized by Mahatma Gandhi (1869–1948) who wrote that our prayer should not be 'God give him the light that thou has given me' but 'give him all the light and truth he needs for his highest development'. He went on further to highlight: 'Pray merely that your friends may become better men, whatever their form of religion'. This equal reverence for all faiths, the readiness to concede to a fellow citizen the right to follow his own light, is the foundation of secularism in India and national unity. The secularist approach not only subserves the physical and moral interests of the minorities but is the basis for social modernization and the building of a civilized society. Secularism can ultimately act as the cement of a new social contract, building together all classes of people living in India.

The national movement also concerned itself with giving expression to a composite cultural identity. The cultural movement was sustained by a new political consciousness. Important national leaders of the political movement, like Tilak, Gandhi, Nehru and Azad, were also cultural leaders; similarly, writers like Tagore, Bharati and Maithili Saran Gupta were also national leaders. In north-east India, the leaders of the national movement like Gopinath Bardoloi, Nichols-Roy, Basant Kumar Das and Fakhruddin Ali Ahmed were considered cultural leaders in their respective areas of influence. The twin processes of cultural renaissance and the struggle for freedom were responsible for the growth and conceptualization of the new framework of values. The basic ideals of these values have found expression in free India's constitution: national unity amidst regional diversity, democracy, secularism, an egalitarian social order, and modernization.

In the context of north-east India, the acceptance of these values *per se* ought to have had no problems as this region, perhaps excluding Manipur and Tripura, had a more egalitarian social order than any other part of India. In economic terms, the difference between the rich and the poor was not marked by the large disparities that characterized other regions. North-East India had a loose caste-structure and was particularly free from the scourges of untouchability and dowry. Most of the tribes managed their polity on democratic lines. Bampfylde Fuller, who was Chief Commissioner of Assam in 1902, wrote as follows about the Khasis:

> Quite half of the Khasi Hills district is administered by a number of little indigenous governments..... The Chief of each State is assisted by a council which he is bound to consult. He holds office, not in simple hereditary right, but by election, being chosen from amongst those who are qualified to succeed by relationship to a particular female line. In some States the electing authority is a college of augurs who belong to a priestly clan: in others secular electors, such as the headmen of villages, have secured representation along with augurs, or have even displaced them: in others, again, election is by general plebiscite.[14]

Various rulers in north-east India had practised secular ideals towards adherents of all religious faiths in matters of jobs and land grants. Above all, the consolidation of secular and democratic forces after Independence could have enabled the diverse sections and communities of the area to be on the road to cohesion.

The biggest countervailing factor was the age-old suspicion that almost every tribe has against the other and between the peoples of the hills and the plains, and the indigenous population against the migrants. This had sustained limited social contacts amongst the inhabitants of the area and created a wall of division between the indigenous population and enterprising migrants. Every tribe or group of people in north-east India developed its own word to denote the outsider. Thus, in the Assam plains, the outsiders are variously called 'Bangals' or 'Bahiragats', in Manipur 'Mayangas', in Mizoram 'Vais', ans so on. These terms are often derogatory or denote contempt and have found a place in folklore and song.[15]

One can appreciate that the tribals, due to their long isolation, view outsiders or plainsmen with suspicion. But when one comes to the Brahmaputra Valley, which has two-thirds of the population of the region and where the freedom struggle was in full bloom, the attitude of the indigenous people towards migrants needs explanation.

The suspicion towards 'outsiders' has its roots in history and certain none-too-happy experiences of socialization. Historically, the distrust originated from the very nature of the relationship between the Ahoms and the Mughal rulers in Delhi. The Assamese rulers loved their independence and were interested in protecting their territory, while the Mughals, as we have already seen were actuated by a strong desire to annex the whole of Assam. The Hinduization of the Ahoms and the neo-Vaishnavite movement led by Sankardev brought in a great attitudinal change. The rule of Rudra Singh (1696–1714) was landmark, for the king had an all India outlook. He deputed Khaunds and Bairagis to important centres in India to apprise himself of worth while traditions and customs, with a view to introducing them in Assam. The records indicate that he invited Bengali priests, scholars, musicians and merchants to his court and sent them back with presents so that his name might be spread in Bengal. Several of the migrants stayed back as the rulers of Assam appreciated the useful role they played in the improvement of agriculture and industry, education and culture, the arts and crafts of Assam. The only condition imposed was that the 'licensed foreigners' had to cut off all connections with places of their origin and, in due course, show their willingness to be assimilated in Assamese society by accepting its language and ways of living.

The Assamese attitude towards migrants appears to have changed with the start of the third phase in Assam's contact with outsiders. This brought a migration in large numbers of clerks and assistants from Bengal, who came in the wake of the British annexation of the region in 1826. These new migrants were wittingly or unwittingly responsible for heightening Assamese suspicions against outsiders in general and Bengali-speaking people in particular. The Assamese language, which had produced a poet, dramatist and reformer of the stature of Shankardev lost its position in its own land in 1837; Bengali became the language of administration and instruction, along with English, and it was only in 1873, thanks to the support given by the American missionaries settled in Sibsagar district and a few British civil servants, that the process was reversed and Assamese replaced Bengali as a language of administration and instruction. The jobs in government service, the tea and oil industries and in central undertakings like the railways and posts and telegraphs went to an increasing number of Bengalis and the trend continued after Independence as well. Cultivators from East-Bengal deprived the Assamese of large tracts of land and, in some cases, the plains' tribals and even caste Hindus had to surrender their villages in favour of the migrants and move to other places.

Despite the rise of a powerful Assamese middle class in the twentieth century, which came to control the levers of political power after Independence and important administrative positions that were previously the monopoly of Bengalis, the attitude of suspicion and hatred has not ebbed but further hardened for a variety of reasons. First, the Bengali factor is still real. Secondly, the Assamese intelligentsia fears that Muslim cultivators from Bangladesh, who have declared Assamese as their mother-tongue before a succession of census officials since 1951, are likely to declare Bengali as their mother-tongue in the next census. Finally, the Assamese have always resented Marwari control over Assam's food trade and the Punjabis from Delhi and Punjab for their domination in the field of consumer articles and the industry of the State. The presence of a work-force from Bihar and Uttar Pradesh, primarily as rickshaw pullers, agricultural labourers, road and embankment labourers is also disliked. All these groups remit their incomes outside the region.

The political movement since 1979 against 'aliens' in Assam has to be viewed in this larger background of an age-old suspicion and dislike of 'outsiders'. Although the leaders of the movement have clarified a number of times that their concern is the expulsion of foreigners or non-Indians, this attitude is not widely shared. In fact, it would be a positive contribution of the anti-alien movement in Assam if the suspicion of 'outsiders' is channelled only against 'foreigners', or non-Indians, for it would then help fuse the indigenous and migrant population from other parts of the country.

Besides, a number of things have occurred since Independence which have also had an adverse impact among the people of north-east India. The central government has not always paid adequate attention to the region, given its many other urgent. preoccupations. Besides, the sanctity of the ballot box suffered a great deal as a result of the election boycott in Nagaland in 1952. Loyalty to the social order largely accounted for the impressive continuity of the major social institutions in the region over many centuries. However, all these age-old values did not allow the growth of loyalty towards the political notion of the State, particularly in areas unaffected or only partially affected by the new winds of nationalism. Thus, in north-east India today, the primordial loyalties of class, tribe and religion demanded and still receive far greater loyalty than the idea of the State.

In recent years there has been a genuine and meaningful concern to give the people of Assam and north-east India a new deal in order to foster a durable nation-building process nourished by sound economic principles. There are, however, several debilitating factors, such as the lack of infrastructural facilities (particularly underdeveloped communications), primitive agricultural practices, unscrupulous exploitation of natural resources as well as misutilization of scarce materials. There is no regional centre and the elites are divided and lack a common perception. The sheer distance from New Delhi prevents the national capital from effectively supervising the critical tasks of economic development and the promotion of equity in the seven political units that constitute the region.

In the normal course, it would have been reasonable to expect that the planning process and expansion in State activity would gradually help national values to take strong roots even in remote parts of the region. But the failure of the national planning process to usher in an egalitarian social order is already having an adverse impact. The growing tendency among the national elite towards conspicuous expenditure and moral irresponsibility, is transparent in the behaviour of the ruling elites in north-east India as well. The middle class of the region has come to consider misutilization of scarce developmental resources in collaboration with the migrant business-class as a legitimate economic activity. Various

groups of people are used by politicians to thwart moves for rapid
industrialization in the region. For instance, in Meghalaya, the
construction of a 32 km railway track from Gauhati to Burnihat
has become the subject of controversy that exploits the cultural
and economic sensitivities of that State for narrow political objectives. Meghalaya currently has no rail link, but the construction
of the railway line is dubbed the 'greatest insult to the tribals of
Meghalaya'. The opposition to the project is based on the fear
that the railway line 'would open the floodgates for outsiders' and
thus affect the population structure of the State.

This attitude towards modernization is shared by a number of
people in north-east India. A senior journalist of Gauhati has said
that it is appropriate that the people of Meghalaya should oppose
the extension of the railway line into their state. The argument
advanced was that for smaller groups a few years of backwardness
may be preferable to the exploitation of the resources of the State
by others from outside. He went on to observe that it was a 'pity'
that the other states of the region were 'unable to evince the same
wisdom'. Fortunately, there is a section of people, particularly
among the indigenous youth, who would like rationalism to
inform various aspects of life in north-east India. In a signed article in the *Assam Tribune,* an Assamese intellectual posed the basic
choice that the people of north-east India have to make: The basic
question, therefore, if we are to survive and flourish, hinges on two
alternatives: either to master the art, the science and the commerce of a fast moving world and acclimatize ourselves to it or die
of the luxury of barren rumination.'[16]

The conflict between these two choices is unresovled at present.

CHAPTER III

The Middle Class, the Elite and Regional Consciousness

Although in India, including the north-eastern region, there existed a class of traders who operated over large areas, the traditional political system and the control of the state or community over land meant that a significant middle class did not grow till the advent of the British on the Indian scene. Even after the British annexation, traditional patterns of economic and educational development had their influence in determining the evolution, the nature and the size of the middle class in the region. Among the people of the plains who were closely linked with the rest of India, the middle class grew more rapidly than in the hill areas which were on the periphery of the greater Indian civilizational process. However, largely due to the influence of Christianity, Western economy and modernization, a middle class in the hills did eventually form and it began increasingly interacting with its counterparts in the plains. The middle class of the region not only played an important role in the freedom struggle but also had a major say in the evolution and management of a variety of political activities. It is instructive to delve into the role that the middle class plays in north-east India and its capabilities, both in terms of modernization and the integration of the region with the Indian society at large.

During the British period the middle class grew from the external compulsions of conquest and the need for playing a role, even if subservient, in the conqueror-conquered relationship at several strategic but still comparatively minor points. As a result, only those middle class groups which were necessary for this contact came into being, such as the professional groups of lawyers, doctors and salaried earners like clerks and teachers; in Assam, the intake of even these groups from the local societies was limited in view of the migration of both professionals and salaried personnel from neighbouring Bengal. In this growth process, the commercial intermediaries became less important. The growth in the tea and oil industries also did not lead to the development of an innovative Assamese middle class as in these areas Marwari traders played more important roles as bankers and foodgrain dealers than the local petty traders and businessmen. A small group of indigenous entrepreneurs were involved in the tea industry and the business in forest materials, but did not have much of influence on the economy. In fact, the middle class, being derivative in character, could not play an innovative role in the process of socio-economic change.

After Independence, politics as a career became fashionable amongst the middle classes all over the region and particularly in the Assam plains, where the freedom struggle had attracted a large number of young and educated persons. One of the significant achievements of the political leadership in the initial years of their management of the polity was in the establishment of new centres of education to train local youths for jobs in administration as well as in such professions as medicine, engineering and architecture. Actuated by a strong desire to subserve the interests of the expanding indigenous middle class the political leadership was expected to give preference to local talent as far as employment was concerned. As a result, the various middle class elements of the region concentrated on wresting the control of district and state administrative organs from the earlier dominant groups, mostly outsiders. The migrant middle class, however, continued to retain as well as expand its control over central government agencies and also had a major say in the utilization of development funds, thanks to a variety of historical reasons and its ability to go along with politicians and civil servants of other states.

As regards the middle class in tribal areas, two developments after Independence made an important impact on class composition. In the first place, the annual governmental expenditure had a decisive influence in converting *jhumia* cultivators into a class of contractors, traders, businessmen and middle-men between the politicians and migrant entrepreneurs. The amount of money injected into the tribal economy was several times greater than the total local revenue. It is, however another matter that in the initial years the local economy could not absorb the total allocations and their consequent generation of surpluses, which led to a transfer of wealth to areas outside the region. Secondly, due to the policy of reserved seats in legislatures and posts in the government, many educated tribals entered the Assemblies of their respective states, union territories as well as Parliament. The younger members of the various tribes not only joined the State services but also the all-India and the central services. The elected posts in the newly set-up district councils in tribal areas as well as administrative positions in development agencies provided fresh opportunities to the expanding indigenous middle class. Also, restrictions on the movement of outsiders in some tribal areas protected the interests of this new class.

Over the years, the new middle class in north-east India has come to consist of: (a) a group of tea planters; (b) the body of merchants, agents and proprietors of industries like jute, tea, forest goods, etc., along with contractors, foodgrain dealers and shop-keepers; (c) salaried personnel, like managers, inspectors, supervisors and the technical staff of private firms, public sector corporations and banks; (d) the main body of civil servants, both of the all-India services and the State services; and (e) members of professions — lawyers, doctors and teachers. The growth of the middle class, however, has followed different patterns in different areas. Some of the significant features of this development are summarized below.

During the Ahom period of governance in Assam (1228-1826), the Ahom nobility—the descendants of Sukapha and the seven original families that had accompanied him in the annexation of Assam— constituted the highest class. In terms of social prestige there was the class of priests and teachers, government officials and *satradhikars* who were exempted from personal service and were also entitled to keep slaves. The rest of the population rendered compulsory service to the state under the *khel* system. It was a feudal order and the middle hierarchy of this social system cannot strictly be treated as a 'middle class' in terms of an economic category. Similarly, in the hills, society comprised the tribal chiefs and the mass. The principal means of production, i.e, land and labour, were under the control of the community[1].

It was only after the annexation of Assam by the British that the region was opened to new ideas and institutions. Several factors led to the rise of a middle class in Assam. A middle class had already taken root in neighbouring Bengal and the British, led by David Scott, came to Assam after its annexation, with a band of Bengali clerks, officers and traders. The British introduced an education policy in Assam which helped produce administrators and clerks from among the indigenous Assamese. The gradual monetization of the economy by raising the land revenue and the introduction of the tea and oil industries brought in a class of merchants and entrepreneurs from outside the State, mostly from Rajasthan, who spread over the entire region and played an important role in the economy of north-east India even though generally in conflict with the indigenous population. The land administration of the British did not, however, create a zamindari system in the area, as a permanent settlement was confined to Goalpara and Cachar districts and the rest were either under the tribal or ryotwari system.

The efforts of British administrators like Major Jenkins to create a class of landed proprietors to take lead in agricultural and industrial undertakings had failed years before Independence. The resurrection of such a class was against the philosophy of the freedom struggle and it did not therefore occur in the Brahmaputra Valley. A typical representative of the Assamese middle class was Anandaram Dhekial Phukan (1821–59), a civil servant, who in a memorandum to the British government articulated the aspirations of the nascent Assamese middle class and later exhorted the people in the Brahmaputra Valley to emulate the Englishman's knowledge and diligence in the advancement of agriculture, industry and commerce[2]. The Assamese middle class was however particularly small in the pre-Independence era.

The spread of education after Independence swelled the ranks of both the professional groups of lawyers, doctors, etc. and salaried civil servants. The development funds and plans to construct flood control embankment, railway lines, national highways, industrial undertakings in the areas of oil, jute, paper, sugar, fertilizer and forest goods helped proliferate a class of indigenous contractors who overnight acquired wealth and a middle class status in society. New opportunities in the fields of transport, entertainment centres like cinema houses, consumer industries like soap, glass, match-boxes etc. also benefited this class.

However, in every productive activity the indigenous middle class was dependent upon its migrant counterparts and even on outside business houses. Thanks to a variety of historical and cultural factors, there never emerged a genuine coalition between the indigenous and migrant middle classes. The migrants always had the advantage, despite political power being in the hands of the indigenous Assamese middle class. In the early 1970s, I had the opportunity of witnessing a familiar pattern of relationship between the indigenous and migrant middle class in the distribution of a then scarce raw material, paraffin wax. The grant of permits for this commodity was a prerogative of the State government and always went to members of the indigenous middle class; but the permits were invariably sold to migrant entrepreneurs on a premium which provided only a short-term benefit to the seller. This kind of relationship is still prevalent in several fields of economic endeavour in Assam and elsewhere.

The inability of the indigenous middle class to run its affairs to its exclusive advantage has generated in it an inferiority complex as well as resentment. The sense of inferiority arises from the fact that the middle class of the region has capitalist aspirations and would like to see itself in the role of entrepreneurs and top executives. But its comparative lack of skills and the non-availability of capital in its hand gives it a subservient position in managements which are controlled by big business houses. The resentment of this class is a by-product of its semi-feudal and tribal attitude and its nostalgia for a past, when Assamese played a dominant role in every aspect of the socio-economic life of the Brahmaputra Valley. The more youthful members of this class have found fault both with the central government and the local political leadership for this phenomenon. While some of the movements, like those in Assam and Manipur have decried their politicians, the central government is always singled out as the principal culprit. In a situation where it feels hemmed in, the various movements led by the middle class have all been against the central government on the one hand, and, on the other, it has demanded protection for local or regional economic interests by that very central authority that it has been decrying[3].

In Manipur, the rule of the Maharaja led to the growth of a class of officers in the army, but it was a small group. The unorganized mass, like their counterparts in Assam during the Ahom period, gave free service to the Maharaja for ten in every forty days under the *lalup* system. The situation did not change much during the British period, as the State remained inaccessible and the old pattern of administration and management of the economy was not altered as in the Brahmaputra Valley. After Independence, a middle class grew both in the hills as well as in the plains While the educated youth in the hills benefited from reserved jobs due to their scheduled tribe status, the Hinduized Meiteis were denied this protection. It has to be appreciated that the Manipuris who dwell in the plains are of the same stock as the surrounding hill tribes, except that the former embraced Vaishnavism and those in the hills became Christian or remained animists. Limited economic opportunities, a large number of degree colleges and widespread corruption amongst politicians, civil servants and the indigenous as well as migrant middle classes in Manipur have greatly circumscribed the role of its middle class both as the agent of change and integration.

In Tripura the monarchical system was always manned by tribals and the army consisted of people drawn from various tribes. The earlier Hinduization of the tribes led to the migration of Bengali Hindu peasants from neighbouring east Bengal districts. In the social structure before Independence a middle class of army and civil officers, priests and landlords was above the masses and below the king and the tribal chiefs. The liberal encouragement of migration under the Tripura kings, the influx of Bengali refugees immediately after Partition and in subsequent years have reduced the tribals, who once constituted a majority in Tripura, into a minority. After Independence, the educated tribal middle class has strongly resented this development. Violent clashes have occurred and the economic developmental processes have been impeded, although the base of the middle class is growing on account of the rapid spread in education and developments in the fields of agriculture and industry: but a coalition between middle class tribals and middle class Bengalis is yet to emerge.

A special characteristic of social structure in north-east India is that the new middle class is virtually the highest class in the social order in Meghalaya, Nagaland, Mizoram and Arunachal Pradesh. In Meghalaya, the children of Khasi *syiems* (tribal chiefs) and Jaintia kings are in the middle class by virtue of their ownership of land, entry into the services, contract work, etc.[4] A class of indigenous moneylenders joined the middle class by acquiring property in urban areas. In the Garo Hills, the emergence of a middle class was a late event in view of the primitive character of its agriculture and its distance from Shillong and Gauhati. It was, in fact, urbanization around Tura that attracted the attention of businessmen and contractors. Earlier, petty shopkeepers and moneylenders from Rajasthan and some parts of north-India constituted the lower middle class. The situation started changing in the 1970s and in the Garo Hills the middle class is perhaps as significant today as its counterpart in the Jaintia Hills.

The growth of the middle class in Nagaland was intimately linked up with the spread of education and was not based either on a landed aristocracy, which never existed, or on commercial activity, which came only with the introduction of English education. Even here the middle class is the dominant group. It comprises the bureaucracy, businessmen from contractors to shopkeepers, and those belonging to independent professions, such as law and medicine. The migrant middle class is a product of the massive expenditure on development schemes dating back to the 1960s and consists of contractors, shopkeepers, foodgrain dealers, etc., from North India. They are mainly concentrated in Dimapur, which is outside the purview of 'inner-line'.

In Mizoram the middle class is largely a product of post-Independence years and the expansion in state activities, particularly after 1972 when Union Territory status was conferred on the erstwhile Lushai Hills district of Assam. The spread of primary and secondary education in Mizoram thanks to the efforts of Christian missionaries has provided a base for the growth of the middle class. The presence of outsiders, and the control of foodgrain trade, transport and other instruments of commerce by Silchar-based traders is resented in Mizoram.

In Arunachal Pradesh, which on the eve of Independence was 'a jumble of densely forested, sparsely inhabited roadless mountain⁵, a middle class is slowly developing with the tribal youth who have joined trade, politics and the services. There is no aristocracy in Arunachal Pradesh and there are signs that the middle class here will be innovative and likely to change the face of primitive society in the years to come.

In short, the middle class phenomenon in north-east India has four distinctive features: (1) the absence of a traditional bourgeoisie or capitalist class; (2) the contradictions and conflicts between two easily identifiable groups—the indigenous middle

class and the migrant middle class; (3) the control of the indigenous middle class over the apparatus of the State, including the
bureaucracy and agriculture, and of the migrant middle class over
industry and trade; large-scale and heavy industries, however, are
in the hands of the State or business houses located outside the region and in the agricultural operations of the Brahmaputra Valley,
Muslim cultivators from East Bengal constitute an important
influence; and (4) the economic leverage commanded by outside
economic forces.

Elite

Most civilized societies have relied at some stage on an elite or
inter-related groups of elites to provide a cohesion through their
codes of conduct, values and leadership. Different societies
evolved different types of elites; Japan was led by its warrior-
knights or the Samurai; China was held together by her mandarins
or scholar-administrators, and Britain by her landed aristocracy.
What are the chief characteristics of the elites in north-east India?

Uneven economic and educational developments have their
own impact on the attitudes and responses of indigenous elites. In
the north-east administrative headquarters like Shillong and
Gauhati and trade centres for newly found oil and tea like Dibrugarh, Jorhat and Tezpur were developed during the British
period and schools and health centres established. The spread of
Christian missionary activity in parts of Meghalaya, Mizoram
and Nagaland made primary education fairly widespread in these
areas. On the other hand, in Arunachal Pradesh, parts of Manipur, Tripura, Meghalaya and Assam, education as well as modern commerce could make rapid strides only after Independence.
As a result of this historical legacy, the level of consciousness
greatly varied between the elites of one area and another.

Different political units in north-east India have different elites
and a common elite group for the entire region has yet to emerge.
The economic interdependence amongst industrialists, businessmen and bankers, the regional planning forum of the North-
Eastern Council, the common High Court, the professional bodies
of doctors, lawyers, administrators and voluntary workers and the
operation of national political parties with comparable national

aims may, over the years, lead to the emergence of strong links bet-ween the various social elites of the region and, consequently, to greater understanding and integration in the society of the entire region.

In view of the dominant role of the state in north-east India, the political and administrative elites have a crucial function. They act in close co-operation with the elites that represent two social forces — ethnic and linguistic. Thus the recognized elders of various communities, authors and office bearers of such bodies as the Assam Sahitya Sabha and other linguistic organizations have a tremendous influence on government decision-making in their respective areas.

In pre-British times, the ruling classes in Assam held economic as well as political power. With the spread of the national movement political activists as well as theorists came to have the upper hand in Assamese society and hold the reins of political power. But the landed class of zamindars and *mauzadars*, and the cream of university graduates, who joined the Assam civil service, could no longer be ignored in view of their important administrative functions and a nexus thus formed among these groups. A few Assamese planters, a growing class of industrialists and businessmen have also played a supplementary role and helped further the consolidation of this indigenous elite.

It is interesting to highlight the relationship of the ruling class in Assam with those who control production, state power and ideology. Its relationship with the dominant landed group in Assam is very close. It favours small-scale industries by indigenous entrepreneurs. However, it does not have a close relationship with tea-plantation industry, which is largely in the hands of multinational companies and Indian capitalists based outside Assam. Similarly, the oil, paper and pulp industries are controlled by national-level public sector corporations and thus the State apparatus generally has a marginal say in them. The same is true of the railways, banks and post and telegraph organizations. The ruling class has, however, complete control over State power and its bureaucracy, including the all-India services. Its ideology is basically nationalist in character, but with the Assamese language and culture playing a very important role. The ruling class views itself as part of the national elite, but it has a distinctive or sub-regional outlook despite its affiliations with national political parties, the all-India services, the national bourgeoisie and capitalist class.

The ruling elites in Assam, like their counterparts elsewhere use their control over State power to ensure continuity of their dominant position in its apparatus, economy and administration In the face of an imminent threat to its continued hold over rep· resentation in the legislature—political power— the ruling groups of Assam started an agitation over the 'foreign nationals issue in 1979 demanding identification of aliens in Assam, their deportation to Bangladesh or dispersal to other states of India Similarly, in the early 1970s, in the face of growing unemployment among the educated youth of Assam, the State administration for· mulated employment policies to ensure jobs for local people in the public and private sectors[6]. The ruling class has also used its social power to repress through violence or coercion or local excommuni· cation all those who pose a threat to its dominance, as indicated by the numerous clashes with Bengali and Marwari traders.

The ruling class shares the ideology of the party in power at the centre, but depends on and draws strength from linguistic and ethnic forces. Whenever its regional interests seem to be in jeopardy, it has asserted itself more forcefully, as Gopinath Bar· doloi—the leader of Assam did against the Cripps Mission's grouping scheme in 1946, or B.P. Chaliha did in respect of the lan· guage issue in 1960, or with handing over of the control of law and order to the sub-state of Meghalaya in 1968. Whenever the Assamese ruling class has had a high representation in the Union Cabinet, as during 1971–7, the centre has had a greater say in Assam's affairs —as shown in the re-organization of Assam in 1971 or the treatment of minorities at the hands of the ruling class during 1973–7.

There has been a convergence between the interests of the mid· dle class and the traditional ruling elites or bourgeoisie in the north-east. By and large, this combined group has felt confident enough to control the levers of State power through the instrumen· tality of universal suffrage. Whenever it has felt threatened, whether in Nagaland, Mizoram or Assam, it has created situations where the holding of elections has been very difficult. What is the special strength of this group? The answer obviously lies in the politicization of ethnic ties which have no parallel elsewhere in the country. This essentially extra-economic system of 'influence' on the ballot box cuts across the class-system and, at the same time, reinforces it. There has never been a socio-economic revolution from the bottom in any part of north-east India and most of the social reformers and even insurgency leaders, have come from the upper echelons of their respective societies. In the absence of a social upheaval, an ethnic group has become transformed into a political group, and we thus find more ethnic conflicts than class conflicts in north-east India. Only when ethnic loyalties clash with national-level capitalist groups or national political leadership do violent clashes occur between ethnic groups on the one side and the state's security forces on the other. The most ethnic groups have maintained their hold over the levers of political power through their membership of the Congress party or, in the case of Bengalis, with the dominant group in Calcutta.

However, the traditional ruling elites are losing their independence in Assam not because of pressures and interference from the Centre but because of (a) increasing influence of capitalists, traders, contractors, and businessmen over the State's administrative decision-making process; and (b) the State's inability to accommodate the aspirations of the youth of hitherto suppressed groups of tribals and Muslims who are beginning to demand a central place in the economy and polity of the region. The rapid socialization between business, the services and politics in north-east India is a phenomenon that is noticeable even to visitors to the region. The ruling elites in each political unit of north-east India are facing challenges from all those groups which are numerically powerful and progressing with the spread of education—Muslims and the plains' tribals in Assam, the Garos and Jaintias in Meghalaya, the Meiteis in Manipur and tribals in Tripura.

It has also to be appreciated that the existing dominant class has neither the opportunity nor the capability for formation and consolidation outside the state and/or the region and in the circumstances it would naturally depend upon ethnic links and at times manipulate ethnic discontents and even trounce democratic rules-of-the game in the pursuit of victory and continued hold over reins of economic and political power. The need for the national elite to interact with the various groups of the region and accommodate their genuine aspirations are thus greater.

Regional Consciousness

The term regionalism 'properly represents the regional idea in

action as an ideology and as a social movement"[7]. North-East
India is not under the grip of such a regional philosophy or move
ment. The majority of the people inhabiting the area are still com
posed of a traditional social order where people have a sense o
belonging only to a village, a hill tract or a valley. The Nagas or th
Mizos are more attached to their hills than most other things. Th
modernization process is enlarging their spatial consciousnes
beyond a village, a hill or a valley to that of the north-east or th
nation, and in certain respects the participation of the some o
groups of the area in the national movement created a consciousnes
of belonging to a nation. But this was confined largely to the plains.

For most tribes 'regionalism' is even narrower than 'north-east'
It essentially denotes ethnic, linguistic or caste groups and these
qualities are placed higher than national interests or values
Nationalism would perhaps curtail tribal, clan, religious or feuda
loyalties and simultaneously spread secularism and loyalty
towards the nation-state. Some conflicts between regional con
sciousness and national consciousness are possibly implicit in a
large and varied country like India, but the essence of India's
national integration lies in unity and diversity not being mutually
exclusive but complementary to each other.

Looking at the situation from this perspective, say in Assam, we
find that, like an average Indian, an average Assamese is wel
aware of both his regional and Indian identities. The importan
difference is that an average Assamese, unlike an average Indiar
of Bihar or U.P., is more uncertain about his future. He naturally
wants the security and comfort that speaking Assamese brings to
him. He abhors confrontation and desires to be left alone. In thi:
setting, he considers the Brahmaputra Valley solely his possessior
and resents the entry of non-Assamese into the region and view:
them as intruders. Only a very small percentage of those educated
outside are comfortable when socializing with 'outsiders'. Foi
others, government service, contracts and business made availa
ble since Independence have helped create new demands and a
noticeable craving for consumer goods. If this narrow outlook pre
vails amongst the Assamese community, who have historicall'
been the chief exponents of Indian cultural unity in north-eas
India, the aspirations and preferences of small tribes can well b
imagined. Some of them were not touched by the national move
ment and are now facing exposure not only to modernization and

education for the first time, but also to international propaganda and intrigue.

The reorganization of States on the basis of language gave an impetus to regionalism in the country. The primacy of Assamese in Assam was formalized by the State legislature in 1960, but in an area so diverse it only aggravated existing misgivings concerning suggestions to have a single state of Assam covering the entire north-east region. This was, indeed, unfortunate as over the years the Assamese plainsmen, had acted as the torch bearers of ideas in the north-east and spread the Ramayana–Mahabharata tradition in the region through the Assamese language. This cultural unity of various races in the north-east was evident in their folklores, songs and rituals and bound them to the rest of India. After Independence, many officials and anthropologists genuinely believed that further assimiliation of the hillmen could be advanced through the Assamese language, a language which was particularly familiar to several tribes and was increasingly viewed as the regional lingua franca. The efforts of Assamese leaders like Bishnuram Medhi were misunderstood as the Assam government formulated schemes which envisaged posting plains' officers in the hills and vice versa and the insistence that tribal officers learn Assamese. And the later induction of Hindi in place of Assamese caused a functional alteration in the medium of communication which had operated for centuries in the hills. The implications of their change were far from conducive to the integration of the hills and the plains. Over the years, the language issue in north-east India, and particularly in Assam has become highly emotive and controversial and is a major political factor.

There is also a psychology of isolation which has been perpetuated by the 'inner-line' system. The 'inner-line' was originally devised to curb an impetuous British administration and greedy tea planters from disturbing the tribal ecology in Arunachal Pradesh, Nagaland and Mizoram. Today, the inner-line is being widely demanded and this restrictive system is regarded as the only effective mechanism for the protection of the tribal 'identity' and 'culture'. There are many who would like to see this line over the Brahmaputra Valley as well. This has largely been a reaction to the massive influx of foreign nationals in north-east India, large-scale alienation of the land of the plains' tribals in Assam and Tripura, and exploitation of the local people not only by their own socially rich but also by the merchants, moneylenders and others from Bengal, Bihar, Rajasthan and Punjab. The faith of the regionalists in laws to obstruct the physical movement of population and the acquisition of land by outsiders is such that they do not appreciate the power of those who have already rendered in-effective the inner-line system in the tribal belts and blocks of the Brahmaputra Valley. In Nagaland, students in 1982 detected or a single day several hundred violators of inner-line permits in Kohima, the capital of the State.

Another factor which has helped isolationist and chauvinis ideas to flourish in north-east India has been decline in the role o voluntary organizations in socialization and development tasks In ancient times Hinduism was the uniting factor between the var ious groups of people inhabiting north-east India. During the British period the role of the Church in the spread of education and health cannot be overemphasized. Hindu institutions and the Church are still active in north-east India, but they no longer ac in concert with the State. This is a logical corollary of India's faith in secularism, and, despite the many virtues of the new order, the impact of religious foundations in social programmes has been emasculated.

Mahatma Gandhi's constructive programmes and various workers' organizations in the fields of education, health and khad and village industries was a very viable substitute for the Church and Satras in the socialization process. In the 1950s, when Bhoodan, Gramdan and Sarvodaya workers engaged in the task o social reconstruction, working in close co-operation with the Con gress party which, in turn controlled the State apparatus all over the country including north-east India, things moved very wel under Vinoba Bhave's leadership. After the Chinese aggression in 1962, Vinoba Bhave set up Maitree Ashram in North-Lakhimpu for the promotion of friendship among the tribes and plainsmen He also sent voluntary workers to the hills to spread his message of love to the people of Tibet and China through voluntary con tacts. As a district officer at North-Lakhimpur (during 1966–8), i was my privilege to have been associated with voluntary workers of the Ashram in the task of social upliftment and co-operation Over the years, various organizations were formed and it seemed possible that integration and economic development could be facilitated through Gandhian workers. The Sarania Ashram a

Gauhati, economic development centres at Kumarikata and Dhamdhama in Assam, the various Shanti-sena Mandals in Arunachal Pradesh, the Peace Centre at Kohima, the organs of the Bhartiya Admjati Sevak Sangh and Khadi & Village Industries Commission all over north-east India and several other organizations were deeply involved in social reconstruction. The failure of the Bhoodan movement and, much more importantly, the split in the Sarvodaya movement over the question of direct political action under the banner of Jayaprakash Narayan's ideas of total revolution in 1974, broke the understanding between voluntary organizations, the Congress party, the governments at the centre and in the states almost completely. The reconstruction of this understanding during the Janata administration was short-lived. From 1980 onwards there has been a steady decline in the activities of voluntary organizations and a total lack of interaction between the State and social workers. This tendency is likely to continue and thus deprive the nation-building tasks in north-east India of a major source of voluntary assistance. There is no doubt that some organizations of the Christian missionaries and the Vishwa Hindu Parishad are working in the region along with those of the Ramakrishna Mission, Sankar Mission and a few others, but there is a lack of overall direction and co-ordination. The point of contact of these organizations with the State is confined merely to the grant or renewal of residential permits, arms licences, the allotment of scarce materials and, at times, land.

The forces of regionalism and isolationism will decline with national attention being focussed on the north-east. There has, of late, been a rapid growth in communications and transport in north-east India. One hopes that modern agriculture and industrialization will follow this development. The most hopeful feature, however, is widespread literacy and the knowledge of English in the region. It holds the great potential of making various ethnic groups see and achieve equality of opportunity in the services and every sphere of economic development and, in the process, to gain a vision of India.

CHAPTER IV

The Political System

The Indian political system is an amalgam of two pre-Independence administrative and political patterns. One is the old administrative-governmental process charged with the regulatory functions of maintenance of law and order and the collection of revenue; and the other is the comparatively more recent politicization of a fragmented social structure brought together under the leadership of the Indian National Congress with the avowed goal of attaining independence and political and economic equality. After Independence, while political parties assumed the role of manning the legislature and running the government, the administrative system was entrusted with the additional responsibility of planned development. It has been mentioned earlier that in several parts of north-east India administration was merely symbolic during the British period, even in respect of its regulatory tasks. Similarly, the Congress, which was a vibrant public movement in the plains of Assam, was not known in many of the hill areas. The growth of political organizations was slow in the hills[1]. Not surprisingly therefore, in the early years after Independence several areas of north-east India witnessed a clash between attempts towards a greater integration and forces representing communitarian, tribal or ethnic consolidation. It must, however, be said to the credit of the national political parties, particularly the Congress, that they succeeded in a substantial measure through the efforts of their workers and opinion leaders in spreading political reforms, values and ideologies amongst the various ethnic groups inhabiting the entire length and breadth of north-east India. The civil servants, too, moved fast and dotted the landscape with institutions of development, communications and law and order to carry out the new tasks.

Development activity and elections generated almost a new kind of socialization process where talk about electricity, roads, health centres and whom to vote for were accorded an important place, almost side-by-side with the traditional songs, dances, rituals, etc. Hindi and, later, Assamese and Bengali films and the radio network helped the spread of new ideas and modes of consumption; linguistic loyalties were strong elements of the social character and also deeply influenced the political process leading to the growth of local or regional political groupings. There is no denying that national political parties showed appreciation of and concern for local customs and sensitivities. As a result, both national parties and local or regional groups seek mandates from the electorate, with regional forces concentrating more on representation to the State legislatures[2].

Against this backdrop, it is instructive to study the election results during thirty years (1952-82) in Assam, and particularly from 1972 onwards, when Assam was reorganized[3]. For our purposes, we club independents and regional political groups together and consider them as representative of regional forces. It is also instructive to note not only the political affiliations of candidates who won the elections but also the percentage of votes polled by the national political parties and the regional forces[4].

Assam had twelve representatives in the Lok Sabha during 1952-62 and fourteen thereafter. In the first general elections to the Lok Sabha in 1952, Assam sent 11 Congressmen and 1 Socialist; in 1957 there were 9 Congressmen, 2 Socialists and 1 Independent; the 1957 performance was repeated in 1962. In the 1967 elections, Assam sent 14 members to the Lok Sabha: 10 Congressmen, 1 Communist, 2 from the Praja Socialist Party (PSP) and 1 Independent; in 1971 there were 13 Congressmen and 1 Independent. This suggests a decline in the influence of the socialists and communists by 1971 as far as representation to the Lok Sabha was concerned. The regional forces got no representation in 1952, but consistently had one member from 1957 onwards. So far as the percentage of votes is concerned, the regional forces polled 22.7 per cent of the votes in 1957, 25.73 per cent in 1962, 22.85 per cent in 1967 and 24.43 per cent in 1971.

The story in respect of elections to the Assam Legislative Assembly during 1952-72 is, however, different. The regional forces secured greater representation to the Assembly and a larger percentage of the total votes polled than in the Lok Sabha elections. In 1952, in a house of 108, Independents and others secured 26 seats and polled 32.2 per cent of the votes as against 76 seats secured by the Congress, 1 by the Communist Party and 5 by the PSP. In 1957, in a house of 108, Independents and others secured 25

seats and got 26.80 per cent of the votes as against the 71 seats won
by the Congress, 4 by the Communist and 8 by PSP. In 1962, the
national political parties fared better as far as total representation
was concerned: the regional forces secured only 20 seats, although
they p' ''ed 30.73 per cent of the votes, against 79 seats secured by
the Co.,gress and 6 by the PSP. In 1967, the strength of the Assembly was raised to 126 and the regional groupings got as many as 35
seats and 31.48 per cent of the votes as against 73 seats that went
to the Congress, 3 to the Swatantra Party, 7 to the Communist
Party, 5 to the PSP and 4 to Socialists. During 1967, the Congress
lost the elections in several states in north-India and SVD
(Samyukta Vidhayak Dal) governments were formed in some.

The reorganization of Assam, as stated earlier, was in pursuance of the demands for separation from Assam by various tribal
groups. Hence it is necessary to analyse the nature of political representation in all seven political units of the region from 1972
onwards, particularly in respect of the Assembly elections. This
analysis will also help us view the future of the political system in
the region:

Assam has been the main centre in the region of political debate.
The statistical projections given below show sizeable support for
regional forces in the State.

Assam has always witnessed two contrary pulls—a national
integrating ethos, and a regional or 'Brahmaputra Valley' outlook. The conflict between the Brahmaputra Valley and the
Surma Valley or between Assamese and Bengalis, continued into
the post-Independence years and buttressed local chauvinistic
feelings. On the other hand, the involvement of the people in the
freedom struggle and efforts to improve socio-economic conditions
under the aegis of the Congress made them view themselves in an
all-India framework of values and aspirations. From many angles,
it would be appropriate to conclude that national forces succeeded
in giving a lead to socio-political change after Independence,
although chauvinstic and regional feelings did not die but were
only kept under manageable proportions. One significant result of
this phenomenon was that the regional parties in the
Brahmaputra Valley consistently failed to become deep-rooted.
The rise and fall of the Assam Jatiya Mahasabha in the 1930s, the
Ahom Sabha, the United People's Party and the Samadal Party in
the 1940s and 1950s, and the Peoples Democratic Party in the

1960s convey the same story. During the 1983 elections to the Assembly, Muslim domination in the Congress and other national parties became obvious: out of 110 constituencies in which elections were held, as many as 32 Muslims were returned to the Assembly.

Elections to the Legislative Assembly

4.1 Assam

S.No. Name of Party	Year of General Elections					
	1972		1978		1983	
	% of votes	No. of seats	% of votes	No. of seats	% of votes	No. of seats
A. *National Parties*						
1. INC	53.29	95	8.78	8	51.54	91
2. Socialist	5.77	4	–	–	–	–
3. KMPP.	–	–	–	–	–	–
4. C.P.I.	5.6	3	4.09	5	1.81	–
5. Jan Sangh	0.27	–	–	–	–	–
6. PSP	–	–	–	–	–	–
7. Swatantra	0.53	1	–	–	–	–
8. SSP	–	–	–	–	–	–
9. CPI (M)	2.59	–	5.63	11	3.82	2
10. RPI	–	–	–	–	–	–
11. INC (O)	0.47	–	–	–	–	–
12. INC (I)	–	–	23.62	26	4.18	2
13. Janata Party	–	–	27.55	53	–	–
TOTAL	68.52	103	69.67	103	61.35	95
B. *Regional Parties*						
14. PTCA	–	–	–	–	3.80	3
15. Other Parties	1.73	–	4.66	–	–	–
16. Independents	29.75	–	25.67	23	19.23	10
TOTAL	31.48	11	30.33	23	23.03	13
GRAND TOTAL	100	114	100	126	84.38	108

Source: Report on General Elections 1982–3, Statistical, p.638 [In the 1983 Assembly elections 4 seats were uncontested and, thanks to violence, no elections were held in 17 constituencies.]

The agitation over the aliens issue in the Brahmaputra Valley during 1979-85 has fully exploited the xenophobia inherent in the Assamese psyche, and the weakness of the Congress in these years has allowed the people to undergo an intensely regional experience. Leading Assamese intellectuals and even civil servants have presented the movement before the masses as a 'life and death issue' in the struggle to retain the cultural identity and language so dear to them. Also, the failure of the all-India parties to assert themselves in the Brahmaputra Valley as effective spokesmen of the genuine fears of the people further strengthened the regional forces in Assam. A predictable political development was that regional feelings would later be manipulated to explore the possibility of forming a combined regional party. In the beginning of 1984, the All-Assam Students Union (AASU) was authorized to explore the possibility of merging regional parties, such as the Asom Jatiyatabadi Dal (AJD), the Purbanchaliya Lok Dal (PLD), Karbi-Anglong People's Conference (KAPC), and the Plains Tribal Council of Assam (PTCA). The various organizations spearheading the agitation over the aliens issue as well as the existing regional parties share the belief that a regional party can only best serve Assam's interest as an equal federating partner of the Indian Union and free the state from the colonial exploitation by the Centre[5].

There is also widespread feeling that the local leadership of the all-India parties pays little attention to local problems since it owes its position in the party as well as the government more to its equation with the central leadership than the support of the local people. It is believed that the central leadership, preoccupied with national and international issues, has little knowledge or appreciation of regional interests, no matter how important these interests might be for the cultural identity of the region or its economic growth. Meanwhile, the nationalist forces have been resurrected with the emergence of a strong Congress party on the scene managing the affairs of the State government under the leadership of Hiteswar Saikia in 1983. The response of the people in future elections to regional and nationalist parties will be interesting to watch. This aspect has been dealt with in the Epilogue.

Nagaland

Nagaland has been the principal centre in north-east India of narrow ethnic loyalties and secessionist thinking. The position changed slightly after the 1974 elections; after the 1982 elections the Congress formed a government in Nagaland. The following table shows the party position:

4.2 Nagaland

S.No. Name of Party	Year of General Elections					
	1974		1977		1982	
	% of votes	Seats	% of votes	Seats	% of votes	Seats
A. *National Parties*						
1. I.N.C.	–	–	20.44	15	32.08	24
TOTAL	–	–	20.44	15	32.08	24
B. *Regional Groups*						
2. United Democratic Front	30.01	25	39.21	35	–	–
3. Naga Nationalist Organization (Supported by the INC)	35.71	23	–	–	–	–
4. National Convention of Nagaland	–	–	11.86	1	32.01	24
5. Independents	34.28	12	28.49	9	–	–
6. NNDP	–	–	–	–	35.91	12
TOTAL	100.00	60	79.56	45	67.92	36
GRAND TOTAL	100.00	60	100.00	60	100.00	60

The success of the institutions of parliamentary democracy in Nagaland is of relevance to all people who seek to establish principles in the management of human affairs, principles that oppose the forces of traditionalism, insurgency and deep mistrust. A brief historical sketch will help in understanding this phenomenon. The evolution of parliamentary institutions in Nagaland fall into three periods, namely 1950-62, 1963-73 and 1974 onwards.

During the British period, the major part of the present Nagaland was a district of Assam. After Independence, this arrangement was continued, notwithstanding the opposition of an important section of Nagas who wanted an independent, sovereign state for themselves. Under the Sixth Schedule of the Indian Constitution, the Naga Hills became an autonomous district of Assam, with a district council for their local administration. The Naga Hills were allocated three seats in the Assam Legislative Assembly and one in the Lok Sabha. In the first general elections of February 1952 the electoral process could not take root in Nagaland as, at the instance of Phizo the Naga people did not seek election either to the State Assembly or the Lok Sabha and none voted although arrangements had been made by the Election Commission to hold the election. The second general election of February 1957 was preceded by a split in the Nagaland National Council and a new group led by T.N. Angami declared its intention to participate in the elections. This group became a political party called the Naga Nationalist Organization (NNO) and in the elections three of its candidates were elected uncontested to the Assembly and one to the Lok Sabha. The growth of parliamentary institutions was at best halting and lacking in promise.

   The second half of the 1950s witnessed a fierce armed conflict between the underground Nagas and the security forces on the one hand, and a well-meaning search towards enlargement of their democratic rights by the Naga people on the other. The Central government, supported by nationalist moderate Nagas, found an honourable solution by granting a separate state to the Nagas. Accordingly, Nagaland was carved out of Assam and made into a State on 11 December 1963, even though it then had a population of 0.3 million only. The first election to the Nagaland Legislative Assembly was held in January 1964 and candidates of the NNO (a party close to the Indian National Congress) and the newly formed Democratic Party competed for forty-six Assembly seats and one seat for the Lok Sabha; the NNC, led by Phizo, boycotted the elections as before. The NNO, led by Shilu Ao, formed the first government in Nagaland. However, the elections and consequent formation of a Government did not usher in either a fully participating democracy or peace in Nagaland. The forces of insurgency articulated the proud and independent character of the Nagas even as the forces of democracy had used the tradition of democracy in Naga society to make it participate in elections. The results were mixed. On the one hand, the new State administration chartered an ambitious plan for development, and, on the other the underground Nagas organized more determined violence which made them clash with the security forces. The Democratic Party was dissolved in 1964 after the elections.

The second Assembly elections in Nagaland were held in February 1969 and the contest was mainly between the NNO and the United Front, a group of political activists which included erstwhile underground elements, dissatisfied elements of the NNO and Independents. The elections attracted more than 75 per cent of the voters and witnessed lively debates about the policies and programmes of the two main parties. The NNO, led by Hokishe Sema formed the government. Although the electoral process aroused tremendous interest during 1963-73, democracy was yet to become a fully participatory system in Nagaland and there was widespread belief that the civilian government at Kohima was a 'stage-managed' show by the rulers at New Delhi.

The most crucial test for the survival of democracy in Nagaland took place immediately after the results of the February 1974 elections were announced. In this the United Democratic Front (UDF), a party composed of NNO dissidents and persons who were sympathetic to, and in touch with, the underground, emerged as the single largest party with 25 seats (in a house of 60); the NNO won 23 seats and there were 12 Independents. At the time of reckoning, the NNO secured the allegiance of only 5 Independents while the UDF had the support of 7, bringing its strength to 32. There were several powerful interests that genuinely felt it was advisable for the Centre to impose President's Rule rather than risk national security by appointing a UDF ministry. The Governor of Nagaland had a most difficult decision to make, placed as he was between the claims of his oath to the Constitution and a possible harsh verdict from history for having played with the integrity of India. L.P. Singh, the Governor, acting in consonance with the oath that he had taken, invited the leader of the UDF., Vizol Angami, to form the government. The gravity of the situation is aptly described by L.P. Singh himself:

> How could I pre-judge the possible behaviour of the UDF when their leaders had been declaring for months that they would act within the limits of the Constitution and the law? It appeared to me that it was better to act honestly in the spirit of the Constitution and to find later that one's trust had been misplaced, than to discover later that it had been a serious mistake to act on distrust. It seemed to me that our duty

being to get the Indian constitution, and its democratic processes, fully
accepted by the Naga people,it would be utterly self-defeating, if I,
having taken an oath to uphold the Constitution, were to give a deadly
blow to the Constitution in Nagaland of all places. I could also see
that if I did not act constitutionally, large sections of Naga people
would lose faith in the sincerity of our constitutional and democratic
professions, and our credibility in general would be destroyed. One of
the first consequences, I was certain, would be eruption of large-scale
violence which we could, no doubt, control but only at a fearsome loss
of life[6].

The 1974 experiment brought home to the underground that the
constitutional system can reflect the genuine desire of the electorate
and that, once it was expressed, the Constitution enjoined upon all its
instruments. The very fact that the NNO which was close to the Congress, could become an opposition party after remaining in power for
a decade because the Naga people willed it so helped establish respect
for the democratic process in Nagaland.

The subsequent elections in Nagaland in 1977 and 1982 have
helped to normalize the functioning of the democratic system. The
merger of the NNO with the Congress in February 1975 marked the
evolution of a regional party seeking to bring national-level policies to
Nagaland and was a precursor of the merger of the All-Party Hill
Leaders' Conference (APHLC) of Meghalaya with the Congress in
1976. That the political system in Nagaland is not free from defections
and other evils of patronage only proves that the nature of democracy
in this State is similar to that of other States in India! There is a small,
disgruntled group in Naga society, within the State as well as outside,
who consider democracy a 'sham' and would like Nagaland to secede
from the Indian Union. But such elements are losing support as
democratic processes are gradually integrating the Naga people into
processes of economic development and modernization. The nation
could reasonably be proud of a moderately stable constitutional culture in Nagaland, particularly against the backdrop of the earlier violence.

Meghalaya

For Meghalaya, statehood itself was a product of a regional movement under the banner of the APHLC. But over the years, and as
a result of the merger of regional groups with the Congress, politi-

cal power ultimately came into the Congress fold. The statistics
are as follows:

4.3 Meghalaya

S.No. Name of Party	Year of General Elections					
	1972		1978		1982	
	% of votes	Seats	% of votes	Seats	% of votes	Seats
A. *National Parties*						
1. INC	9.89	9	1.44	Nil	28.97	25
2. CPI	0.57	Nil	0.62	Nil	0.69	Nil
3. INC (I)	–	–	28.96	20	–	–
4. Janata Party	–	–	–	–	0.03	Nil
TOTAL	10.46	9	31.02	20	29.69	25
B. *Regional Groups*						
5. All-Party Hill Leaders Conference	35.67	32	24.92	16	24.09	15
6. Hill State People's Democratic Party	–	–	19.24	14	19.62	14
7. People's Demand Implementation Committee	–	–	–	–	4.93	2
8. Independents	53.86	19	24.82	10	21.67	4
TOTAL	89.53	51	68.98	40	70.31	35
GRAND TOTAL	100.00	60	100.00	60	100.00	60

Manipur

Manipur has been under the persistent grip of regional forces. A
majority of representatives from regional parties were elected to
the Assembly in 1972 and 1974. The elections in 1980 no doubt
brought the Congress to power through several permutations and
combinations, but political instability and infighting within the
Congress are recurring features in the political management of the
State. The Meiteis' revolt and the disenchantment of youth with
the electoral process are portents which strengthen ethnic movements even at the cost of national interest. In the 1984 election, the

rebel leader, Biseswar, was elected to the Assembly. The table below shows the position in perspective.

4.4 Manipur

S.No. Name of Party	Year of General Elections							
	1972		1974		1980		1984	
	% of votes	Seats	% of votes	Seats	% of votes	Seats	% of votes	Seats
A. National Parties								
1. INC (I)	30.02	17	27.62	13	21.63	13	NA	30
2. Congress (O)	2.37	1	1.47	–	–	–	„	–
3. Jan Sangh	0.22	–	–	–	–	–	„	–
4. CPI	10.13	5	5.54	6	7.26	5	„	1
5. C.P.M.	0.66	Nil	0.56	–	0.57	1	„	–
6. Socialist Party	5.35	3	5.93	2	–	–	„	–
7. Janata Party	–	–	–	–	19.84	10	„	4
8. Janata Party(S)	–	–	–	–	2.83	–	„	–
9. INC (U)	–	–	–	–	9.48	6	„	–
TOTAL	48.75	26	41.12	21	61.61	35	„	35
B. Regional Groups								
10. Manipur People's Party	20.17	15	22.55	20	6.59	4	NA	3
11. Kuki National Assembly	–	–	–	–	2.82	2	„	1
12. Other Parties	–	–	12.32	14	–	–	„	–
13. Independents	31.8	19	24.01	5	28.98	19	„	21
TOTAL	51.25	34	58.88	39	38.39	25	„	25
GRAND TOTAL	100.00	60	100.00	60*	100.00	60	„	60

Tripura

Tripura has always been dominated by the national political parties. Even under the heat generated by clashes between tribals and

Bengalis, the people of Tripura returned the Marxists to power in 1983. It should be possible for the national parties to remain the centre of political adjustment in the years to come. The facts are as follows:

4.5 Tripura

S.No. Name of Party	Year of General Elections					
	1972		1978		1983	
	% of votes	Seats	% of votes	Seats	% of votes	Seats
A. *National Parties*						
1. INC	44.83	41	17.76	–	30.51	12
2. Jan Sangh	0.07	–	–	–	0.06	–
3. CPI	3.04	1	0.84	–	0.82	–
4. CPM	37.82	16	47.00	51	46.78	37
5. Forward Bloc	1.14	–	1.04	1	–	–
6. R.S.P.	–	–	1.66	2	1.64	2
7. Janata Party	–	–	10.46	–	0.06	-
TOTAL	86.90	58	78.76	54	79.87	51
B. *Regional Groups*						
8. Tripura Upajati Juba Sangh	1.17	–	7.78	4	10.47	6
9. Other Parties	–	–	9.20	–	0.70	–
10. Independents	11.93	2	4.26	2	8.96	3
TOTAL	13.10	2	21.24	6	20.13	9
GRAND TOTAL	100.00	60	100.00	60	100.00	60

Mizoram

The insider-outsider syndrome has always generated considerable heat and occasional violence in Mizoram. The induction of national parties into Mizoram's polity was difficult, although both the Congress and Janata obtained substantial support in the 1979 elections. The government of the People's Conference has been acting in concert with the policies of the central government. The representation of regional forces in the legislature is likely to increase if the MNF participates in the electoral process. Meanwhile, the Congress was given a clear mandate to rule Mizoram in the 1984 elections. The table below shows the position:

4.6 Mizoram

S.No. Name of Party	Year of General Elections							
	1972		1974		1980		1984	
	% of votes	Seats	% of votes	Seats	% of votes	Seats	% of votes	Seats
A. *National Parties*								
1. INC (I)	30.91	6	–	–	23.88	5	39.82	19
2. Socialist Party	1.54	–	–	–	–	–	–	–
3. Janata Party	–	–	–	–	13.09	2	–	–
TOTAL	32.45	6	–	–	36.97	7	39.82	19
B. *Regional Groups*								
4. People's Conference	–	–	37.47	22	32.67	18	35.54	8
5. Independents	67.55	24	62.53	8	30.36	5	24.64	2
TOTAL	67.55	24	100.00	30	63.03	23	60.18	10
GRAND TOTAL	100.00	30	100.00	30	100.00	30	10.00	29

Elections for 1 seat were held on 27 June 1984, and it was won by the INC.

Arunachal Pradesh

Despite regional proclivities, those elected in Arunachal Pradesh have always endeavoured to bring their people into the mainstream of national life. The administration in Arunachal Pradesh has helped increase the tempo of literacy in this Union Territory which is inhabited by some of the most primitive tribes in the world. The political representation here was as follows in 1978 and 1980:

4.7 Arunachal Pradesh

S.No. Name of Party	Year of General Elections					
	1978		1980		1984	
	% of votes	Seats	% of votes	Seats	% of votes	Seats
A. *National Parties*						
1. INC	–	–	42.58	.13	NA	21
2. INC (U)	0.45	–	4.90	–	,,	–
3. Janata Party	42.08	17	–	–	,,	–
4. B.J.P.	–	–	–	–	,,	1
TOTAL	42.53	17	47.48	13	,,	22
B. *Regional Groups*						
5. Peoples' Party of Arunachal	30.24	8	40.98	13	,,	4
6. Independents	27.23	5	11.54	–	,,	4
TOTAL	57.47	13	52.52	17	,,	8
GRAND TOTAL	100.00	30	100.00	30	,,	30

The Lok Sabha election results during 1972–83 show that in 1977 Assam elected only one person representing regional forces, and none out of only 2 seats for which elections were held in 1980. No person representing regional forces was elected to the Lok Sabha from Manipur and Tripura during the 1977 and 1980 elections. In Nagaland and Mizoram, on the other hand, the national parties drew a blank both in 1977 and 1980. In 1977 Arunachal Pradesh and Meghalaya sent one person each to the Lok Sabha who represented regional forces. In 1980, the Congress won both the seats in Arunachal Pradesh and one in Meghalaya (no election was held for the other seat in 1980). In 1983, the Congress won all five Lok Sabha seats for which elections were completed. This, however, does not mean a decline in the influence of regional parties or groups, for they had decided to boycott the elections in Assam and in this act they were supported by two national level parties—the Janata Party and Bharatiya Janata Party.

The regional parties in north-east India are prone to break-up like many national political parties. Since the regional political parties are deprived of a remote central body like the High Command of a national party, which plays a decisive role in maintaining party unity in the face of personality clashes, the regional parties break-up more easily and become weak and ineffective. The break-up of the APHLC, a regional party which was primarily responsible for the creation of Meghalaya, is a classic case in point. In this collapse, Captain Williamson A. Sangma and his Garo supporters joined the Congress; Hopingstone Lyngdoh and his followers resurrected another party called HSPDP; and B.B. Lyngdoh formed an APHLC of his own image and following. There are various other regional groups in Meghalaya seeking popular support. The personality clashes that arise from the relentless pursuit of capturing power to the determinent of public interest characterizes most disorganized, regional groups. Except for the People's Conference in Mizoram, regional parties in Arunachal Pradesh, Manipur, Tripura and Assam have split-up on account of this factor. In Assam, the break-up of the AAGSP, leading to the expulsion of its leader Nibaran Bora in 1982, was a similar event.

There was a major attempt in 1976, to merge the regional parties of north-east India with the Indian National Congress and the All-India Congress Committee Session held at Gauhati in November 1976 was a landmark in this direction. However, the experiment, did not succeed and the defeat of the Congress at the Centre and its break-up in 1978 led to its disintegration in northeast India as well. In 1980 a regional body of the Congress was formed for north-east India with Captain Sangma as convenor, but it is not free from the usual internal squabbles. Thus, its capacity to give political back-up to the North-Eastern Council is very limited. Various leftist parties have formed a coalition that has been in power in Tripura for a second term commencing in 1983. There is a similar alliance of leftist parties in Assam as well. The regional forces in north-east India are also making concerted efforts to unite themselves. In December 1983 a meeting of regional parties was held at Gauhati to provide greater harmony of action among 'like-minded' regional parties in order to meet 'common problems'. But it did not consolidate unity. Any unity among the regional parties seems to be a remote prospect (despite common and similar challenges thrown up by the logic of development and certain specific issues) largely thanks to the lack of socialization among the people of the region, personality clashes among the leaders of local parties and basic differences relating to ethnicity and culture.

Purely from the point of view of the hold of national political parties on the political system in north-east India, there is no reason for anyone to be a pessimist. There are doubts, however, about the ability of the system to be fully participatory. In each State and Union Territory, there are powerful forces articulating significant political aspirations outside the system. To these forces neither the Constitution of India nor the democratic processes are sacrosanct. These forces never accepted the creed of ahimsa. On the face of it, the insurgency and armed rebellion that started first in Nagaland and later spread to Mizoram, has reached Manipur and Tripura. There is considerable dissatisfaction in Assam over the handling of the 'foreigners issue' by the political system and what is considered to be the imposition of elections prior to a solution of the problem. An echo of the agitation over the aliens issue can be heard in Meghalaya and Arunachal Pradesh as well.

Regional parties and forces are not injurious to national integrity in themselves if there is a convergence of thought between the regional and national consciousness. North-east India is not sufficiently unified to have a regional personality or identity in terms of ideals, customs, language or religion: different tribes in the area and the various communities have their own heritage, customs and language. The requirement, therefore, is to help the forces which are operating in favour of integration between these groups side-by-side with their convergence with the national personality. The process is in progress and in this context the national political parties can play a more constructive role than a regional party of each tribe and each community.

The challenges to this integration are not fully reflected in election statistics, as various ethnic groups or a large section of people have from time to time opted out of the political system. This phenomenon has also enveloped Assam as the agitation over foreign nationals has been conducted outside the purview of the State political system. Integration between the seven political units of the region is also being sought by the secessionist or chauvinistic forces, but their objective is to detach north-east India from the Indian Union. More than nationalist, regional parties, it is the national political parties that can effectively fight this phenomenon of a limited but divisive convergence of political views, with strength derived from their all-India character. It is in this context that the important role of national and regional forces in the working of the political systems in the seven states of north-east India has to be seen and appreciated.

The complex character of society and the undeveloped state of various political organizations in north-east India make it particularly difficult to forecast the status of national and regional parties in the next decade or so. But it is clear that important elements within the ruling middle class in the region would prefer the Congress rather than any other political party or group of parties to be in power as the Congress continues to symbolize in their eyes stability and the status-quo. This preference will only alter in the event of the Congress forfeiting its claims to rule from New Delhi. In the Surma, Manipur and Brahmaputra Valleys the Congress was a party of the freedom struggle and, as such, has an edge over the regional parties in these areas. In Meghalaya, Mizoram and Nagaland, where statehood was attained after a long struggle under the leadership of regional parties, the national parties will continue to face powerful challenges from regional forces. The merger of a regional with a national party, as occurred in Nagaland and Meghalaya in the 1970s could, of course, tilt the balance in favour of a national party. In the Brahmaputra Valley, where regional feelings have been forcefully articulated in recent years by students, it is quite likely that regional forces will pose a challenge to national parties for some years. There is, however, no charismatic regional leader in the Brahmaputra Valley like those in Nagaland or Mizoram. One thing is clear in the post-Independence era, student leaders in the Brahmaputra Valley, barring a few exceptions, have generally settled down in petty business or contract work and in low-grade employment. Above all certain inherent limitations face the organizers of regional parties in the Brahmaputra Valley. These are: (1) the tradition of the freedom struggle and the long innings of the Congress as the centre of 'conflict adjustment'; (2) the polyglot nature of the State's population; and (3) the history of failure of regional forces.

As regards the wider question of the efficacy of the political system and the importance of political power in north-east India, some characteristics clearly stand out. First, the various governments in the region have come to believe that the local people's sanction alone is not sufficient to sustain the validity of their rule unless there is sufficient backing from either the Central government, including its coercive machinery, or some other outside prop. The State governments manned by regional parties look to the Central government for support as much as Congress governments did. Similarly, the leftist government in Tripura draws its strength from that in West Bengal in ideas as well as personnel. Second, even though the political system is not yet fully participatory it is definitely stabilizing amidst forces of revolt, unrest, agitations and organized violence. The electoral process is gaining respectability even in areas where the sacred character of the ballot box was in doubt, as in Nagaland and Mizoram. The trouble in the Brahmaputra Valley vis-a-vis the functioning of the electoral system could be resolved with deft handling and the passage of time. Finally, politics is gaining ascendancy in relation to other forces in north-east India. In its evolution, political power has tended to ascribe to itself absolute capacities; there are signs that even ethnic or religious developments will increasingly revolve around political power in the coming years. This has forced individuals to identify themselves with increasingly smaller segments of society for the promotion of their particular interests.

CHAPTER V

Attractions of Political Reorganization in Assam

All societies are characterized by conflicts and north-east India is no exception. Most of the movements in north-east India are based on ethnic demands and have a revivalist temper, as each tribe or clan at a given point of time was a ruling race and enjoyed unfettered authority. None the less, there is an essential difference between the nature of conflict in the hills and the plains of the north-east from the point of view of political management. The revolts in Nagaland and Mizoram are aimed at separate nationhood. The unrest in Manipur and Tripura is concerned not only with greater autonomy of these States but comprises a set of complex socio-political demands. Each revolt or unrest is well-organized, with a political machinery to carry out its goal and a military wing attached to the political organization to implement its dictates—all have the trappings of a tribal political order but are presented in modern language and supported by modern weapons.In the ethnic conflicts in Assam, however, all the groups are agreeable to resolving their differences within the national constitutional framework.

The socio-political landscape of Assam is characterized by eight social and ethnic groups whose political responses, with varying degrees of difference, emanate from ethnic value-systems and the desire to promote them. The ethnic groups are:(i) caste-Hindu Assamese; (ii) immigrant Muslims, (iii) Bengali Hindus, (iv) tea-garden labour, (v) a migrant Hindi-speaking population, (vi) the Ahoms, (vii) the Bodo-Kacharis, and (viii) Other Backward Classes (OBC). The Ahoms and Bodo-Kacharis not only clamour for socio-cultural, political and economic rights for their members, but, unlike other groups, also agitate for a separate state for themselves, to be carved out of Assam. The prolonged agitation over the 'foreigners' issue has given fresh life to earlier ideas that Cachar should be separated from Assam, a measure that would be supported by certain elements of both the Assamese and Bengali linguistic groups. The OBC factor has been important in state politics since 1971. All these conflicts have tempted many scholars and politicians to view the familiar and tried methodology of the political reorganization of Assam as a reliable solution for present problems as well.

Demand for a Separate Cachar

In any study of the fears of the Assamese community, the fear of Bengali domination over them would stand out as the single most notable feature in the entire history of twentieth-century Assam. This 'fear' has not declined despite very active participation by Assamese caste-Hindus in the national freedom struggle and their control over the apparatus of the Congress. On 28 November 1937, the predecessor organization of the present All-Assam Students Union (AASU), then styled as the Asamiya Deka Dal, presented a memorandum to Jawaharlal Nehru pleading for his intervention in saving the Assamese identity and culture. It demanded implementation of the following six points:(1) the transfer of Sylhet to Bengal; (2) total ban on Bengali immigration to the Brahmaputra Valley for a period of twenty years; (3) strict naturalization laws for resident Bengali immigrants; (4) outlawing all anti-Assamese organizations in the Brahmaputra Valley; (5) a ten year moratoriam on agricultural indebtedness; and (6) exclusion of the planters bloc from the legislature.[1]

In fact, the fear of Bengali supremacy has been consistently haunting the Assamese mind since Assam's annexation by the British in 1826, which resulted in the replacement of Assamese *dangariyas* in government jobs by the Bengali *bhadralok* and relegated the Assamese language to dialect status up to 1873.

The restoration of the Assamese language to the status of an official language and the medium of instruction in educational institutions after its suppression during 1837-73 no doubt reassured the Assamese, but the territorial reconstitution of Assam on 6 February 1874 and its constitution as a separate Chief Commissioner's Province, as against the earlier arrangement whereby Assam was a part of Bengal, did not really help reduce the fear of Bengali supremacy. The incorporation of the Bengali speaking district of Sylhet into Assam on 12 September 1874 made the Bengali speaking community in Assam a majority and exacerbated these fears. So long as Assam was a part of Bengal (1826-73)

Assamese speakers were in a majority within a specific area, even though Bengali was the language of administration and education. During 1874-1931, however, Assamese speakers were in a minority in Assam.[2]. Thanks to an understanding with migrant Bengali Muslims on the language issue (through the help of Congress leaders and the leader of the Muslim League, Saadulla) Assamese speakers once more became a majority in Assam under the 1931 census. However, an overwhelming majority in Sylhet, Cachar, and Goalpara districts looked to Bengal and considered its language and culture superior to those of the indigenous people of Assam, which played a critical role in the politics of the State and became a convenient instrument in the British game of 'divide and rule'.

In 1874 the people of Sylhet had protested against their separation from Bengal and thereafter wanted a re-union. Later, the people of Cachar and Goalpara—the other two Bengali-speaking districts of Assam, resented any proposal to transfer Sylhet to Bengal unless the scheme also envisaged the inclusion of Cachar and Goalpara in Bengal. On the other hand, the Assamese-speaking people of the Brahmaputra Valley always demanded the transfer of Sylhet to Bengal to give the Assamese a numerical superiority in Assam. In the wake of the partition of India, the fate of Sylhet was left to be decided by a referendum of the people of the district, which had a majority of Muslims. The communal argument, however, did not weigh heavily with Assamese caste-Hindus of the Brahmaputra Valley. Notwithstanding their public pronouncements, the Brahmaputra Valley Congressmen were pleased with the results of the referendum of 6th and 7th July, 1947, in which Sylhet opted for Pakistan by a margin of 55,578 votes —2,39,619 votes went in favour of Pakistan and 1,84,041 for the status-quo. The Bengali Hindus of Sylhet were unhappy about this result and blamed the Congress leadership as well as the administration for it. But the impact of the separation as well as the continued acceptance of Assamese as their mother-tongue by the remaining migrant Bengali Muslims was dramatic. The proportion of Assamese speakers in the post-Independence State which constituted only 31.42 per cent of the total population in 1931, rose to 56.69 per cent in 1951, while the corresponding percentage of Bengali speakers declined from 26.79 in 1931 to 16.50 per cent in 1951. ;

The transfer of a major portion of Sylhet. to Pakistan was vie-

wed by several political analysts in the Brahmputra Valley as a
step which lent a degree of homogeneity to an otherwise most
diverse linguistic and cultural region of the Indian subcontinent:
it allowed the Assamese-speaking population of the State to dominate electoral politics. Over the years, however, largely due to
a massive influx of a Bengali-speaking population from erstwhile
East Pakistan and now Bangladesh into Assam, the anxieties of
the Assamese have been revived. The untruthful response of Bengali Muslims as regards their mother-tongue before successive
census enumerators have added to the Assamese fear psychosis as
regards their identity, language and culture.

Over the years, Cachar district in Assam has acquired both linguistically and culturally a distinct Bengali personality with
nearly 90 per cent of its 2.5 million people speaking Bengali; the
language of the district courts of administration is Bengali, as is
the medium of instruction in most educational institutions in the
district. Once Cachar's schools are delinked from Assam Board of
Secondary Education and the district's colleges from the University of Gauhati by conceding a separate Board and a separate University, the educational system of the district will become unilingual and separate from that in Assam. The separation of Cachar
from Assam is, in fact, considered by many as a possible answer
to the Assamese quest for identity. The idea is attractive to some
politicians and scholars who are willing to buy peace for ten or
twenty years and is emotionally appealing to the Assamese-speaking people in the Brahmaputra Valley. The latter see in the lack of
support of Cachar's people over the aliens issue, proof of the unwil-
lingness of the Bengali-speaking population of that district to
share the sufferings of the Assamese.

Would the separation of Cachar from Assam help solve any
problem? In other words, is a further political reorganization of
Assam a solution to its social, cultural and economic problems?
Several answers have been offered to these questions, but three
will be discussed here. First, V. Venkata Rao, a noted academic of
Gauhati University holds that 'the only possible solution to the
problem of language is the separation of Cachar and Goalpara from
Assam'. He has advocated that Cachar be constituted into a union
territory. He writes; 'it has all the qualifications to be a union territory, being densely populated, with a well educated community and
an effective leadership'. Alternatively, he feels it could be

attached to Tripura, which has a Bengali majority. I suspect however, that the Bengalis and tribals of Tripura may not welcome the Cachar Bengalis and so the only alternative is the conversion of Cachar into a Union Territory. Venkata Rao would like this separation to take place at the earliest and is hopeful that, after Cachar's constitution as a union territory, the Bengalis of the Brahmaputra Valley may change their attitude towards the Assamese and accept that language as the medium of instruction and examination at all levels.[3]

Secondly, in a letter of 29 March 1983 to the Editor of the Indian Express, J.L. Chowdhury, a teacher, has demanded a separate university for Cachar. The circumstantial logic for this emanated from the fact that, in the wake of agitations over the foreign nationals issue, the various examinations conducted by the Board of Secondary Education, Assam and the universities of Gauhati and Dibrugarh were postponed during 1980-84, thus leading to the loss of precious academic years. As the students of Cachar never supported the agitation, Chowdhury argued that they should not be made to pay this 'heavy price' and a separate system of secondary and university education for them could solve the problem. Chowdhury reveals his sympathies when advocating that 'colleges in the Brahmaputra Valley run by linguistic minorities and tribal people may be given the option to affiliate themselves with the proposed Cachar University which will also settle the most sensitive and emotive issue—the medium of instruction—once for all.' In other words, while the Bengalis would not demand the separation of Cachar from Assam, they aim to promote Bengali linguistic identity in Assam.[4] Finally, the Assamese view Cachar as a financial liability on Assam's resources and, as such, most of them would welcome the separation as good riddance[5]. This view, however, is changing, and Satish Kakati, a journalist and author, is right in expressing the sentiments of the Assamese elite when he says that the 'notion of all problems disappearing if Cachar is taken out is too simplistic'. He feels that the whole issue needs to be viewed in the context of the continued affiliation of the Hill districts (Karbi Anglong and North Cachar) with Assam and the claims of the tribals in the plains for Udayachal. Kakati concludes that 'the separation of a part of Assam is no panacea for the ills that afflict either the state or the breakaway unit' and that 'instead of thinking of further truncation', attempts should be made to settle the problems by preserving the present geographical character of Assam[6].

I maintain that a separate Cachar would leave the common people where they were and many internal conflicts—both with religious and ethnic variants—within the present Cachar district would gradually assume unmanageable proportions, hampering, in turn, the process of any meaningful economic development. How would Bengalis in the Brahmaputra Valley react to the separation of Cachar, would they accept the Assamese language and culture or organize themselves into a small group with a separate Bengali identity and look up to Bengali as the sole means of preserving that identity? Notwithstanding what V. Venkata Rao feels, the Bengalis, particularly Hindus, would never give up their language in favour of Assamese. There is no denying that the Assamese and Bengali languages are closer to one another than any other two languages in the country, but in the Brahmaputra Valley, thanks to a number of historical, geographical and attitudinal factors, the Bengali linguistic personality is not likely to yield place to the Assamese as it did when adopting Hindi in Bihar or U.P. In view of this prognosis, the separation of Cachar is likely to lead to fierce hostility between Assamese and Bengalis in the Brahmaputra Valley[7]. Such a situation would lead to the complete vivisection of Assam, in the light of the demands for Udayachal State and Ahom State. Let us examine the latter demands.

The Ahoms have not prospered ever since they lost their right to rule over Assam in 1826. The British no doubt granted meagre pensions to a large number of ex-rulers and nobles, but their decline continued. Economic blows were administered by the abolition of slavery in 1841 and the withdrawal of the free labour that the Ahoms were entitled to under the *Khel* system. The Ahoms also erred in not sending their wards to English-medium schools and, as a consequence, lost jobs in the administration to Bengalis and, later, to local Hindus who had once served the Ahoms as clerks. During the entire period of British rule, from 1826–1947, Bengalis held the dominant positions in administration. The turn of Hindu Assamese came only in 1946 when Gopinath Bardoloi succeeded Saadulla as premier of Assam. Caste Hindu domination over politics, administration and, consequently, over economic opportunities continued up to 1971. In January 1972, with the appointment of Sarat Chandra Sinha as Chief Minister, political power shifted to the Backward Classes, but caste Hindus

retained their hold over the administration and economy of
Assam. The Janata Party's rule in Assam briefly restored political
power to caste Hindus and the struggle for political power in
Assam has penetrated the agitation over the 'foreign nationals'
issue.

The proposal for the reorganization of Assam floated by the
Central Government in 1967 led to the assertion of a socio-ethnic
personality by various groups for separate States not only in the
Hills but also in the Brahmaputra Valley. The most striking
expression of this was that of the Ahoms in upper Assam, who had
ruled over Assam for 600 years and accepted the Assamese language and Hinduism. The Ahoms and allied ethnic groups
pleaded with the Central Government for protection of their culture and tradition from the 'political and cultural domination' of
'outsiders', which included, amongst others, caste-Hindu
Assamese whose forefathers had been priests, teachers and officials of the Ahom rulers. On 28 May 1967, in a representative
meeting of the Ahoms held at Garhgaon, the capital of the Ahom
Kings, a resolution was adopted demanding a 'separate autonomous unit of upper Assam'; and a year later the demand was converted into one of separate statehood. The political organization of
the Ahoms which is seeking acceptance of these demands is styled
the Ujoni Assam Rajya Parishad (UARP).

The Ahoms came to form part of the OBC, but have always held
a distinct position in view of their heritage and also simultaneously
promoted the idea of separate statehood for themselves. While
demanding separation they have been pragmatic enough to seek
the status of 'Scheduled Tribes' to get the benefit of reservations in
jobs and government contracts. One of the results of Ahom pragmatism is seen in the fact that, while the UARP has not met with
significant success at the polls, Ahom representation in the ruling
parties—Janata during 1977-79 and the Congress (I) thereafter,
has been considerable. The Chief Minister of Assam, Hiteswar
Saikia, was an Ahom. It is reasonable to conclude that, so long as
the Ahoms are given important political positions in government,
the demand for a 'Ahomland' or the like will not be strongly pres-
sed, even if it remains alive.

'Udayachal'

The demand for 'Udayachal State' seeks a separate political unit based solely on ethnic considerations for the Bodo-Kachari tribes in Assam. Geographically it is expected to comprise the northern parts of the Lakhimpur, Goalpara, Kamrup and Darrang districts of Assam. The leadership of the movement is in the hands of a tribal political organization styled the Plains Tribal Council of Assam (PTCA). The PTCA has always had greater representation in the State legislature than the UARP. At the same time, the Bodo-Kacharis, like the Ahoms, have also had a fair amount of representation in the Congress (I) and, over the years, been represented in the State Cabinet. The Bodo-Kacharis constitute a large ethnic group in Assam and the 1971 Census shows their number at half a million.

Nowhere in India has language been as contentious a political issue as in Assam. As soon as Assamese was declared the official language of the State in 1960, in addition to protests by Bengalis and the hill tribes, the Bodos also joined the fray and demanded the use of Bodo in the areas where they were concentrated. The Bodo Sahitya Sabha (formed in 1952) became active, and, as a result of its efforts and that of its political organ, the PTCA, the Bodo language—a fairly developed one—became the medium of instruction in the region up to secondary level in April 1968. A major development, however, which will have a long-term impact on the assimilation process in the Brahmaputra Valley, was the refusal of Bodos to accept the Assamese script and their insistence on the Roman script—a demand which, the Bodos gave up on the intervention of the Prime Minister of India on 12 April 1975; instead, they accepted the Devanagari script. While the Devanagari script will help the Bodos to keep their own language distinctive from Assamese and also bring them emotionally closer to the Hindi-speaking region, it has certainly impeded the assimilation of the Bodos in the composite society of the Brahmaputra Valley.

The Bodos are essentially agriculturists and did not show any interest in British education, producing their first graduate as late as 1936. The Bodos are exercised over the alienation of their land to immigrant Muslims, Assamese caste Hindus and migrants from Nepal and other States of India. In a memorandum to the Central Government in 1972, the PTCA complained that the plains' tribals have been uprooted in a systematic and planned way from their own soil and that 'the step-motherly treatment of the administration, dominated by the Assamese-speaking people, have reduced them to the status of second class citizens of the State'. In August 1983, the PTCA leaders impressed upon the Prime Minister that the massacre of tribals in February 1983 in the Brahmaputra Valley had convinced them that they had no place in Assam and that they must have their own separate Union Territory, consisting mainly of the plains' tribal population.[7]

The existing provisions of the Assam Land Revenue Regulations for tribal belts and blocks, which puts restrictions on non-tribals acquiring surplus government land, has not met with any success. The formation of tribal belts and blocks immediately after Independence gave institutional expression to the felt needs of the plains' tribal population and had been very thoughtfully conceived by the indigenous leadership. These provisions were added to the Assam Land and Revenue Regulation in 1947 with a view to stopping the process of alienation of tribal lands into the hands of the outsiders and preventing the plains' tribals from being further driven to the interior. Despite this however, tribal land has passed on to immigrant Muslims, Nepalese and caste Hindu Assamese with impunity. The violence that erupted with the announcement of general elections in Assam in February 1983 was largely due to land alienation to the Assamese. This provoked the Bodo-Kacharis of Gohpur in Darrang District to kill a large number of Assamese caste Hindus in a situation surcharged with pro-and anti-poll compaigners. Similarly, the Lalungs—a plains' tribe supported by the Bodos, and caste Hindu Assamese massacred immigrant Muslims at Nellie in Nowgong district on a scale unknown in the histroy of Assam. The land alienation process needs a close look.

Briefly stated, the root of the problem lies in the tendency to live in colonies and compartments with one's own kind. People tend to seek jobs in their own communities, to restrict their social life to their own group, etc. There is a need to expose the elites to wider ideas so that, when they speak of an Assamese culture they understand it as a live, innovative process of development of a mixed society. The issue of language is another major bone of contention. The caste Hindus in the Brahmaputra Valley would like the plains' tribals to adopt the Assamese script. The Miris have adopted the Roman script, while the Bodos have chosen the Devanagari. The rejection of the Assamese script has dismayed the Assamese who, without the support of the tribals, become a minority overwhelmed by the Bengali-speaking population. A meaningful relationship between the Bodo Sahitya Sabha and Assam Sahitya Sabha would help bring about a closer relationship between caste Hindus and Bodos. It is true that the plains' tribals have a grievance against the Assamese elite for having ignored them. A Bodo school teacher from Kokrajhar district told me that the issue of Udyachal is whipped up to gain greater attention and better facilities for the Bodos. Left to themselves, most Bodos are neither conscious of the need for a separate State for themselves nor willing to sever relations with the Assamese caste Hindus.

The OBC Factor in Assam

English education had been a major source of change in Indian society in the nineteenth century. After the British annexation of Assam in 1826 the ruling elite of Assam—the Ahoms, Chutias, Morans, Matakas, Rajbanshis, and Koches, perceived English education as a symbol of their subservience and subjugation and withdrew themselves and their children from the new system of education. This 'royal complex' had adverse economic results on the communities involved, leading to future social backwardness and distance from the new centres of power. The problems of terrain and the determination of these ruling elites to withdraw from the socialization process initially frustrated even the educational efforts of enterprising missionaries. However, by the beginning of the twentieth century a new generation of the erstwhile ruling elites was attempting to convince their kinsmen to send their children to missionary schools and also place their demands concerning the amelioration of their backward conditions before the district officers.

The movement for independence helped consolidate the resolve of these groups to seek social advancement.[8] Article 340 of the Constitution of India, which provides for the development of the Backward Classes, is an expression of this. A Backward Classes Commission was set up at the national level in 1953 and its report submitted in 1955. The Commission listed as many as 23 communities as the 'Other Backward Classes' in Assam, this number has since been raised to 30 by the Government of Assam.[9]

The categorization has a social significance and several

nuances. First, the erstwhile elites who had ruled over different
parts of Assam ranging from a decade to over six centuries were
reduced within a century and a half to a socio-economic level
where they needed statutory reservations in the services and protection in other avenues of life. Second, the Assam government
declared 7 of these 30 backward classes including tea garden
labour as 'more backward', and included as many as 5 erstwhile
ruling elites in this category, leaving only the Ahoms in the category of 'Other Backward Class'. Finally, the Scheduled Castes were
raised in the social scale and made members of the Other Backward Classes.

The formalization of the Other Backward Classes as a pressure
group to protect and further the interests of their members took
place in 1952 when at a meeting in Dibrugarh, the Backward Classes Association was formed. The first annual conference of the
Other Backward Classes of the entire State was held at Dibrugarh
on 3 February 1959 and the Backward Classes Association was
rechristened the All-Assam Other Backward Classes Association
(AAOBCA). The new Association started work on the consolidation of the various classes within its fold with great zeal and annual
sessions were held at Nowgong in 1960, Shillong in 1961, Sibsagar
in 1966, and Kokrajhar in 1969. It stepped up its activities and in
1971 the Association pointed out that, despite the OBC population being around 70 per cent in the State, the share of OBC gazet-
ted officers in the State government was merely 3.63 per cent, and
for Grade IV employees 32.6 per cent. The Association demanded
corrective measures for the removal of these 'discrepancies', prop-
ortional reservation of seats for the OBC students in institutions of
engineering, medicine, and agriculture, proper representation in
democratic institutions from village panchayats to parliament and
preferential allotment of land to the landless OBC. In a sudden
move by the central leadership of the Congress, the Chief Minis-
tership of the State passed from a caste Hindu, Mahendra Mohan
Chaudhury, to an OBC Rajbanshi, Sarat Chandra Sinha at the
start of 1972.

The political domination of the OBC was resented by the caste
Hindus in Assam. The state services, which were manned by caste
Hindus, were initially reluctant to support the new Ministry.
There was hostility from the local press, again in the hands of caste
Hindus. The language agitation all over Assam in 1972 was widely

believed to be a bid to oust the OBC Chief Minister on grounds of inefficiency and inept handling of a sensitive issue. The OBC leadership has so far always chartered a different course from the Ahoms, another member of the OBC. But in the new politics in the State there was a convergence of views between the Ahoms, represented in the Cabinet by Hiteswar Saikia, and others of the OBC, led by the Chief Minister, Sarat Chandra Sinha. In Dibrugarh University the domination of caste Hindus came to an end in 1974 when the student leadership passed over to the Ahoms. The caste Hindus who dominated the student group of Gauhati University, were humiliated when the district authorities of Kamrup ordered the police to flush out the university hostels in mid-1974 for the maintenance of peace.

The OBC consolidation in State politics was encouraged by the caste Hindu Assamese politician, Dev Kanta Barooah, who was a Central Minister and the President of the Congress during the eventful years of 1972–7. It is widely held that he was the originator of the idea of politicization of the OBC factor in State politics.

The defeat of the Congress in the election of 1977, the break-up of the party in 1978 when the OBC leaders parted company with Indira Gandhi and joined the rival Congress, and the defeat of the Congress (I) in the Assembly elections of 1978 led to this group losing political power. It also led to cleavages within the OBC and Ahom combination.

The OBC factor is important in Assam politics and could be viewed as a politically stabilizing force in a society full of ethnic diversities. The OBCs are composed of various elements and since caste structure has never been very strong in Assam, unity among the various castes comprising the OBC is unlikely to be as strong as in Bihar, U.P. or Karnataka. However, members of the OBC are now more aware of the modern trends and there is greater socialization between one group of it and the other as a result of developments during 1952-72 and the wielding of political power during 1972–8. In view of similar attitudes of caste Hindus and OBCs over language and religion, one can visualize the growth of a common approach in political and social matters forming over the years. OBC sensitivities have to be taken into consideration in the political management of Assam and perhaps, herein lies the key to political stability in the State.

CHAPTER VI

Administrative Philosophy and Institutional Framework

Historically, two principal characteristics of the administrative philosophy in north-east India have been (1) separate administrative organizations for the hills and the plains; and (2) uncertainties about the future of the administrative framework, particularly for the Hill areas after the Second World War. Both these characteristics have influenced the evolution of administrative policy as well as the institutional framework of the region all these years and, in several ways, have hindered the growth of a uniform administrative pattern for the entire north-east region. Nonetheless, after Independence and particularly after the reorganization of Assam in the 1970s, three administrative institutions, namely, the North-Eastern Council, the common High Court and, until recently, a common Governor imparted a certain uniqueness to the pattern of administration in the region. The future efficacy of these institutions will have a considerable bearing on the management of change in the region.

The divergence in administrative policy and organization in the hills and the plains of north-east India is a fact of history and has always prevailed even when there was a single political unit. The plains, overwhelmingly populated by people who came from north India, have been subjected to greater administrative supervision and control than the Hills, which have a majority of tribals. The policy response has been to regulate the affairs of the plains' people more or less as in the rest of India and to allow the hill tribes to practice their own traditional codes of life. All the principal ruling elites of the region—the Ahoms and the British in particular—followed this policy.

After their conquest of Assam in 1228 the Ahoms set up their headquarters in the Brahmaputra Valley and not in the hills. They ruled the plains for the next six centuries with direct authority and exacted compulsory service from their people both in peace and in war under the *Khel* system; towards the tribes in the hills their policy was one of conciliation and non-annexation. A knowledgeable Assamese historian has summed up Ahom policy as follows. 'Conciliate these tribes by promising to furnish them their necessaries as far as possible. If they indulge in wanton pillage, pursue and capture the miscreants, but never overstep the limits.[1] The Ahoms realized the impracticability of conducting expeditions in the hills and one of their pragmatic generals compared this task to that of 'an elephant entering a rat-hole.'

British rule (1826–1947) followed the basic features of this dual policy. However, the British brought in certain changes in keeping with their all-India pattern, security considerations and economic objectives. Unlike the Ahoms, the British annexed the Hill areas, included them in Assam and kept their headquarters first at Cheerapunjee and, later, at Shillong, both in the Khasi Hills[2]. They also viewed the administration of the plains of Assam as different from that of the rest of India, and of the Hills adjoining the plains of the Brahmaputra and Surma Valleys as different from that of the plains. This was accomplished by providing the Hills as well as the plains an administrative system that was paternalistic in character and of a non-regulation type. The two special characteristics of the non-regulation system were: (a) that no legal enactments were to be considered in force in these areas except when specially adopted; and (b) that all executive and judicial functions were concentrated in the executive head of the district. This system was adopted for Assam because it was a province with little revenue, scanty population, and generally backward. The system was paternal because, with this extreme concentration of power in the district head, the success of the system depended upon his personality, maturity, drive and vision. However, to accommodate variations in the Hill areas, while the Lushai Hills had a Superintendent as its head, each division of the North-East Frontier Agency had a Political Officer. The idea was to give more discretion and authority to a Superintendent or a Political Officer, who normally functioned in remote areas, than to a Deputy Commissoner in the plains. In fact, NEFA and the Tuensang areas had non-resident Political Officers. The Political Officers lived in the foothills and their main function was to 'show the flag' from time to time and lead occasional punitive expeditions against tribal raiders of the plains; this was similar to the practice followed by the Ahoms.

Even the introduction of a Legislative Council after 1905 did not alter the dual pattern of administration. Under the 'dyarchy' introduced in 1919, the administration of tribal areas was among the reserved subjects' left to the special care of the Governor of Assam and outside the purview of Indian ministers. This continued, under the Government of India Act of 1935.[3] The Simon Commission had earlier clearly maintained that the stage of development reached by the inhabitants of the hills prevented the possibility of applying to these areas methods the representative institutions adopted elsewhere. The Commission felt that the tribals did not ask for self-determination, but for security of land tenure, freedom in the pursuit of the traditional methods of livelihood and the reasonable exercise of their ancestral customs.[4]

The dual pattern of administration was given formal shape under two codes: the Bengal Frontier Regulation, 1873, and the Assam Land and Revenue Regulation, 1886. The first brought into being the 'Inner Line' in some districts of Assam—a 'Line' beyond which no British subject could proceed without a pass from the Deputy Commissioner. The Regulation also laid down rules regarding the possession of land, trade, etc., beyond the line. Not long after the Inner Line was promulgated, another, 'Outer Line', was drawn for official guidance, though it was not publicized. The Inner Line was administratively significant as it was then explained that 'up to the inner line, administration was to be conducted in the ordinary way while between the inner and outer lines it was to be administered only politically'. In actual practice this meant that the political officers whose jurisdiction was beyond the Inner Line were to exercise only a loose political control in the affairs of the frontier hills, to collect a reasonable poll-tax or house tax, and to take such measures as could be conveniently enforced for the preservation of forests. The tribals attracted reprisals only on account of raids on and damage to the plains' people, their cultivation and cattle; and for practising human sacrifice. The Inner Line regulation was made applicable only in NEFA, the Lushai Hills and the Naga Hills.[5]

The administration of the plains was carried on in accordance with the other code, the Assam Land and Revenue Regulation,

1886. The Regulation laid down in great detail procedures for survey of land, various types of land and the rights of landholders,
procedures regarding land settlement, the functions of the revenue
authorities, and so on. The application of civil, penal and criminal
codes in the plains brought their administration very close to the
British pattern elsewhere in India.

With the partition of India in 1947 and consequent transfer of a
major part of Sylhet to Pakistan, the dual pattern of administration in north-east India did not alter. The principle that Hill
administration had to be separate in form and content from that of
the plains was well accepted.

After the Second World War, there were grave uncertainties
about the future political management of north-east India. In July
1944, the Viceroy and the Governor of Burma, entertained the
idea of grouping the tribal areas in Burma, Assam, and possibly
Bengal, into a separate unit to be administered directly either by
the Governor-General or by the Governor of Burma, depending
upon the political settlement with India and Burma.[6] On the eve
of Independence, the Government of India in a position paper
summed up the main aspects of the problem of accommodating
widely different groups of mainly animist tribes in a future Indian
constitution; and the specific problem of the 'McMahon Line'*
between Assam and Tibet. It was felt that the means of welding
the Hill areas into the body politic of India would have to bear in
mind the need for 'protection of tribal institutions and way of life
for full-scale development', and also the maintenance of 'the integrity of an external boundary—at present with Tibet but foresee-
ably with expansionist China'. The administrative policy to be followed was left as wide as the 'inter-meshing of Central and Provincial machinery' and recommended prudence in dealing with the
tribes and, in particular, the Nagas who 'would not tamely yield to
exploitation or too wide an infringement of their "Way" and would
be capable of creating a very considerable local security problem,
the liquidation of which would be a long and costly process'.[7]

At the local level, there was considerable divergence of views
between the Governor of Assam, Robert Reid (1939–42) and his
successor, Andrew Clow (1942–7). Reid favoured the idea of a
North Eastern Frontier Province 'embracing all the hill fringes
from Lushai land on the south right round to Balipara Frontier

*Named after Sir A.H. McMahon, Foreign Secretary of British India.

Tract on the north, embracing on the way, the Chittagong Hill
Tracts of Bengal and the Nagas and the Chins of Burma and
perhaps their Shan states too... The members of this federation
shall not be subject to constitutional changes introduced in the
Provinces of India'.[8] Clow, in a more incisive analysis, confined
the choice of reorganization to two possibilities, namely, a merger
of the hills and plains of Assam in a manner which will conserve
tribal rights and will recognize in an effective manner the different
needs and outlook of the two areas; and 'the constitution of separate provinces for the hills and the plains, with some links on the
administrative side'. Clow wrote in 1945 that 'if a choice had to be
made now, the balance of advantage seems to lie with the first of
the two alternatives'. He argued that on a long-term view it was
difficult to see any future for the Hills as a separate province.
While the Hills were by no means without resources, they were
'too heterogeneous to form a satisfactory unity and too small, even
if fully united, to sustain a healthy and progressive life of their
own'. He concluded that 'the ultimate interests of both plains and
hills lie in fusion'.[9]

If the British policy prescriptions for the future were far from
definitive, the various ethnic and political groups within the region
entertained all kinds of ideas about future polity management.
Khasi society was divided and some of its elite wanted separation
from India and of a separate sovereign State for the Khasis. There
were others who wanted merely separation from Assam or a federated status within Assam. The Nagas were divided as well between demands for autonomy and independence. Under the banner of the Mizo Union, some of the more educated leaders of the
Lushai Hills entertained thoughts of separation from India, while
others wanted 'local autonomy'. The Mikirs were veering towards
the idea of being a district of Assam with autonomy in the management of local affairs. The Garos wanted the Hills to be linked to the
plains with a common government. In Manipur, the hill dwellers
had a different perception than those of the Manipur Valley. The
Maharaja of Manipur who had only titular authority over the Hill
areas was not in favour of a federation with Assam but wanted a
separate political personality for Manipur. The politically conscious people of the northern Hills demanded educational facilities
and representation in political bodies. Important leaders like
Gopinath Bardoloi and J.J.M. Nichols Roy had differing views

about the future of the region. While Bardoloi wanted a composite Assam, Nichols Roy favoured a Khasi and Jaintia Federated State within Assam.

Although at the national level the political leadership was deeply concerned with the impending partition of India and in minimizing its adverse impact on the region and the country at large, Jawaharlal Nehru had a vision of north-east India in which the tribals would be allowed to develop according to their own genius and Assam a great centre of contact between the civilizations of India and China. Nehru visited Assam in December 1945 and on his return journey to Calcutta on 21 December 1945, obvserved: 'Assam has the look of great reserves of strength and potential power...I have no doubt that great highways by road, air and rail, will go across her, connecting China with India, and ultimately connecting East Asia with Europe. Assam will then no longer be an isolated far away province but an important link between the East and the West'.[10]

Against the background of all these ideas, the task of providing an institutional framework was entrusted to the Constituent Assembly, which was charged with the responsibility of formulating free India's Constitution. The Constituent Assembly constituted a sub-committee styled the North-East Frontier(Assam) Tribal and Excluded Areas Sub-Committee. Bardoloi was its Chairman while J.J.M. Nichols Roy and Rup Nath Brahma, a plains' tribal from the Brahmaputra Valley, were members; there were two other members on the sub-committee from outside the north-eastern region.

In the formulation of its recommendations, the Bardoloi Committee was guided by principles of extending democracy and universal adult franchise throughout the region, and the important social and economic realities unique to it. The Committee found that (1) 'the fact the hill people have not yet been assimilated with the people of the plains of Assam has to be taken into account'; (2) the assimilation process has least advanced in the Naga Hills and in the Lushai Hills and 'the policy of seclusion has ...tended to create a feeling of separateness'; and (3) the various tribes in the foothills under the administrative jurisdiction of one frontier tract or the other were closer to the plains' tribes through family as well as economic bonds than with their Kinsmen in the hills.[11] The Committee wished to safeguard tribal institutions so that new political organizations could take root on old foundations. The distinct features of the tribal way of life pertaining to land, forests, *jhumming* and dispute settling were sought to be preserved; changes would emanate 'as far as possible from the tribe itself'. Members of the Constituent Assembly were asked to view the uniqueness of the tribal scene: whereas elsewhere in India the tribal population has assimilated to a considerable extent the life and ways of the plains' people and tribal organizations had largely disintegrated, in north-east India the tribals are 'divided into fairly large districts inhabited by single tribes or fairly homogenous groups of tribes with highly democratic and mutually exclusive tribal organizations and with very little of the plains'.[12].

Keeping in view all these considerations, the Bardoloi Committee recommended that (1) the Khasi and Jaintia Hills District (excluding Shillong town), the Garo Hills District, the Lushai Hills District, the Naga Hills District, the North Cachar Hills and the Mikir Hills excluding certain plains' areas be made autonomous districts with wide ranging powers vested in the District Councils for the administration and development of these areas; (2) the Sadiya and Balipara Frontier Tracts, the Tirap Frontier Tract and the Naga Tribal Area should be non-autonomous areas and responsibility for their all-round administration and development should be vested in the Governor of Assam; and (3) the plains' tribals of Assam should be recognized as a minority and be entitled to all the privileges of a minority, including representations in legislatures and in the services and that their land should be protected.[13] All these recommendations were accepted and provisions were made in the Constitution and the laws framed thereafter. Manipur and Tripura retained their individual identities in the new constitutional set up.

The District Council was an administrative innovation to meet the political aspirations of the tribal people by giving them a decisive role in their economic development through the instrumentality of district planning. The District Council found its place under the Sixth Schedule of the Constitution, which highlights the importance that the national leadership attached to this socio-developmental organization.[14] It was a democratic framework as seventy-five per cent of the councillors were directly elected. It was also significantly traditional as twenty-five per cent of the councillors would be nominated by the government from among ex-tribal chiefs, village headmen and social workers. The decentralization of administrative and financial powers to District Councils was more substantial than either to the panchayati raj institutions or to municipal bodies elsewhere in the country. There were also several ingredients in the scheme of District Councils to counter any possible trend towards the isolation of tribal peoples from the mainstream of India's social and political life. It was provided that the executive authority of the Government of Assam would encompass the autonomous district; the Assam Legislature and the national Parliament, which would have representatives from the tribal areas, would also have the power to legislate for these areas, subject to a few exceptions, and the onus would be on the State Government to establish the rationale for the non-applicability in the region of any law passed either by the State Legislature or Parliament.

The inauguration of Distirct Councils was hailed as a great landmark and voting days for election to these Councils, the Legislature, and Parliament were marked by gaiety and festivity. At the same time, the national leadership was giving final shape to a policy framework and the most authoritative documentation on tribal policy is found in Jawaharlal Nehru's foreword of 9 October 1958 to the second edition of Verrier Elwin's *A Philosophy for NEFA*. Nehru reflected the philosophy as follows:

We cannot allow matters to drift in the tribal areas or just not take interest in them. In the world of today that is not possible or desirable. At the same time we should avoid over-administering these areas and, in particular, sending too many outsiders into tribal territory. It is between these two extreme positions that we have to function. Development in various ways there has to be such as communications, medical facilities, education and better agriculture. These avenues of development should, however, be pursued within the broad framework of the following five fundamental principles:

1. People should develop along the lines of their own genius and we should avoid imposing anything on them. We should try to encourage in every way their own traditional arts and culture.

2. Tribal rights in land and forests should be respected.

3. We should try to train and build up a team of their own people to do the work of administration and development. Some technical personnel from outside will, not doubt, be needed especially in the beginning. But we should avoid introducing too many outsiders into tribal territory.

4. We should not over-administer these areas or overwhelm them with a multiplicity of schemes. We should rather work through, and not in rivalry to, their own social and cultural institutions.

5. We should judge results, not by statistics or the amount of money spent, but by the quality of human character that is evolved.[15]

There were, however, ominous signs from the day the District Councils, were inaugurated in 1952. A District Council could not be constituted for the Naga Hills as the Nagas boycotted elections to it, with some demanding full statehood while several others clamoured for independence. The Chinese claim over a large chunk of territory in Assam's northern areas in 1959 and China's subsequent agression in 1962, and the grant of statehood to Nagaland the same year did not allow the District Council of the region to establish itself firmly in the local political soil.[16] There were other complicating factors: the language policy of the Government of Assam created suspicion in the tribal mind about Assamese intentions regarding their identity and economic independence; the failure of the Assam administration to depute its senior and best officers to work in the District Councils both for the formulation as well as implementation of the plans, and so on. The most important destabilizing factor came from the tribal elite who were proficient in English and accepted western dress and modes of liiving, but were keen to become chief ministers and ministers of their own lands.

Nehru was receptive to the new wind blowing in the north-east and in his meeting with the Hill leaders on 5 October, 1963 suggested that a Commission could go into the demands of the Hill people. A Commission headed by H.V. Pataskar was constituted after Nehru's death, on 16th March 1965 to suggest 'a full measure of autonomy for the hill areas, subject to the preservation of the unity of the State of Assam'.[17] The recommendations of the Pataskar Commission were discussed in various forums but did not satisfy anyone except Assam. Several new suggestions were floated: a federal plan conferring upon the Hill areas equal status with the rest of Assam;[18] a regional plan on the Scottish pattern where there would be a cabinet of the plains to advise the Governor in matters relating to the plains, and a cabinet of the Hills which would advise the same Governor in matters relating to the Hills[19], and the Asoka Mehta plan, which maintained the integrity of Assam but granted full autonomy to the Hill areas.[20] Finally on

11 September 1968, the establishment of an autonomous State of Meghalaya within Assam was announced, with the proviso that public order and the police would remain with Assam, along with certain financial and taxation matters. The new autonomous State of Meghalaya was born on 2 April 1970 with a new Legislature and a new cabinet.

The experiment, however, was short-lived. It did not fully satisfy the tribal elites of Meghalaya nor was it a really workable proposition. As the functional head of the Personnel Department of the Assam Government, I saw the clamour by hill leaders for the deputation to the Hills of able and senior officers, and the equally strong refusal from the Assam administration. As a result, the new State's administrative apparatus was headed by an officer from Madhya Pradesh. Tribal officers were allowed to go on deputation to Meghalaya. The situation in Manipur and Tripura was not quiet either. Once statehood was granted to Nagaland, it was difficult to refuse the larger populated Manipur and Tripura a similar status. All this called not only for a new look at the political and administrative arrangements of the 1950s, but also speedy reforms. The process of political evolution, cultural-linguistic heterogeneity and meeting popular aspirations demanded a redrawing of the administrative map in north-east India. It was only appropriate that Parliament passed the North-Eastern Areas (Reorganization) Bill, 1971 despite the turmoils in neighbouring East Pakistan in 1971. As a result, at the start of 1971 north-east India came to have seven political units and a nascent regional planning authority – the North-Eastern Council, a common Governor, and a common High Court.

During these years of trial, one can in retrospect, single out some encouraging features. Indira Gandhi, the then Prime Minister of India, inherited Nehru's philosophy and sympathetic approach towards the problems of the people of north-east India, as well as her own personal and first-hand knowledge based on long years of association with the region. She received unfailing support and assistance from B.K. Nehru, the Governor of Assam, L. P. Singh, the Home Secretary in Delhi, K. C. Pant, the junior Home Minister, B. P. Chaliha[21], the farsighted and compassionate Chief Minister of Assam and F. A. Ahmed, who had richly contributed to the secular ethos in north-east India and rose to become the President of India.

The reorganization of Assam in 1971–2 changed the dual pattern of administration in decisive ways. The grant of separate statehood or union territory status to the Hill areas took away the duality in approach and enabled the principal tribes to have their own council of ministers. There were other fundamental changes that Indira Gandhi brought in : (1) the role of the Zonal Council was eliminated ; (2) the North-Eastern Council not only replaced the Zonal Council but introduced in institutional form the concept of regional planning; and (3) the north-eastern areas became an administrative concept. In the task of administrative integration, the North-Eastern Council, the common Governor and High Court were expected to play a leading part. How has this arrangement worked during 1972–84? What are the lessons for the future? Have the political and administrative systems helped consolidate these reforms, and have they given the administration sufficient vitality for the smooth and orderly management of a region in almost 'perpetual turbulence'?

Let us look at the regional institutions: the North-Eastern Council, the High Court, and the Governor.

North-Eastern Council

At the time of the reorganization of Assam in 1971 the need to have a forum where an integrated and co-ordinated view of the entire region could be taken was strongly felt, both for reasons of security and development. The arrangement, however, had to fit the federal structure of the Constitution and, accordingly, it was provided that the North-Eastern Council (NEC) would be an advisory body and not, in any way, infringe upon the political autonomy of the constituent units. Two policy innovations were made in the constitution of the NEC and the administration of north-east India. In the first place, the concept of a 'regional planning authority' with a separate plan and outlay was envisaged. The regional plan was to be formulated by the Council by bringing together schemes which would be of common importance to more than one constituent unit of the Council, thus covering the residuary area between the Central and State Plans. The Plan was to be executed under the supervision of the Council even though it could not assume direct responsibility for execution as it was an advisory body. The Plan was to be financed by the Council out of funds made available to it by the Central Government, as the Council has no financial resources of its own. Secondly, the Council was given the task of being a source of ideas for 'the development of the region for human welfare' as well as the 'maintenance of security and public order'. It was a novel formulation which emerged out of years of thinking, consultation and discussions.

It needs to be clearly stated that the North-Eastern Areas (Reorganization) Act, 1971 and the North-Eastern Council Act, 1971 were twins born out of a new vision for the north-east. The reorganization formula was welcomed by the new political units, and even Assam, out of which Meghalaya, Mizoram and Arunachal Pradesh were carved, gave its 'willing agreement' to the creation of the new States and Union Territories. However, this ·vas not so in the case of the North-Eastern Council. Nagaland refused to participate in it, Manipur and Tripura were not enthusiastic. Meghalaya welcomed the Council, for its headquarters were to be at Shillong. Assam was reluctant, and the position was summed up by a member of the Lok Sabha from Assam on 22 December 1971 as follows:

> The North-Eastern Council has been approached by the people of Assam with a certain amount of reservation. The reservation arises not because of the objects of the Bill, but because there is a feeling in the minds of the people that this Bill will curtail the autonomy of the State of Assam, and secondly, the feeling is also prevalent that this Bill will not be able to achieve the objects for which it has been brought forward but will be another exercise in futility.[22]

Assam gradually changed its stance. Manipur and Tripura also joined the Council. Nagaland became a member in 1976. But differences of opinion continue as to who should preside over the Council; the two Governors by rotation, the seven chief ministers in regular succession, or the Governor of Assam. Ideologically, the difference is one of bureaucracy versus democracy. From the very inception a voice was raised to rid the Council of the control of bureaucrats and substitute it by a vibrant political leadership. This school does not want the Governor, a titular head and an agent of the Centre, to preside over the Council. It feels that the job can be done better by the chief ministers in rotation. Its fears are that the Central Government, and particularly the bureaucracy through the Governor, will whittle down the autonomy of the states of the region through the Council. Another school of thought gives pragmatism more weight. It believes that the Council will be weakened if every chief minister is afforded an opportunity to act as Chairman, as chief ministers would not have sufficient time for the Council, and the frequent changes that this arrangement would entail would not be conducive to the health of the new organization. This school of thought worries about the divisive forces in the country and considers bifurcation of the office of a common Governor and Chairman of the Council a setback.

Let us look at the two roles of the Council: development and security.

Development and The NEC

While inaugurating the North-Eastern Council on 7 November 1972 the Prime Minister of India said: 'The primary purpose of this Council is the development of the region for greater human welfare... I am glad to inaugurate this Council which is promising innovation in regional planning. May it fulfil the hope we have invested in it'.[23] In terms of this goal, the Council has a charter of duties and an institutional arrangement to help achieve the tasks. The principal functions of the Council are: (a) formulation of a unified and co-ordinated regional plan in regard to matters of common interest; (b) fixation of priorities of projects and schemes and their phasing from the point of view of implementation; (c) deciding upon the location of projects and schemes; (d) recommending the allocation of benefits and expenditure to the member units with regard to the projects in the regional plan; (e) reviewing and co-ordinating the implementation of these projects; and (f) recommending the initiation of surveys and investigation of projects in the regional plan. The Council is thus expected to help accelerate the economic growth of north-east India as an integrated whole through the voluntary co-operation and mutual understanding of all the units and with the generous assistance of New Delhi. This should not even remotely suggest that the component units cannot develop themselves. Far from it, they are to be encouraged by the Council to be self-sufficient in meeting the basic requirements of their 'people' by co-operating with their neighbours.

The Council commenced its task with a few schemes involving a modest outlay of Rs 28 lakhs during the closing years of the

Fourth Plan. The approved outlay under the Sixth Plan was Rs 340 crores. The annual position, as far as outlays and expenditure are concerned is briefly as follows:

6 NEC. Plans

Year	Outlay (Rs. Crores)	Actual expenditure (Rs. Crores)
1974–75	10.00	4.87
1975–76	10.00	6.69
1976–77	16.50	15.86
1977–78	28.61	26.51
1978–79 1979–80	82.85	65.33
1980–81	64.40	50.86
1981–82	70.00	64.29
1982–83	80.86	87.30
1983–84	95.00	81.23
1984–85	107.75	101.66
1985–86	125.00	96.46
1986–87	145.00	144.13
1987–88	150.00	150.00
1988–89	185.00	—

(Source: Planning Commission Records)

The above statistics reveal that the Council has been trying to avoid the spending-spree that has characterized the management of State Plans. It also highlights the severe infrastructural constraints in the execution of various schemes, even if money is available.

The Council has accorded priority to improvement in communications and manpower development of the region. Apart from its role in extending railways, the Council sponsored and helped in the construction of 1500 kms of inter-State roads during the Fifth Plan at a cost of Rs 56 crores and about 1700 km of road at a cost of Rs 80 crores. In addition construction of about 1600 km of roads of economic importance was taken up during the Sixth Plan at an outlay of Rs 120 crores.

There is an acute paucity of trained administrative staff and entrepreneurial and technical talent in the region. The Council has conducted a study of manpower requirements of the region, identified the areas from where they can be drawn, set up training institutions to train personnel to the required levels and, meanwhile, had some people trained outside the region. There are genuine fears in the north-east that the exploitation of natural resources will bring an influx of people from the more advanced States of the country. This fear can only be removed by the systematic training of local people in agricultural and industrial fields and by reducing dependence on other parts of the country.

The objective of development also demands that the Council effectively co-ordinates not only the State Plans and the Plans of Central Ministries but also has a link with organizations involved in survey and research and committees like that of Ministers at the Centre charged with the task of giving an extra impetus to development projects and programmes of the region.

Security and the NEC

While introducing the North-Eastern Council Bill in the Lok Sabha on 11 May 1970, the then Home Minister of India stated the objectives of the Council plainly: 'When the proposal for reorganization of Assam was considered, it was thought that there should be a forum where a co-ordinated and integrated view of the entire eastern India can be taken. There are two aspects which need co-ordinated action: one is the security aspect and the other is the development aspect'.[24]

The role of the Council was to be advisory but, not like that of the traditional variety of advisory bodies in the country. It was to be something novel, significant, permanent. While participating in a debate on 11 May 1970, a member of Parliament advocated the need for providing legitimate opportunities to the various groups in the north-east to express themselves 'so that nobody feels dismayed or suffocated, but side by side it is necessary that these personalities are brought together, not only woven together into a web of developmental relationship but, what is more important, exposed to common problems of security'. He went on further: 'Let us bring these units into some kind of a meaningful whole because this whole has to be defended sometimes against multiple attacks from different frontiers. At such a time it is necessary that there is a focal point where people who are administratively divided are not emotionally but rationally, and in terms of economic and security considerations are closely brought together'.[25] In the very logic of things, the Council became a significant planning and security organ on India's territorial frontiers with Burma, Bangladesh, Bhutan and Tibet.

As stated earlier, the Council did not receive a cordial welcome from its constituent units. Its advisory and recommendatory role in respect of 'maintenance of security and public order'[26] was viewed with suspicion, reservation and even open hostility. Consequently, the development of the Council as an advisory security organ of the north-east had been slow, hesitant and poor. The Council periodically held conferences on security matters by calling senior civil and police officers of the seven units, but only with the reluctant concurrence of the State chief ministers.

What is the security set-up in the north-east? To protect the eastern borders, the Eastern Command of the Indian Army with headquarters at Calcutta is assisted by two corps headquarters, one located at Tezpur and the other near Siliguri. The army is assisted by the Border Security Force and Assam Rifles in its border patrolling and policing duties. To contain and eliminate insurgency, the Army has deployed several divisions in Nagland, Mizoram, Manipur and Tripura and is assisted by the Central Reserve Police and Assam Rifles. It operates directly under the control and guidance of the Eastern Command. In both these tasks, the Army gets air support from the Indian Air Force, whose eastern headquarters are located at Shillong. The services of the C.R.P., B.S.F., and the Army are frequently requisitioned by State Governments for the maintenance of law and order and the Army and Air Force render help and support to the civilian population in times of flood, which are a common occurrence in the region. While insurgency is technically the responsibility of the law and order agency of a state, over the years the Union Home Ministry has been playing the role of the senior partner and co-ordinator. The North-Eastern Council does not have a direct say, but much depends upon the personality of the Chairman and his equation with the Home and Defence Ministries, senior politicians of the States and Centre, and the esteem in whch he is held by the local population. Similarly, the intelligence agencies—the Intelligence Bureau, the Special Branch of the States, and those of the Army, the Air Force and the para-military forces—neither regularly report to the Council nor look upon it as the intelligence co-ordinator of the region, notwithstanding the fact that the Chairman is kept informed of important developments bearing on the internal security of the region.

Given this position, various questions come to mind. Is not a decade suffiicient time to give the Council a role in security matters that Parliament intended for it? Is there the need for a separate command of the Army and Air Force for the north-east? Should we not move towards developing a unified intelligence machinery, at least for internal security and accord a proper role in this task to the North-Eastern Council?

There is a need to have a look at the institutional set-up of the Eastern Command. Its jurisdiction extends to all the States and Union Territories of the north-east; plus Sikkim, West Bengal and Orissa. It might be functionally more appropriate to have a separate command for the north-east incorporating Sikkim and the north Bengal districts of West Bengal. This would enable the new Command to give exclusive attention to insurgency, protection of the eastern borders of India as well as meeting the defence obligations of Bhutan. If the headquarters are shifted to Siliguri, Gauhati or Shillong (in order of preference), it would also bring the command headquarters nearer to the North-Eastern Council. The security role of the council could be enlarged to cover Sikkim as well.

As regards the intelligence set-up, the first requirement is to have an institute for defence, insurgency and ethnic studies as a wing of the North-Eastern Council. It is admitted the world over that more than seventy per cent intelligence flows out of books, periodicals, magazines and newspapers. A proper compilation and evaluation of these would be of tremendous help and value in the north-east. There is also the need to strengthen the Intelligence Bureau set-up in the region as the nodal agency of intelligence collection, analysis and dissemination. All the other agencies should regularly feed the Intelligence Bureau. The sources of information should be shared, at least at senior levels, so 'professional sources' do not lull the administration into the false confidence that a piece of information is credible only because various agencies have corroborated it.

Despite clarification from various quarters that the Council will not qualitatively alter the relationship of the member units with the Central Government, doubts have persisted on this front and the Chairman of the Council in almost every meeting has had to highlight this fact. Psychologists would say that any suspicion can be removed only with the passage of time and that the Council should so conduct itself that it does not in any way hurt the sensitivities of member units and make them feel like second class states in the Indian federal structure. To a political scientist, however, much depends upon the management and strengthening of the Council as an instrument of economic betterment of the people and as an additional forum for the expression of the personalities of the north-eastern political units. The Council could help bring their ideas to the notice of the press and the leadership of the country which, currently hears only of the noises and troubles of the region and not of its economic and social advancement.

Several constraints have become evident in the Council's first decade of working. There is no doubt that the Council comes in conflict with the political ideology of greater autonomy to the federating units – a vociferous demand in all the north-eastern states. However, in view of the distance from Delhi, and the legacy of all round non-development or under-development in the region, a regional planning authority, which the Council essentially is, must be accepted as a necessity. The Council has already come to be recognized by the constituent units and the people of the region as a forum for solving regional problems and an institution for projecting these problems before the Central Government.

The unique nature of the task of inter-State co-operation in the realm of planning and security, with which the Council was entrusted, is slowly being appreciated as useful and relevant. As stated earlier, the Council has succeeded in bringing to the region additional investment and expertise without really infringing upon the internal autonomy of the constituent units. It has thus established itself as an economic organization of considerable value for its constituent members. It has helped in the initiation of an era of scientific and planned development. Between the constituent units and the centre, it plays the role of an 'honourable lobby'. The Council, however, has not been able to project its role in the arena of internal security, notwithstanding the plethora of revolts in the region and the obvious requirement for deep study of the various social, ethnic and economic factors that bear on peace and stability. The continued denial of the Council's role in the security affairs of the region is not conducive to the security of the country in this region.

Gauhati High Court

There is a common High Court for the five States and two Union
Territories of north-east India, with Gauhati as its principal seat.
The Gauhati High Court is widely acclaimed as an integrating factor in the administration and life of north-east India. The fact that
the laws applicable to different units differ but are being administered by one High Court has led to common concepts of justice and
equity developing and informing the decisions and orders of judicial courts. A former Chief Justice of the High Court has aptly
observed: 'The judicial map of the north-eastern region is not
merely a conglomeration of scattered political entities, but presents a composite picture of unity in diversity. The common High
Court is the single emblem of that unity. It has to be properly
maintained and nursed. How one wishes it to be a massive plank
to rest man's profound faith in man in more ways than one, start-
ing a reverse process against the present crisis of confidence in
almost every walk of life. If the common High Court succeeds in
justifying the great trust reposed in it by the people of the entire
region, it has done its duty.'[27]

The underdevelopment of administration in north-east India is
nowhere more marked than in administration of justice. Despite
the establishment of a separate province of Assam in 1874, the judicial administration of the area remained under the Calcutta High
Court. In December 1937 a motion for the establishment of a High
Court in Assam was carried in the local Legislature, but it was not
implemented. Only after Independence, on 5 April, 1948 was the
Assam High Court established at Gauhati. Today, it has benches
at Imphal, Agartala, Shillong and Kohima, and benches at
Itanagar and Aizawl may not be very far off.

The administration of justice in north-east India is a fusion of
two different systems, the modern and the traditional. The modern
system has been amplified in the codes of Civil and Criminal Procedures, the Evidence Act, the Indian Penal Code and numerous
laws enacted by parliament and the State legislaures of the seven
political units of the region. The traditional system comprises a tribal heritage of customary laws and practices and has been given
constitutional recognition. The administration of justice is carried
on in terms of these customs and practices, even to the exclusion of
various codes and parliamentary enactments. This is in recogni-

tion of the different levels of development of the legal systems of north-east India, and in tune with the philosophy that a legal framework divorced from history and the spirit of the people whose law it seeks to enforce cannot either be effective or able to meet the changing needs of society. Accordingly, at present, central Acts are applicable only to the Brahmaputra and Surma Valleys of Assam, Manipur and Tripura. Nagaland and Meghalaya and the two Union. Territories of Mizoram and Arunachal Pradesh are governed by customary laws and only the spirit of the codes of Criminal and Civil Procedures apply to these political units.

The laws which govern people in this region are diversified and different. Various tribes are governed by their own religious or social practices and customary laws and procedure; these are duly protected under Article 317(a) of the Constitution of India. To add to the complexity of the situation, the various areas of this region are in different stages of development in the matter of codification of their laws, rules and regulations. Under the Sixth Schedule of the Constitution of India, powers have been given to the District Councils to make laws regarding the appointment of chiefs and headmen, inheritance of property, marriage and social customs, besides other subjects. Some of these customs have come in for elaboration or comment in the judicial pronouncements of the Gauhati High Court and the Supreme Court. Very little, however, has been done to bring all these to print and provide a synthesis and codify the laws in the interests of clarity, understanding and perhaps uniformity. In 1973, a Law Research Institute was established and appended to the Gauhati High Court, but the Institute is not getting the attention and wherewithal it needs.

Despite a common High Court, each State has its own cadre of members of subordinate judicial institutions and very little has been done to form a common cadre of judicial officers for northeast India. There is no organization worth the name to look after the training requirements of judicial officers. Similarly, all the States have opened new sub-divisions and districts but there are inadequate housing facilities for the courts essential for their security, sanctity and respect not to mention housing for judicial officers, a *sine qua non* for their efficiency, impartiality and non-corruptibility. Why is it not possible to move in the direction of giving a united, institutional strength to the administration of justice? It appears that interaction between the High Court and State Executives is far from satisfactory. An overall view is unfortunately not available and, in the absence of this; public support is not forthcoming and a sense of drift continues from year to year.

However, there are several positive factors in north-east India which could be articulated to improve the administration of justice in the region. The establishment of benches has contributed not only in the expeditious disposal of cases but also in the development of legal talent in the region. Judicial officers and the members of the bar find an important place in the middle class and the elite of the region. As a supplement to this, there is widespread faith among the tribals and Bengali Hindus in the impartiality of Assamese judicial officers. We should, therefore, move in the direction of a cadre of judicial officers of north-east India under a common High Court pending creation of an All-India Judicial Service. It should be possible to produce within a reasonable time-frame volumes of the laws and customs which govern the people of north-east India for wider reading, analysis and codification. Are we really moving in these directions at a speed that the needs of the people and national integration demand? We cannot any longer take shelter in the past story of unconcern and neglect. All these measures can be initiated by the judicial officers, members of the bar and other administrators of the region.

Common Governor

For nearly a century (1874–1972), north-east India, with the exception of Manipur and Tripura, shared a common administrative head styled variously as Chief Commissioner, Lieutenant-Governor and, finally, Governor.[28] With the reorganization of Assam in 1972, while Manipur and Tripura were added to the charge of the common Governor, the newly created union territories of Arunachal Pradesh and Mizoram had a Lieutenant-Governor, each directly accountable to the Union Home Ministry. The 'seven sisters' of the north-east India, however, meet in the North-Eastern Council presided over by the common Governor of five states. In actual practice, too, the two Lieutenant-Governors looked to the common Governor for guidance. However, the demand for more than one Governor, had started as soon as Nagaland became an independent state, in 1963. Nagaland's logic was that a common Governor makes Nagaland an inferior State. After 1972, various arguments were advanced for the appointment of separate governors. In the first place, it was widely held that the office of the Governor of the north-eastern States was not only a challenge to the administrative capabilities of the occupant of this office, but also to his physical and mental health, in view of the heavy workload. He was under obligation to address the first session of the five legislatures every year, of swearing in the Council of Ministers of each State and all additions to it, and of assuming the responsibility of administering a State in case of a breakdown of its constitutional machinery, a widely prevalent feature in the north-east.[29] Secondly, the need to know and comprehend the complexities of the multi-ethnic societies of the region, the senior civil servants of the States and the civilian and military officials of the Government of India presents the Governor with a stupendous task. Finally, the argument against common Governorship has been supported on the political grounds of autonomy. The senior partner, Assam, has wanted a separate Governor for itself and various political parties have passed resolutions to this effect. Nagaland's point of view for a separate Governor has been reiterated from time to time, and Manipur and Tripura have also wanted more than one Governor for the region.

The insurgency situation enveloping Manipur, mass-killings in Tripura in June 1980, and the stresses and strains generated particularly in the wake of the agitation over the 'foreign nationals issue' in Assam hastened the creation of another Governorship for the north-eastern States. There is now one Governor for Assam and Meghalaya, with headquarters at Shillong, and another for Manipur, Nagaland and Tripura, with headquarters at Imphal. This bifurcation materialized in August, 1981.[30]

Was it really necessary? Admittedly the task of the common Governor was heavy, but it could easily have been reduced by entrusting the swearing in of various ministers to a judge of the Gauhati High Court. Similarly, in the event of the President's Rule in a State, senior officers could be appointed as advisers to the Governor to relieve him of day-to-day responsibilities and leave him free to concentrate on matters of high policy, direction and control. In any case, in a democratic set-up, the Governor is an agent of the Centre and a ceremonial head of a State. He steps in and assumes the executive power only when no party or coalition commands a majority in a legislature. Notwithstanding this 'fire fighting' utility of the Governor in times of constitutional peril, it will be undersirable to have people with political ambitions as Governors in the north-east, for this would surely hamper the growth of responsible public life and stifle its effectiveness.

What is the impact of the bifurcation of Governorship on the process of nation-building in the north-east? Over the years, and in all forums, the common Governor was viewed as an important factor for integration in the north-east. The bifuraction has snatched away the common link among the States and, to that extent, it has hampered the development of a common personality of the north-eastern States. Further, the north-eastern States have serious border disputes. In times of stress armed police units of the two States have clashed with each other, as has happened between Assam and Nagaland in 1978 and subsequently. A common Governor becomes a centre from where the contending parties can get advice, understanding and be restrained. Above all, another significant role of a common Governor is related to his role as Chairman of the North-Eastern Council—a nascent organization which demands the leadership of an able person for a reasonable period. After the appointment of a second Governorship, the post of the Chairman of the Council remained vacant for nearly a year, to be filled ultimately in June 1982, by the Governor of Assam and Meghalaya. There has been no indication or otherwise as to whether this is a permanent arrangement. If the Chairmanship of the Council is rotated among the two Governors or among the Chief Ministers, as is demanded by various people, the growth of this organization will be seriously hampered.

On balance, it seems appropriate to revert to the previous practice of a common Governor. The argument that the heavy workload requires two governors cannot be carried too far, for otherwise it should be suggested that the office of the chief minister of U.P. should be split, or even that of the Prime Minister of India!

CHAPTER VII

Policy Perspectives:
Points of View

An analysis of the policy framework against the backdrop of recent recent history is essential if we are to draw the correct inferences. While doing so, certain questions come to one's mind. Is there a need to drastically alter the policy 'to allow the tribes to develop according to their own genius'? Was it a mistake to extend the administration even to remote areas, in deviation from the British policy of merely 'showing the flag'? Will the rapid development of an economic infrastructure, like roads, railways, power and communications really integrate north-east India with the rest of the country? Has the Government reorganized north-east India too frequently, which may have caused confusion and bewilderment amongst the people as well as administrators? In future, should the tasks of national integration and economic development demand strengthening the existing political and administrative structures rather than fresh innovations?

The perpetually turbulent scenario in north-east India has prompted several politicians and social workers to decry the policies pursued by the Central Government since 1947. Its critics have denounced the 'inner-line' policy and restrictions and the belief that the tribes be allowed to develop according to their own genius. They feel that attempts to keep the tribes as they are, to preserve them as 'specimens of anthropological museums', will hold up their development and eventual integration with the people of Assam and, ultimately, with the people of the rest of India.

The politicians' viewpoint was aptly summed up by D.C. Goswami, then a Congress member from Assam, while participating in a debate in Lok Sabha on the North-Eastern Areas (Reorganization) Bill on 15 December 1971. He said: 'In the entire north-eastern region, the Britishers followed a policy of divide and rule between one tribe and another as they did between the Hindus and the Muslims in the rest of the country. The member contended

that 'even after Independence we have pursued more or less the
same policy'. He went on to clarify: 'on the advice of Dr Verrier
Elwin a policy was pursued that to maintain their cultural identity, the tribal people be kept isolated. The result was that there
was never emotional integration in the north-eastern region'.[1]

In a paper for a seminar on 'Social Work in the Himalaya' held
at Delhi University in 1967 a social worker, Radhakrishna wrote:
'In areas like NEFA, Verrier Elwin's philosophy, which has been
the Government of India's philosophy for nearly a century, has
kept them isolated from the rest of India.' He went on to say: 'It
was argued by its supporters that it saved the tribals from exploitation by civilized people; it undoubtedly did, but it did not protect
them from the exploitation which was in-built in their own primitive tribal organizations.' He further asserted: 'Arguments about
philosophy and culture apart, the borders can be secured only if
the border people know that they are Indian and that they are
defenders of the farthest outposts of this land. And this they can
feel only when they are a part of India's national life and when they
derive their vital breath from its stream of consciousness. So far
they have been out of this current and their image of India is that
of a distant neighbour whose inhabitants periodically invaded
their areas in order to exploit them. This image must change. The
Sarvodaya workers are determined to reduce the imbalances
created by faulty planning and history, and heal the rifts'.[2]

But this is certainly not the whole story. One of the principal
architects of the tribal policy, Verrier Elwin, and Christophe von
Furer-Haimendorf an anthropologist who had the opportunity to
oversee the various aspect of tribal development in the region,
have written favourably about the virtues of leaving the tribes
'alone to run their own affairs'.

In *The Tribal World of Verrier Elwin*, Elwin made a very relevant point: 'in every conference, at every committee, in every
speech, people feel it their duty to discuss over and over again the
old controversy of Isolation, Assimilation or Integration, forget-
ting, that it has been put completely out of date'. The major factor
responsible for this phenomenon, according to Verrier Elwin, was
the induction of community development blocks, which encompassed the whole of India. He also decried the overzealous
assimilators.

It is said that if we allow the tribal people to retain their language, dress or social institutions, we keep them separate from the rest of India, and if we want to integrate them as quickly as possible and smooth them out, as it were, they will be exactly like everybody else. The fallacy in this is that the people of India as a whole are marked by great variety and that there is no standard culture, religion or language to which we can adapt the tribes. In practice, too it is just those tribesmen who have smoothed themselves out and adopted a way of life that is indistinguishable from that of their neighbours who have been most clamorous for separation from the rest of the population. They have realised that they are losing their identity and are desperately anxious to preserve it. Many of the Naga rebels have taken to a western way of life and dress in western clothes. The hill people of Assam proper who want a separate state are just those who have been most completely assimilated. It may well be that in the long run all tribes will lose their distinctiveness and sink into a drab uniformity possibly dominated by the overpowering American civilization that is so rapidly spreading across the world. But it seems to me foolish to accelerate this process in the interest of integration, for this does not and will not work.[3]

But did the society of the region really remain static?

After a visit to Subansiri and Tirap Districts in 1962, Christoph von Furer-Haimendorf wrote:

When I first travelled in the Subansiri region in 1944, the local tribes, the Apa Tanis and Daflas, had virtually no contact with the government. By 1962 there was an administrative centre in the Apa Tani Valley, linked by a motorable road with the Brahmaputra Valley, and attached to it were a hospital, schools, co-operative stores, and various other amenities open to the tribesmen. More impressive than these developments, however, was the fact that the local tribesmen seemed to be deriving considerable economic advantages from the activities of the administration without suffering any apparent damage to their cultural and social life.[4]

The damage to the tribal pattern of life was avoided as no outsiders were allowed to acquire land. The introduction of modern means of communication, like trucks and jeeps, induced the Apa Tanis to learn to drive. Haimendorf gave credit to a policy which provided 'a measure of isolation combined with a systematic and imaginative policy of a progressive administration'. Democracy and rapid industrialization, however, have violated the sacrosanct character of the policy. Haimendorf has lamented that, except in a few areas, such as NEFA, 'these principles have seldom been put fully into practice'. Writing in 1967, the author feared that there are indications that 'Nehru's extremely liberal ideas regarding the rights of the tribals and preservation of their cultural heritage may not be shared by all of the present leaders of the Congress party, and it is likely that pressure for a speedier and more complete assimilation of the aboriginals will gradually increase and lead to changes'. Have the policy directions really undergone such changes as to justify Haimendorf's fears? In a more recent work, published in 1982, Haimendorf reflects as follows:

> There can be no doubt that the establishment of vast industrial enter-
> prises in tribal zones lends urgency to the extension of protective mea-
> sures to all tribals whose rights and way of life have been placed in
> jeopardy. The architects of the Indian Constitution were determined
> that, while the age-old isolation of the Scheduled Tribes would have to
> be ended, they should be saved from exploitation and from the erosion
> of their rights to their ancestral land. It was clear that this aim could
> be achieved only by special legislation, but unfortunately for the tri-
> bals the original idealism of politicians and legislators is wearing thin,
> and while the laws for protecting tribals are still in existence, their
> implementation leaves much to be desired. Even among educated
> Indians, there seems to be a growing unwillingness to face the fact that
> forty million tribal people will for a long time form a separate and
> unassimilated element within the Indian nation. While many concede
> that there is also a widespread feeling that any privileges enjoyed by
> tribes were required only for a period of transition, and that within a
> span of ten or twenty years the integration of the tribes within the
> mainstream of the population should be completed, whereupon there
> would be no more justification for the continuation of scheduled areas
> and privileges for scheduled tribes.
>
> This new trend in public opinion represents as great a threat to the
> future prospects of tribals as the greed of land-grabbers does to their
> present well-being. The manner of the intergration of the tribal into
> the wider Indian society will ultimately be determined by political
> decisions, and these will be made on the basis of moral evaluations. It
> thus seems that, unless the intellectually leading sections of the Indian
> population develop a spirit of cultural tolerance and an appreciation
> for tribal values, even the most elaborate schemes for the economic
> improvement of tribal populations are likely to prove abortive.[5]

Nari Rustomji who spent thirty-five years as a member of the I.C.S. in north-east India, Sikkim and Bhutan and is an eminent author, wholeheartedly supports the original Nehruvian policy.

However, he holds the government's policy and approach responsible for the continuing violence and armed insurgency in the region. According to him governmental responses have been two-
fold: (i) an increasing dependence on military force, which has
taken on 'the semblance of an ever-spreading armed encamp-
ment'; and (ii) a lavish grant of funds to accelerate economic
development. He writes:

> It is unfortunate...that the methods invoked to restore stability have
> generally had, in fact, the effect of aggravating instability. It has to be
> recognized that, while inter-village rivalries and casual skirmishes
> have been endemic in the tribal areas since time immemorial, it has
> been only since Independence and the imposition of a much heavier
> administrative control that violence and armed insurgency have come
> to be accepted as the normal pattern of life. The loss of life resulting
> from the head-hunting raids of former times was negligible in compari-
> sion with the fatalities of the more recent period of political unsettle-
> ment. For the imposition of tighter and heavier administrative control
> has given rise to conditions of continuous and widespread tension,
> with the security forces of government in perpetual conflict with law-
> less elements of the local population.[6]

On this matter, Rustomji commends British policy, which was
one of least possible interference; 'it was the missionary, not the
administrator, who was the main harbinger of change'.[7] As a way
out of the present impasse, he feels that it will take time and pati-
ence to undo the damage brought about by well-intentioned,
though hasty, zeal. But the tribals are an understanding people
and will respond quickly to a change of heart and an approach that
demonstrates not an attitude of superiority and condescension but
a spirit of equality and mutual self-respect.[8]

There are others who lament the failures. B. K. Roy Burman, a
noted demographer, has blamed 'the political operators and
bureaucrats' for the slowness of the integrative process. He writes
that 'the initiative to give shape to the political vision of the found-
ing fathers passed on to the political operators and bureaucrats.
They failed to recognize that the Autonomous District Councils
were symbols of the emergence of supra-tribal entities in the process of articulation within a national society. They tried to treat
the Autonomous Councils merely as subordinate organs of the
State. This contradiction only helped those who were inimical to

the process of integration of the hill areas with the rest of the country'.[9]

While Goswami and Radhakrishna would have us believe that all the uncertainties have been caused by the wrong or inadequate policies of the Nehruvian era and subsequent years, Verrier Elwin, Haimendorf, Roy Burman and Rustomji have supported the policy framework but find serious faults with subsequent government approaches in the matter. Haimendorf suggests that the Nagaland crisis arose because, unlike NEFA, which was accorded a special status, all parts of Naga territory were brought under an administration run by the Assamese. The Nagas viewed the Assamese as 'new rulers intent on depriving them of the virtual self-government the tribesmen had enjoyed in the British days'. The massive insurgency in Mizoram in 1966 was caused, according to Roy Burman, by the 'failure of the State to create an institutional framework for augmenting the productive forces and modernizing the land-use pattern without impinging on the system of ownership'. The spread of insurgency to Manipur and Tripura are variously described as similar failures of government policy and approach. This school of thought would have us believe that a repetition of similar mistakes over the 'alien's issue' in Assam is going to finally alienate the people of the Brahmaputra Valley from the national political system.

A well-known Assamese historian, H. K. Barpujari, views the situation in the context of the strategic importance of north-east India and considers a move towards an India-China detente as an essential prerequisite to peace and stability in the region. He writes: 'even if it may not be possible to have a return to the Hindi Chini Bhai Bhai, a settlement of the boundary question will normalize relations between the two neighbourly but unfriendly countries and tend to do much towards peace, stability and security of the North-East Frontier'.[10] As regards the internal policy, Barpujari feels that the slow and cautious Nehruvian philosophy of development in NEFA has already paid dividends. The number of insurgents in Nagaland and Mizoram is on the decline. He recommends that 'endeavours need be made to bring them to reason and make them feel the fundamental unity of India in spite of the congeries of so many states of diverse ethnic groups having different languages, cultures and traditions; their fortunes are inextricably interwoven with their neighbours in the plains and a settlement of their problem could be made only with the Government of India and, that too, with compromises and not with confrontation. The aspirations of Mizos, Nagas or any other ethnic group need be considered with reason and sympathy, but not at the cost of disintegration of the country'.[11]

V. Venkata Rao, the widely respected scholar of the region emphasizes the need for conceptual clarity in formulating policy. The main question, according to him, is whether to establish unity by 'integration' or by 'assimilation'. Assimilation, being based on the principle of *matsyanyaya* (the big fish swallowing the small) would mean a total loss of cultural life and identity of the group that is being assimilated and its absorption into the dominant group on the latter's terms. This would lead to 'antagonism, tension and increasing alienation of each from the other'[12]. In the circumstances, he feels that 'we should admit that for building a strong state, cultural identities of the groups need not be eliminated. Instead of emphasizing cultural differences, economic interdependence should be encouraged'. The political reorganization of Assam in the recent past or even in future is acceptable to Venkata Rao.[13]

B. K. Nehru has found the causes of insurgency in the rise in the level of local consciousness and 'the sudden exposure of relatively primitive societies to the complexities of the modern world which they did not understand at all and from which they tried to protect themselves through their traditional and instinctive reaction of violence'. B. K. Nehru does not make scapegoats of the bureaucrats. He says: 'But one point certainly needs to be made. These changes which have caused the reaction were not imposed from outside because of the theoretical ideas of uniformity-loving bureaucrats. The demand for these comes from the tribal people themselves; they are no more willing to live without modern education and the material benefits of modern civilization in the constricting framework of a traditional society. And yet the new framework which requires a much extended base is not always accepted'.[14]

Was the management of north-east India really so simple a matter that had 'political operators and bureaucrats' done their jobs properly, everything would have been fine? If the government makes a genuine effort to revert to the old British pattern of administration and stops 'interfering' and treats the tribals with 'respect', is it really possible that even today things would again become quiet and orderly? It seems unlikely that it is within the competence of the Central Government to plan and execute such a policy in a vastly changed national security environment.

In fact, there are certain compulsions of international politics in a sensitive border area. The north-east is no longer a part of an empire which was feared in Tibet and Russia, when Burma was a part of that Empire, when China was weak and had not made claims over vast tracts of Indian territory nor garrisoned its troops on India's borders, and the USA had no geo-political interests in South Asia.

An agreement with China regarding the international boundaries would be a stabilizing factor, but the role of India's security forces even in that event has to be accepted as a permanent feature in north-east India, almost analogous with the situation on the western frontier. Similarly, any political convulsion in Burma will be of considerable significance to north-east India and the impact of such an event would depend upon whether political power is grasped by the Burmese Communist Party, which owes allegiance to the Chinese Communist Party, or remains with the army and nationalists. An interaction between the Indian security forces and the tribes cannot, therefore, be avoided. The impact of development within Bangladesh also cannot be ignored. Any large-scale persecution of Hindus in Bangladesh always puts tremendous pressure on the system to stop migration to India from that country. In recent years, the Chakmas, a Buddhist tribe in the Chittagong Hill Tracts of Bangladesh, has had to enter Mizoram as a result of Bangladesh Government's policy of throwing open tribal lands to Muslims. The Chakmas number half a million and their exodus to Mizoram or Tripura could cause grave social and economic strains in these territories. The instability in the Chittagong Hill Tracts benefits Mizo rebels in giving them a safe sanctuary adjacent to Mizoram.

Even the large-scale influx into India of Muslims from Bangladesh cannot be ruled out in view of the economic compulsions in Bangladesh. In a recent study on unemployment and underemployment in agriculture in the Phulpur police station area of Mymensingh district of Bangladesh, Muhammad

Masum[15] has brought out the prevalence of massive disguised unemployment in that area. In fact, Bangladesh is a classic case of a labour surplus economy, with a 3 per cent growth rate in population and a rural population accounting for 94 per cent of the total population, with the agricultural labour force estimated at about 84 per cent of the total labour force. Any famine or economic distress in Bangladesh leads to an influx of population into north-east India and the presence of relations and friends in the region only induces Bangladeshis to cross over regardless of the international frontier.

The induction of the army into Nagaland or Mizoram is, however, a different matter altogether. Historically, it was not the presence of the army that caused the rebellion but the insurgency of the rebels that led to the army's presence in Nagaland, Mizoram, Manipur and Tripura. The threat to national integrity has to be met and the administration cannot abdicate its responsibility here. Similarly, it is debatable whether a slowing down of the tempo of economic development would be welcomed by the tribals themselves. Most tribals have long been exposed to the radio and cinema and now to television, and there has been a rapid spread in education in recent years, even among the primitive tribes of Arunachal Pradesh. All these have created new demands and even fanciful consumption habits. Each member of the tribal community, like people elsewhere, wants a measure of fulfilment of his own dreams and every failure to fulfil personal desires leads to frustrations. In such a fast-changing environment, any move to push a tribal community or communities back to a traditional order would be resisted by the tribes themselves and is bound to fail. The change is thus inevitable.

It has to be appreciated that while articulation of the issues of language, religion, ethnicity and convergence and conflict are manifestations of the problems of the people at various stages of economic and political progress, the degree of change has definitely heightened the crisis. Broad-based, participatory political and economic organizations that could have steered the course of change in smooth fashion are undeveloped in the region. This phenomenon is a legacy of history and human failure to build powerful institutions. Historically, the inability of the national level parties, including the Congress, to involve the hills' people in the freedom struggle, and the segregationist policy of the 'inner-line

system' of the British prevented political organization from growing. The growth of most regional political organizations after
Independence, whether in Nagaland, Mizoram, Manipur, Tripura or Assam has contributed to conflict and violence rather than
to resolution and peace. The economic organizations that took
root during the British period, particularly in the tea and oil industries, failed to integrate with the indigenous economy, and this
trend notwithstanding, certain notable developments to the contrary have continued even after Independence. Thus, despite the
educational and economic backwardness in Bihar or Madhya
Pradesh and the existence of alien economic control to an even greater extent than in some States of north-east India, the problems
of change have been less acutely felt by the people in these states;
Bihar and Madhya Pradesh are gifted with more powerful political organizations and a more homogenous social structure than
the states comprising north-east India.

The close interaction between the middle class, the elite and the
several movements for regional identities in north-east India is far
too evident to go unnoticed. All the movements for regional identity so carefully promoted by the elite and middle class in each unit
of north-east India, cannot be summarily dismissed as the emotional and irrational outbursts of primordial loyalties. Behind
every agitation, whether over language or aliens, there are the
well-planned designs of the elites of that region aimed at maintaining control over the levers of power and the economy through the
involvement of mass support. The emerging socio-economic forces
have contributed towards the formation of new groups among the
peasantry and minorities and these groups in turn are demanding
their share in the economy and polity, leading to conflicts and the
emergence of new relationships.

There is a school of thought which believes that eventually all
variety, colour and culture of tribal life will yield place to uniformity and Americanization, and that the various revolts seeking the
freedom and presentation of the tribal heritage will melt away.
This is a somewhat unreal perception of the situation. What is true
is that, in a fast-changing society, some earlier policies and institutions have lost their shape as well as relevance. The reorganization
of Assam has made several District Councils less relevant; the policy of leaving the tribes alone has not prevented either the widespread induction of modern values in the region or the exploitation

of the less educated and economically poor by vested interests. Similarly, the policy of giving primacy to infra-structural development and modernization in agricultural operations has left Jhumia tribal cultivators at the mercy of the new economic system in which they have been severely exploited (for want of skill and experience).

The reorganization of north-east India has certainly given the tribals a sense of pride in their separate political status, and the local elite and dominant sections of the middle class have greatly benefited in economic and political terms. The benefits of reorganization, however, are yet to percolate down to the masses in a satisfactory manner. Having achieved separate political units the tribal leaders have emerged as ministers and heads of public sector bodies, and over the years some are no longer as honest, active and straightforward as they were. The liberal allocation of finance by the Centre and the growing deviousness of political life have led to the flow of black money in the region and political defections; in Manipur an M.L.A. reportedly defected three times in one day.[16] It may not therefore be very long before (in the face of glaring corruption and manipulations by a few in cornering all economic benefits) the large body of the people get disenchanted with the mere shell of their separate political status. The problems emanating from this perception might well lead to further trouble and threaten the prospects of progress in the region much as insurgency did in the first three decades after Independence. There is thus an imperative requirement to have a fresh look at the policies as well as the instruments of their implementation. These will be discussed in Chapter IX.

CHAPTER VIII

Demography, Culture, Identity Crisis And Economic Development: An Overview

Demographic Changes

One of the principal features of the demographic history of north-east India up to the first half of the nineteenth century was the sparseness of the population, both in absolute terms and in relation to the abundance of land. The population assessment that followed Assam's annexation in 1826 revealed fewer than a million people in the region. The other parts of the north-east were even more sparsely populated. In attempting to enhance the land revenue and augment the exchequer by exploitation of the natural resources of the region, the British found that the shortage of manpower in Assam was the greatest obstacle to the fulfilment of their plans. They thus encouraged and arranged for the migration of population into the Brahmaputra and Surma Valleys from East Bengal, Chotanagpur, Orissa, north Bihar, etc. to clear the jungles and reclaim swampy lands for cultivation, as well as to develop tea cultivation. The process of migration from East Bengal, in particular, continued despite the partition of India in 1947 and official efforts to terminate the inflow of people to north-east India. The results have been alarming.

During the last one and a half centuries the population of north-east India has witnessed an unprecedented increase, from less than one million to a sizeable 26 million people. The population of present-day Assam has risen from 3,290,000 in 1901 to 19,902,826 in 1981, a growth of 505.01 per cent as compared to 186.84 per cent for India as a whole during the corresponding period. The figures in millions for the other states of the north-east from 1901 to 1981 are: Arunachal Pradesh, 0.02 to 0.63; Mizoram, 0.08 to 0.49; Nagaland, 0.12 to 0.77; Tripura 0.17 to 2.05; Manipur, 0.28 to 1.14; and Meghalaya, 0.12 to 1.32. The population growth rate from 1901 to 1981 has thus been 491.71

per cent in Mizoram, 661.48 per cent in Nagaland, 1088.63 per cent in Tripura, 404 per cent in Manipur, and 289.95 per cent in Meghalaya.[1] The impact of this phenomenon on the society, polity and economy of the region has naturally been very significant.

The migrant communities have gained control over land and secondary sources of livelihood, like government jobs and so on. From an ethno-economic angle, there was once a fairly neat division in respect of economic spoils among the migrant communities. Migrant tribal labourers from Chotanagpur and Orissa settled on the tea estates with their families and later occupied wastelands for cultivation to supplement their meagre incomes from tea-garden employment. The other major migrant community, Bengali Muslims from East Bengal, settled initially on fallow land along the Brahmaputra but gradually extended their hold over lands in traditional tribal areas and Assamese villages. Bengali Hindus cornered middle class jobs in Assam, Tripura and Meghalaya, started small businesses and settled in several towns. The impact of migration on politics has been equally significant. In a democratic framework the demographic factor has played a crucial role and brought in spectacular changes in the wielding of political power. The most striking development has been in Tripura. Over the years, thanks to the migration of Bengali Hindus from East Bengal, the tribal autochthones have been outnumbered. The tribal population dropped from 64 per cent of the total in 1874 to 29 per cent in 1971. Bengalis had become 68 per cent of the total population by 1971, and are now estimated to be 70 per cent. Political and administrative power has thus passed from the indigenous tribals to migrant Bengalis. The transfer of land from the tribal population to Bengali migrants proved to be the critical factor in deteriorating social relations and a flash-point was reached in the June 1980 riots at Mandia, when several hundreds lost their lives and 3,00,000 were rendered homeless. There is widespread apprehension in the minds of the Assamese caste Hindus that in the near future their political power will be taken from them by the migrants. The other states of the region also share similar fears.

Limited Nature of Socialization

The question naturally arises as to why migrant communities

were not assimilated in the traditional society of north-east India. Why did the various political units comprising the region fail to evolve participatory and conflict-resolving social orders and polities? There are several factors responsible for this phenomenon.

Geographic factors – steep ridges, deep ravines and dense forests–had kept one hill tribe secluded from another for centuries. This led to the growth of animosities and mutual distrust between the hill tribes, while also facilitating the development of autonomous cultural traits among every tribe. The degree of socialization, however, varied from tribe to tribe; the Khasis and the Garos had more contact with others than the Nagas or the Apatanis. On the whole, the socialization process in the region has been at a very low level compared to areas with more hospitable terrains and easier communications. This is not to suggest that socialization *per se* would have led to assimilation and avoided conflict: it is quite likely that the indigenous people would have resisted massive migration in the initial years of British rule itself and that this in turn might have led to violent ethnic conflicts. But better communications undoubtedly facilitate socialization which in turn, can alone usher in an era of understanding.

During 1228–1826 there was limited, even if organized, migration to Assam and other regions of north-east India. This was well managed by the respective societies, the Ahoms and other ruling elites in the region. The organized migration of outsiders was necessitated by the frequent attacks on Assam by Muslim armies from Bengal during 1205–1682. As the Assamese historian, S.K. Bhuyan, records:

> The Ahom rulers encouraged men from India to come and settle in Assam provided their introduction was of advantage to the country. Artisans, craftsmen, weavers, clerks, accountants, scholars and saints, both Hindu and Moslem, were freely admitted, and occasionally brought by special arrangement with the rulers of Hindustan as there was an inadequacy of such men in Assam. But these licensed foreigners, after having come to Assam, had to cut off all connection with their mother country, and to become assimilated with the Assamese in language, manners and racial sympathy. They became subjects of the Assam government like older inhabitants. The Assamese objected to the admission of foreigners who owed allegiance to other rulers and proposed to reside in Assam as a temporary measure. The Assamese made a sharp distinction between desirable

foreigners who came to stay and became naturalized, and undesirable foreigners upon whom the Assam government could not exercise any degree of control. Europeans fell in the second category, and hence their entrance was almost always forbidden, and their movements closely watched even when they were permitted to enter the Assam territory.[2]

In the slow-moving socialization process over the centuries, the tribals were attracted by Hinduism and seveal tribes were assimilated in the Hindu fold. The advent of British rule in 1826 not only disrupted this process but the new cultural policies and programmes disrupted the spread of the Ramayana-Mahabharata tradition. There is no record of any dialogue occurring between British administrators and the local people about the fresh migration organized to work the tea gardens, on construction works or in local administrative establishments in the north-east.

The commencement of civil war in Assam in the late eighteenth-century and the subsequent Burmese war had also disrupted social harmony. Society in the Brahmaputra Valley in particular was in no position to absorb fresh migrants socially and culturally during the nineteenth century.

Further, besides the induction of divergent groups of people, which the existing social framework could not absorb, there was the entry of a new religion in north-east India: Christianity. Its spread accelerated from the 1860s onwards, to the efforts of a band of dedicated Christian missionaries as well as official British patronage. Over the years, an overwhelming number of people in Meghalaya, Nagaland and Mizoram were converted to Christianity, forsaking their traditional animistic faiths. The spread of Christianity among the migrant population on the tea estates of the plains has also been sizeable. In historical perspective, these conversions meant negation of the traditional process of assimilation between the people of the hills and the plains.

As we have already seen, the cultural renaissance that deeply influenced the consciousness of the common man in Bengal had only marginal influence on the people of north-east India. No outstanding leadership emerged in north-east India and the region was deprived of the mass-movement of unity among different sections of the people that was so refreshingly felt in Bengal. Even the Indian National Congress, which elsewhere united people in the quest for national independence, could not bring the large segments of tribal populations inhabiting the inaccessible hills of north-east India into its fold. The process of political integration initiated by the British no doubt helped in the growth of institutionalized procedures, but this was not enough to usher in an integrated political community in the region: against this background, the re-organization of Assam from time to time reflected the failure to develop an integrated community and continued the dominance of ethnic bonds and primordial loyalties.

Finally, although the exploitation of natural resources did lead to the establishment of oil-producing centres and a massive tea plantation economy, there was no synthesis between the traditional agricultural economy of the rural peasants, artisans and traders with that of the industrial economy, for the tea produced in Assam was either sent to Calcutta or directly to London for sale. This dual-economy pattern has been a major factor in creating a dichotomy in the economic system of north-east India. Even after Independence, such a system has continued, with the wages of migrant labour being remitted to their homes outside the region. Contractors and traders, too, transfer their profits to their home or invest them in more advanced urban centres outside the region. Similarly, and in tune with this ethos, the major companies have consistently kept their headquarters outside the region, leading to the adoption of schemes and projects which disregard the economic growth or ecological balance of north-east India.

Partisan Use of State Power

In a backdrop of limited socialization among ethnic groups, the ruling elites view every development that has a bearing on their control over the levers of political power with great suspicion. The break-up and various divisions of national political parties have given greater importance to ethnic loyalties in electoral behaviour in north-east India. Besides, there is a fairly long tradition among the ruling cities of furthering the interests of their ethnic brethren through the use of state machiney — in securing dominant positions in the economy and educational system of the state. The case of Assam is the most clear-cut here. During the first century of British rule, Bengali Hindus furthered the interests of their kinsmen from within and outside the region in securing jobs and small businesses, to the exclusion of tribals and Assamese caste Hindus. During the 1930s and 1940s the Muslim leader, Saadulla, encouraged his co-religionists to expand and consolidate their hold over agricultural land when he led the administration. After independence, the Assamese caste Hindus widely used the state's apparatus to help their compatriots gain control over various segments of Assam's society through administrative, educational, cultural and economic institutions.

Such partisan use of an administration impairs social harmony and ensures that 'opposite' groups and ethnic communities clamour in turn for political and administrative power. In a democracy it is within no one's competence to allow a community or ethnic group to continue in power in an attempt to ensure static social harmony, for ruling communities rise and fall for a variety of reasons. As the numerical strength of an ethnic or linguistic group is crucial in a democracy all ethnic groups at the helm of affairs in a plural society align themselves with other linguistic, cultural or religious groups. They even allow such groups a major say in political affairs and, consequently, in the management of government. If these political contrivances fail or do not take place, and the ruling ethnic group adopts such measures as to become a numerical majority which drives other groups into leaving the state, social harmony cannot but be seriously impaired. In such eventualities an interventionist role cannot be denied to the central government. The real solution of such a deep crisis, however, would be in the maintenance of order and the simultaneous commencement of dialogue and debate to resolve the conflicting claims of various cultures and political attitudes, the education of the masses and encouragement of the socialization process. It may also be essential to allay the genuine fears of an ethnic community, ruling or otherwise, by providing such safeguards as would be widely acceptable, and then to implement these through the local administration and active support from the national leadership. Such situations have been recurring themes of politics in Assam and Tripura in recent years and are likely to assume critical proportions in Meghalaya in the coming decades.

Population Policy

Notwithstanding the massive agitation over the foreign nationals

issue in Assam since 1979, it has to be appreciated that there can
be no population policy for Assam alone, for the simple reason
that geographical factors prevent it from being effective. Migrants
can move into Assam via Tripura and north-Bengal. In order to
be successful any demographic policy has to take into account: (a)
the powerful Assamese sensitivities towards the presence of Bengalis in the region and the total opposition of the Assamese elite to
any future influx into Assam; (b) the presence of certain elements
in Assam's border districts of Goalpara and Cachar who welcome
migrant populations from Bangladesh; (c) the humane support,
both amongst the people and in the State administrative
apparatus of West Bengal and Tripura for the migration of Bengali Hindu refugees from Bangladesh; (d) the responsibility of the
Central Government to honour international agreements and
national commitments; and (e) the view of various political units
of north-east India as well as the States of West Bengal, Bihar and
Sikkim on the 'aliens' question. Besides, the acute poverty in
Bangladesh[3] and the traditional distrust prevailing there between
Hindus and Muslims cannot be wished away.[4] Whatever the pro-
vocation for the large-scale influx of refugees into India, it should
be the endeavour of Indian diplomacy to ensure that the vulnera-
ble groups are helped within Bangladesh, the responsibility for
this rests with the international community, but the Government
of India could contribute generously for such relief operations.

A population policy for north-east India should not be only a
matter of physical barriers or sealing international borders between India and Bangladesh. It has to be the product of a meaningful consensus between different political units in eastern India
and must adequately reflect the concerns of the local people. Such
a policy alone could be successfully implemented by the governments of the States and the Centre. The concerned administration
would be greatly helped in its tasks if identity cards are expeditiously issued to Indian nationals domiciled in these states; this will
help distinguish them from their neighbours from Bangladesh
and Nepal. Identity cards would be of great assistance in the preparation of electoral rolls, registration in employment exchanges
and admission into educational institutions. Similarly, the registration of births and deaths and compulsory registration of all land
transfers would help the administration attain its objectives of
keeping the region free of 'foreign nationals'.

Cultural Landscape

The cultural landscape of north-east India is characterized by several ethnic groups whose social responses, with varying degrees of differences, emanate from ethnic value-systems and their promotion. Historically, each group developed its own way of life and an identifiable pattern of relationships with the other ethnic groups with which it came into contact. The forces of democracy, politics and modernization that have operated after 1947 have decisively altered age-old patterns of relationships and the spatial consciousness of every tribe or ethnic group. However, in the foreseeable future the tribal factor, the relationship between Assamese Hindus and Bengali Hindus and Assamese Hindus and Bengali Muslims will dominate the cultural equations and politics of north-east India.

Land and Tribal Society

The tribals constitute a majority of the population in Meghalaya (80.58 per cent), Nagaland (83.99 per cent), Mizoram (93.82 per cent) and Arunachal Pradesh (69.82 per cent), and have a significant presence in Tripura (28.44 per cent), Manipur (27.30 per cent) and Assam (11 per cent).[5] Each tribe is different from other tribes, much more so than ethnic groups in the plains. Nonetheless, the tribes in north-east India have also developed some traits and attitudes which are common to each other. These relate to (a) a sense of kinship; (b) an adherence to traditional beliefs; (c) a love for their particular language; and (d) a deep attachment to their land.

A tribe is usually composed of a number of clans, kinship groups and extended families. All its members have a sense of belonging to a community which once had common ancestors. This unit has found its cementing force in the tribal animistic faiths. The tribal dialects, which in several instances, such as with the Bodos and Khasis, have developed into sophisticated modern language, have provided cohesion to the tribal way of life. The proverbial attachment of a tribal to his land is a complex web of relationships, the primary force no doubt being economic. But it is also related to tradition, family ties, religion, and so on. A perceptive author has summed up the position in the context of north-east India as follows:

Land, whether it be homestead land which is the habitat of the family or land for cultivation, constitutes the life blood of tribal community, as much in Christian as in non-Christian villages. Particular locations are considered to be the dwelling place of spirits, good and evil, that have to be periodically placated. Other locations are associated with the shades of devoted ancestors and are held in special respect and reverence ....For a tribal, every corner of his home has its associations. His rice fields may not be extensive, but his co-villagers still talked of the day he offered a Feast of Merit for the community and pointed to the spot where he had sacrificed the ceremonial *mithun*(the gaur, resembling the bison).[6]

The tribals' relationship with their lands in the hills as well as in the plains of north-east India, have been disturbed in a great vartiety of ways since 1947 – notwithstanding government policies and programmes to the contrary. The process commenced in and around Shillong, once the headquarters of the Greater Assam administration and now the capital of Meghalaya. Here, land was liberally leased not only to expanding government offices and the security apparatus, but also for private residential colonies, for influential politicians and civil servants, for markets and business establishments, for churches, hospitals and educational institutions. The same story was more or less repeated in Nagaland after 1963. The regrouping of villages in Mizoram after the insurgency in that area in 1966 and in certain parts of Nagaland earlier, resulted in villagers at communication points being put under the care of the security forces: in the process, they completely lost their ancestral villages, paddy fields and traditional places of worship. The land alienation of the tribals in Tripura was largely caused by the machinations of vested interests, as a result of which the tribals sold their ancestral land to migrant Bengalis and retreated deeper into the hills. In Assam, both in the hills and plains, the tribals have lost their land, and future attempts at social cohesiveness and the maintenance of peace greatly depend upon the way the land problem of the tribals is tackled in coming years. The Assam scenario needs a more detailed analysis in view of the size of its population and its possible impact on other States of the region.

There are separate provisions for the administration of land in the Hill districts (i.e. the North Cachar Hills and Karbi-Anglong) and the plains of Assam. In the Hill districts, the land is owned communally and no individual has a transferable right in land.

Under the Sixth Schedule of the Constitution of India, the authority for land administration is vested in the autonomous District Councils, which run the administration in accordance with the old customs and usages of the region. As regards the plains' tribal areas, tribal belts and blocks – thirty-seven in number – were constituted immediately after Independence under executive orders and the advice of a perceptive indigenous leadership. These executive orders were added to the Assam Land and Revenue Regulation, 1886 through a separate chapter in 1947 with a view to (a) stopping the alienation of tribal lands into the hands of outsiders; and (b) preventing the plains' tribals from being further driven to the interior. Despite this, tribal lands have passed on with impunity to the migrants and indigenous non-tribals in the plains as well as in the Hills.

Despite the importance of land in the economy and way of life of tribal society, no empirical studies were made on this subject in Assam until the 1970s. The three studies made then merit attention and were: (1) that conducted by the Tribal Research Institute of Assam in 1974 and entitled 'The Probelms of Transfer and Alienation of Tribal Land in Assam' (unpublished, but available with the State administration); (2) the Report of the Sub-Committee of the Advisory Council for Welfare of Scheduled Tribes(Plains) on the Settlement of Land in Tribal Belts and Blocks and of Forest Land, 1976; and (3) the Report of the Committee on the Welfare of Scheduled Castes and Scheduled Tribes Relating to Land and Revenue, 1979 presented to the Assam Legislative Assembly on 5 April, 1979.

These studies have revealed that in the two Hill districts of Assam the formal transfer of land to non-tribals is nominal, but that the actual transfer is large. In Karbi-Anglong district, the 1974 report records that 'temporary alienation of lands from the hands of the tribals to the non-tribals in the shape of *Pakis, Sukti Bandhak, Khoi Bandhak, Mena,* etc. is increasing at a very alarming rate'. In this district, tribals practice shifting cultivation and, through the methods mentioned above, non-tribals have raised crops on tribal land and deprived tribals of the fruits of cultivation. The report goes on to observe that, 'within the next few years this temporary alienation of land might lead to complete distortion of the tribal economy if it is not nipped in the bud'. It has been established that neither the Karbi-Anglong District(Transfer of

Land) Act, 1959 nor the supervision of the District Council have stopped the alienation of tribal lands. The failure of the District Councils to protect the land rights of tenants is not because of a lack of authority, for the District Councils have complete authority to prepare the record of rights of tenants, the settlement and use, etc. of land within their territorial jurisdictons. The 1979 Report submitted to the Assam Legislative Assembly has also highlighted 'some very clever devices' employed to deprive tribals of their lands

In the plains of Assam the alienation of tribal lands has been even more marked.[7] Some of the devices employed to deprive tribals of land were the grant by revenue officials of mutation to non-tribals and non-eligible outsiders in tribal lands, in gross violation of the law. Similarly, the registration of sale deeds by registration officials in favour of non-tribals has been done in contravention of the law. The State government itself excluded certain villages from the tribal belt under pressure from encroachers and the forces of urbanization.[8] A former Revenue Minister of Assam allotted a co-operative of educated upper-caste Assamese Hindus a large plot of land in the tribal belt of Darrang district in 1971, showing utter disregard for the rules on the subject.

The administrative failure to protect the sanctity of tribal belts and blocks could be attributed to callousness on the part of officials and social acquiescence of violations of the law. Under the law any non-eligible person occupying land in tribal belts and blocks is to be treated as an 'encroacher' and is liable to be 'evicted'. The 1979 Report has quoted the Revenue Secretary of the State as having testified that he did 'not come across any such instances' of eviction of an illegal occupant of land in a tribal belt or block.

Tribal land alienation, particularly in Assam and Tripura, has strained social harmony and has the potential to create unprecedented damage to it. The incidents at Mandya in Tripura in 1980 were a grim pointer in this direction. The violence that erupted after the announcement of general elections in Assam in February 1983 was largely caused by land alienation and provoked the Bodo-Kacharis in Gohpur in Darrang district to kill a large number of Assamese caste-Hindus in a situation surcharged with pro-and anti-poll campaigners. Similarly, the Lalungs, a plains' tribe supported by Bodos and caste-Hindu Assamese, massacred immigrant Muslims in Nellie in Nowgong district during this period.

'Inner-line' restrictions and the communal nature of land ownership have prevented the problem of land alienation in Nagaland, Meghalaya, Mizoram, Arunachal Pradesh and the Hill districts of Assam from assuming the alarming proportions prevailing in Manipur, Tripura and the Assam plains, where there are no general restrictions on land-ownership rights or the movement of populations. However, as the possession of land is a key factor in the economy of a political unit and has deep economic and social implications involving different ethnic groups with divergent perceptions and at different levels of education and development consciousness, various State governments have adopted different measures. For example, Manipur has prohibited the transfer of land by a member of the Scheduled Tribes to a non-member, unless the permission of the Deputy Commissioner and District Council have been obtained in terms of the Manipur Land Revenue and Land Reforms Act, 1960. Tripura has prohibited the alienation of land and has also provided for the restoration of land under the Tripura Land Revenue and Land Reforms Act, 1974. In Assam, where elaborate provisions were made for the protection of tribal rights in land under Chapter X of the 1947 Assam Land and Revenue Regulation, two separate measures have recently been adopted : (1) under the Assam Land and Revenue Regulation (Amendment) Act, 1981, the previous permission of the Deputy Commissioner of a district is necessary before a landholder can transfer his land even to a permanent resident of the tribal belt or block, unless the person does not belong to the protected class of people duly notified under section 160 of the Regulation; and (2) a Tribal Development Authority for the plains' tribal areas of Assam has been constituted under the chairmanship of the Chief Minster of Assam for the general economic development of these areas under the Assam Tribal Development Authority Ordinance, 1983.

Will these measures help solve the tribal land alienation problem? If past experience of the administration of land is any guide, they may not. A general lack of determination on the part of the administration and society is evident. One could perhaps agree in theory with the authors of the 1976 Report that 'the first and foremost duty of the revenue administration should be to eject all those ineligible encroachments both from *sarkari* as well as *patta* land within all the tribal belts or blocks within a time bound programme', and also that 'all such lands made free from encroachments should be simultaneously handed over for possession to eligible landless persons of the belts and blocks'. But in the prevailing social milieu of Assam, this seems to be a tall order. A more pragmatic approach is called for and governmental decisions should be preceded by empirical studies at micro-levels.

Efforts should be made to find out the various socio-economic factors responsible for land alienation, like the tendency of the plains' and hill tribals to avoid paying land revenue, the expesnses of tribal festivities, their heavy consumption of liquor and the state of their indebtedness. We must know at least in some specific cases as to how the District Councils, composed exclusively of tribals, succumbed to the machinations of vested interests and became party to the alienation of tribal land to outsiders. In respect of tribal belts and blocks, there is an imperative need to ascertain as to whether safeguarding the interests of non-tribal permanent residents, like Nepalis, by the Government in December 1947 encouraged non-tribal ethnic groups to hire away tribal lands, and the like. The study should look into not only the strengthening of existing laws and their stricter enforcement but also some of the following questions: (a) whether exemption from payment of land revenue by the plains' tribals in tribal belts and blocks would help; (b) whether the authority to de-reserve certain areas from tribal belts and blocks should be transferred fromthe State to a quasi-judicial body like the Assam Board of Revenue or to a plains' tribal authority constituted for the purpose; (c) whether tribals should be given land documents through the revenue machinery free of cost; and (d) how to restore land to the tribals. The outcome of such a study on Assam would also be of relevance to the other states of the region.

Politicization of Tribal Society

Post-1947 developments have both modernized and politicized tribal society in north-east India. Whereas in western countries, the democratic system grew out of bourgeois societies and capitalist economies, in the tribal areas of north-east India, democratic political institutions have been transplanted to become instruments of social and economic change.

The tribals, who had no political representation in any legislature before 1937, are today exclusively represented in the Meghalaya, Nagaland, Mizoram and Arunachal Pradesh Legislative Assemblies, making a total of 180 members. Another 43 seats are reserved for tribals in the Assam, Manipur and Tripura Legislative Assemblies. Besides, there are 11 seats for tribals in the Lok Sabha and, at present, there are 6 tribal members from north-east India in the Rajya Sabha. Above all, there are 14 autonomous District Councils in north-east India with at least 24 elected members in each.

The demands of various groups in the region have to be viewed against this background of increased political socialization. The Bodo-Kacharis, who number more than 1.5 million, are demanding through their political organization – the Plains Tribal Council of Assam (PTCA) a separate 'Udayachal State' in which Bodo is the official language. Similarly, immediately after the proposal for the reorganization of Assam was floated by the Central Government in 1967, the Ahoms demanded under the aegis of the Ujoni Assam Rajya Parishad (UARP), a 'separate unit of upper Assam' as well as recognition of themselves as a Scheduled Tribe. The Meiteis' feeling of neglect and deprivation in Manipur, and their demand for recognition as a Scheduled Tribe has to be seen in the light of their deprivation in employment and education vis-a-vis members of the existing Scheduled Tribes. The fears of the Meiteis have intensified thanks to large-scale corruption and a near explosion in the ranks of unemployed university graduates. The demands of the Tripura Upjati Juba Samiti (TUJS), however, go much deeper than politicization and are profoundly rooted in land alienation that has occurred on a scale beyond that in any other state of India since Independence.

Along with politicization, there has been a very sudden exposure of the tribals in remote hill areas in particular to a complex, modern civilization. Head hunters were exposed to writing and debate, scantily clad tribes were initiated into the comforts of tropical and woollen garments, nomadic tribes who had not even handled a bullock cart were trained to drive jeeps and trucks, the practitioners of slash-and-burn cultivation were introduced to permanent cultivation, high-yielding crops and irrigation. And all this in one or two generations. A certain degree of conflict and

violence was thus inevitable in this process of change. As B.K.
Nehru says, 'what is surprising is that these sudden and cataclys-
mic changes have not resulted in reactions of violence among
peoples not noticeably devoted to Ahimsa, more than they actually have'.[9]

North-East India has nearly 4 million of India's 40 million tribals. Over the years, as a result of policies of non-interference in
tribal ways, protection of their land rights, the promotion of education and reservations in employment and education, certain
tribes in north-east India have done better in material terms than
the rest of the population. The high rate of literacy among such
tribes and their willingness to fully participate in the endeavours
of a modern society may pose a threat to ideas about the collective
ownership of land, and to the traditional social order, but it must
be recognized that the tribals are going to play an increasingly
important role in society, politics and the administration of north-
east India and the country at large. There is no political threat to
tribal languages in the Hills and the Bodo language is gradually
getting modernized with publications in subjects like the sciences
and medicine. The need is to handle their cultural and political
aspirations and land rights both in the hills and the plains with
adroitness and sympathy.

The Bengali Factor

The Assamese view themselves as a nationality with the
Brahmaputra Valley as their homeland, Assamese as their language and Hinduism as their religion. They had forged an
alliance with Bengali Muslims on the understanding that the latter would adopt the Assamese language, educate their children in
Assamese schools and play a subservient role to caste Hindus in
the agrarian sector. Similarly, tea garden labourers who are either
Hindu or Christian were treated as neo-Assamese on the understanding that they would accept the Assamese language and support the caste Hindus in politics. In forging this kind of relationship between the Assamese on the one hand and Bengali Muslims
and tea garden 'coolies' on the other, the Indian National Congress has played a crucial institutional role; the leadership of the
Congress in Assam came into the hands of the Assamese middle
class in the 1920s. The plains' tribals have also been accorded a

higher status in the Assamese world view, with the Bodo language given a respectable place as a medium of instruction up to the secondary school level despite the declaration of Assamese as the official language of the State in 1960.

In the growth of Assamese nationalism, the Assamese language was always perceived as the chief instrument of self-assertion and accorded a 'mother' status. A noted Assamese poet exclaimed, *chir senehi nor bhasa janai* ('My mother tongue is my eternal friend'), and this continues to be a popular slogan of the youth in the Brahmaputra Valley. Today, it is difficult for anyone to mix well in the Assamese cultural mainstream without a fluency in the language. In fact, Assamese politics since the nineteenth century has always been concerned with Assamese language and culture. The Assamese psyche seems to have been guided by a philosophy that power and language have a close relationship. If power goes, the language also declines, as happened after sovereignty passed to the British from the Ahoms, and Assamese was replaced by Bengali as the official language.

There is no denying that language is a uniquely powerful instrument in unifying a diverse population. However, some of the very features of a language movement that give unity under certain circumstances become the root cause of disintegration and conflict in a different situation. This has been true of the language movement in Assam as well. In earlier times, the Assamese language helped in the spread of the Ramayana-Mahabharata tradition, Hinduization of the Ahoms and the Koches, integration of several bordering tribes, unity among different peoples in the cause of national independence, and so on. In recent times, however, the language movement has given an impetus to forces which have led to the bifurcation of Assam, violent conflicts between linguistic groups, etc. The process started with the declaration of Assamese as the official language of the State in 1960 and its introduction in phases from community development blocks onwards. The framers of the new language policy failed to realize that the process of making a composite Assamese sub-nationality a durable component of Indian nationhood should not be rushed.

In respect of cultural conflicts with Bengali Hindus in northeast India, several facts clearly stand out. First, Bengali Hindus travelled to most parts of north-east India and cornered administrative positions to the exclusion of the 'sons-of-soil' during the

British period. Second, Bengali Hindus migrated in large numbers to Assam and Tripura after Independence and completely altered the demographic profile of Tripura in their favour. Finally, Bengali Hindus have a sizeable presence in all urban centres in the plains of north-east India as well as in Shillong, the capital of Meghalaya. Of greater significance to our analysis, however, is the belief that Bengali Hindus, whether in Assam or in Tripura, are generally not actuated by any desire nor perceive any compulsion to learn Assamese, Tripuri or any local dialect or language. The attitude of an average Bengali-speaking person towards Assamese, the most developed of the local languages of north-east India, is seen to be far from complimentary or respectful. While some educated Bengalis in north-east India no doubt view Assamese with a modicum of respect, the majority consider the language inferior and dependent upon their own language, literature and media for creativity and excellence. Over the years, Bengali Hindus have set up their own schools in Assam and Shillong, and are no longer required to send their children to local vernacular schools. The result is obvious: their children do not have friends in other linguistic groups, unless educated in English-medium schools which are the exclusive preserves of the elite and the rich. Similarly, in every office there is a sizeable Bengali presence which enables Bengali-speakers to adopt a fairly segregated way of office life. This has hampered the socialization process and heightened the identity crisis of smaller ethnic groups.

Ever since Partition, Bengali Hindus have suffered greatly as a group both in Bangladesh and in several conflicts in north-east India; the fact however remains that the fear of linguistic and cultural domination by the Bengalis in the minds of the Tripuris or the Assamese is not unreal. In Tripura, the Bengali language and culture not only gets demographically superior support, but, over the years, Tripura's educational institutions have been shaped in the light of Bengali culture and values. There is a fear among Assamese-speaking people that they will be linguistically reduced to second place in Assam if the immigrant Muslim decides to declare Bengali as his language.

The linguistic profile of Cachar adds another dimension to the language issue in Assam. Both linguistically and culturally Cachar district has a distinct Bengali personality. Nearly 90 per cent of Cachar's 2.5 million people speak Bengali; the language of the district courts and of administration is Bengali, as is the medium of instruction in most educational institutions. Once Cachar's schools are delinked from the Assam Board of Secondary Education and its colleges from Gauhati University by the creation of a separate Board and a separate university, the educational system of Cachar district will become unilingual and separate from that of Assam. Some Assamese feel that the separation of Cachar would safeguard the rest of Assam's identity, language and culture; but the idea will only buy peace for ten or twenty years if implemented. A further political reorganization of Assam is not the answer to its social, cultural and economic problems. A separate Cachar would leave the common people where they are and many internal conflicts — both religious and ethnic — within the present Cachar district would gradually assume unmanageable proportions, hampering in turn the process of any meaningful economic development. How would the Bengalis in the Brahmaputra Valley react to the separation of Cachar? Would they accept the Assamese language and culture or organize themselves into a small group with a separate Bengali identity and treat their own language as the sole means of preserving that identity? As the latter course is more likely, the stage would be set for yet fiercer hostility between Assamese and Bengalis.

The Muslim Factor

There are several dimensions to the question of the cultural identity of Muslims in north-east India. However, two groups among the adherents of Islam are easily identifiable. The first group arrived in the region during the thirteenth and seventeenth centuries and was assimilated in the local society of Assam and Manipur; these people are now popularly known as Assamese Muslims in the Brahmaputra Valley. The second group came from East Bengal during British rule and later, and they are yet to merge completely in the cultural patterns of the indigenous people; this group is referred to as Bengali Muslims. Muslims are not found in the hills of Arunachal Pradesh, Mizoram and Nagaland, but only in the plains of north-east India, with a heavy concentration in the Brahmaputra Valley.

The Assamese Muslims came from north India as members of the expeditionary forces into Assam from time to time and

belonged largely to Afghan and Mughal stock. Over the years, a
bond between Assamese Hindus and these migrant Muslims
developed. During the Vaishnavite movement led by Sankardev
(1449–1569), the Muslims were assimilated in the local culture. It
is well-established that Chand Khan or Chandsai, a Muslim disciple of Sankardev, viewed Sankardev as an incarnation of God.
Chand Khan, a tailor by profession, once having sighted Sankardev with four arms, made a shirt for his master with four sleeves.
Chand Khan is venerated in Assam by the Hindus and the Muslims alike. Although there are separate Hindu and Muslim villages in Assam, as a result of the Vaishnavite movement several
mixed villages came into being and are still flourishing.

The socialization process between Hindus and Muslims is
unique here, and drew strength from several other facts too. From
the start of the Muslim entry into Assam in the thirteenth century,
Muslims formed a small part of the total population of the
Brahmaputra Valley. They also lost contact with the lands of
their origin in north India, largely thanks to the strained relations
between the rulers of Assam and the Mughals. The Muslims in
Assam remained under non-Muslim rulers for centuries. Besides,
the tolerance shown by Assam's ruling elite towards adherents of
Islam in the medieval period greatly helped the Muslims come
close to the indigenous population. There was no untouchability
in Assam and Hindus and the tribals ate the food cooked by Muslims in the Brahmaputra Valley. This was in sharp contrast to the
general practice in North India.

The Assamese Hindus and Muslims thus forged close links.
The famous historian Shihabuddin, who accompanied Mir Jum-
lah on his expedition to the Brahmaputra Valley in 1662, reflected
on this unity as follows: 'As for the Mussalmans who had been
taken prisoner in former times and had chosen to marry here,
their descendants act exactly in the manner of the Assamese, and
have nothing of Islam except the name; their hearts are inclined
far more towards mingling with the Assamese than towards
association with Muslims.'[10] Today, Assamese Muslims are
proud of the Assamese language and culture, the cultural impact
is so overwhelming in social relations that Assamese Muslims are
closer to Assamese Hindus than to their Bengali co-religionists.
Like Assamese Hindus, the Muslims are monogamous and the
practice of unilateral divorce is unknown among them, as

opposed to the practice among Bengali Muslims. The net result is
that, in cultural terms, both Assamese Hindus and Muslims consider themselves superior to Bengali Muslims, and Assamese
Muslims refer to the Bengali Muslims as *Miyans* in the same con-
temptuous vein as do the Assamese Hindus, who call them
Mymensinghias.

Who are these over 4 million Bengali Muslims in Assam? Until
about the first Muslim invasion by Bakhtiyar Khilji in 1203, they
belonged to various Mongoloid or Mongol-Dravidian tribes and
were Pods, Chandals, Rajbanshis and Koches. During the period
of Muslim rule in the Bengal delta (1203–1765), these groups
were converted to Islam.[11] Physically, they still resemble the
plains' tribals rather than the Muslims of north India who settled
in north-east India. This origin of the Bengali Muslims has
played an important part in shaping their attitude towards language and culture and their spatial consciousness of belonging to
the Bengal delta, irrespective of administrative or national boundaries.

While religion has not obstructed the maintenance of continued unity between the Assamese Hindus and Assamese Muslims, the relationship between Bengali Hindus and Bengali Muslims has been marred by communal disharmony even though
they speak the same language. In the realm of culture, the Muslims of East Bengal have tended to view the Bengal Renaissance
as an extension of Brahminic culture, even if transmitted through
Bengali. An effort was made by Bengali Muslims to orient themselves to Islamic culture and its heritage and, in the process,
Sanskrit words were substituted by Arabic and Persian terms in
the spoken language. The efforts of West Pakistan's rulers to substitute Urdu for Bengali after 1947 was fiercely resented by the
people of East Bengal, but the liberation of Bangladesh in 1971
created another crisis of identity among Bengali Muslims in as
much as the adoption of secularism came to be viewed as the
negation of Islam. In the quest for a separate identity, the Bengali
Muslim elite had earlier perceived their Islamic identity as being
a part of Pakistan. The subsequent philosophy of secularism
made them feel as a part of the Bengali culture of West Bengal and
India. Accordingly, efforts are underway in Bangladesh to construct a Bengali Muslim cultural heritage independent of that of
Bengali Hinduism and Pakistani Muslim culture. The developments on this count will be worth watching.

All these and several other dimensions of cultural incómpatability are present in the cultural make-up of Bengali Muslims in the Brahmaputra Valley. Some salient features of this cultural make-up are: first, the migrant Bengali Hindus and Bengali Muslims are divided on religious and cultural lines, the former being closely linked with the culture of the Bengal Renaissance and Hindu philosophy. Second, the overwhelming number of Bengali Muslims who migrated to Assam were illiterate and had economic expectations from Assamese officials by way of grants of land, jobs, and so on and, almost in exchange, were willing to accept the Assamese language and way of life. As a result of this phenomenon, they sent their children to Assamese schools and declared themselves as Assamese speakers before the census officials.

Third, before Independence, Bengali Muslims had actively supported the idea of including Assam in Pakistan. The 1931 Census mentioned the tensions between Assamese caste Hindus and Bengali Muslims on account of the 'Line System', under which the latter were prevented from acquiring land outside the 'line' earmarked for their habitation and cultivation. Bengali Muslims viewed this as a Hindu-Muslim line, a divide that ran counter to the will of Allah. Interestingly, during the 1930s and 1940s, while every Muslim member of the Assam legislature demanded the abolition of the line, every Hindu member favoured its continuation. The line was thus never formally abolished. Today, while carving Assam out of India does not arise, the control of the Bengali Muslim over the agricultural economy of Assam cannot be wished away.

Fourth, after Independence, some politicians and academicians have assiduously built up the bogey that Assam would soon be converted into a Muslim majority, thanks to (a) migration from Bangladesh, and (b) an alarming birth rate among the Muslims on account of widespread polygamy among them. The Muslim population, whch was only 5,03,670 in 1901 in the present territories of Assam rose to 35,86,840 by 1971. But there was a similar increase among the Hindus as well. In fact, since 1951 the Muslims have never constituted more than 26 per cent of Assam's total population, while the Hindus have never been below 72 per cent. There is little likelihood of the Muslims becoming numerically superior in the coming decades. The birth rate among Muslims is admittedly high. However, as I learnt as Deputy Commissioner in Mangaldai and Barpeta in the 1970s, Muslim women are as willing to undergo tubectomy as their Hindu counterparts. The real cause for the failure of family planning programmes among immigrant Muslims is not religion, but administrative inadequacies and a lack of awareness of even existing facilities. As regards the myth that Muslims have more children because their religion permits them four wives at a time, it needs to be pointed out that there is a general shortage of women in north-east India which makes this impossible. In Assam there were 901 women for every 1,000 males in 1981.[12] In 1951 the number of males of Pakistani origin in Assam was 4,64,440 and that of females was only 3,67,432.[13] Under these circumstances, even if every Muslim had two wives, 60 per cent of the Muslim males would go without a wife! This would cause tremendous social tension. Besides, economic compulsions demand an average immigrant Muslim to content himself with one wife. Above all, it seems unlikely that four women with one husband will have more children than four women with four separate husbands.

Finally, will the Bengali Muslims in the aftermath of the agitation over the foreign nationals issue in Assam get closer to Bengali Hindus and declare themselves to be Bengali speakers before the census officials? Even though both Bengali Muslims and Hindus were affected by the agitation, this question cannot be conclusively answered at this stage. The Bengali Muslims in Assam might be tempted to follow Bangladesh's Islamic cultural policy, just as the Bengali Hindus follow the culture of West Bengal. These are the alternatives available to the Bengali Muslim elite of the Brahmaputra Valley; they are better educated and were modernized than ever before, and will surely see that the community's future lies in a closer link with the Assamese way of life and language. Economic considerations and even the limited socialization between the two communities over the last century should make this feasible. The Assamese will co-operate with the Bengali Muslims, whom they have handled successfully to their advantage in the past. With a fresh political understanding they will again feel confident to do so in the future.

Identity Crisis

An identity crisis is inherent in a society undergoing as rapid a change as in north-east India, particularly amongst its tribes. However tempting it might be, no State system can order or re-order in a chronological fashion the processes of cultural, economic and political change or, in the alternative, keep the social system in static form. One of the lessons of the history of north-east India is that, whenever the State has tried to re-organize the community in its own bureaucratic image—like the regrouping of villages in Mizoram and Nagaland after Independence, or prescribing a language of its own choice over the population as done during the first phase of British rule, in Assam — there have been more problems and the objective of orderly prog-ress gave way to disorder and violence. Similarly, the efforts of certain groups to go back to past practices in dress, food and read-ing habits in the name of caste, tribe and culture, as witnessed in some areas of Assam, Manipur and Tripura in recent years, are bound to fail. For the people of north-east India have already tasted the fruits of science and technology and will not long remain concerned merely with historical nostalgia or in rumina-tions of the past. Besides, in order to remain an Assamese, a Ben-gali, a Tripuri, a Meitei, a Garo, a Khasi or an Ao, it has to be appreciated that revivalism is no answer.

It is essential to realize that the widespread identity crisis in north-east India has been caused by the large-scale migration of population from outside the region during the past one hundred years, and the total dependence of people on the land and the States' apparatus for a livelihood. The phenomenon has made the local population feel outnumbered and swamped by people of dif-ferent cultural origins. The failure of various sections of the mig-rant population to adapt themselves to the local language, cus-toms and traditions has further accentuated the identity crisis. A proper socialization process, which alone could have helped gen-erate understanding among different communities, is frequently impaired in the wake of periodic inter-community clashes and kil-lings and the tendency of each person to confine himself to his own group. The administrative system is always preoccupied with fire-fighting operations, either in containing human tragedies or giving relief to the victims of natural calamities, thereby neglect-ing its role as an instrument of development and a meaningful agent of socializaton and progress. Above all, every single change in identity is not undesirable. The various tribes inhabiting the

Naga hills and the Tuensang area are now all happily referred to
as Nagas—a new identity. Several tribes of the Lushai hills are
called Mizos and many castes in Assam would like to be referred
to as caste Hindus. Similarly, a new respect is being accorded to
local languages. Bodo is widely read, Khasi has developed into a
literary language and Gauhati University, though located in
Assam, has accorded recognition to Khasi in the university cur-
ricula, etc.

As regards religion, of the seven political units, Christianity is
the religion of the majority in Nagaland (66.9 per cent) and
Mizoram (86.1 per cent) and has a near majority in Meghalaya
(46.9 per cent). Hinduism is professed by a majority in Assam
(72.5 per cent), Manipur (59 per cent) and Tripura (89.6 per
cent). A majority in Arunachal Pradesh adheres to animistic
faiths (63.5 per cent). Among the 26 million people of north-east
India, Hinduism is professed by over 66 per cent, Islam by nearly
20 per cent and Christianity by over 9 per cent. Despite the sizeable presence of Christians in three political units, their total
numerical strength does not exceed 2.5 million, while adherents of
Islam (mostly concentrated in Assam, followed by Tripura, Manipur and Meghalaya) exceed 5 million.[14] As matters stand, it
seems that religion will not play a major role in the 'identity crisis'
in north-east India. Religious revival and decline may be a recurring theme in the region, but it will not be a major force in issues
concerning development or national integration.

V. Venkata Rao has advocated the traditional philosophical
approach of the Buddha and Asoka to overcome the problem of
identity. He writes:

Identity is a myth created by politicians to serve their interests.
North-east India is a polyglot area. India throughout its history is
multi-lingual. The Buddha, looking eternally young, seated on a lotus
of purity, clad in yellow robes chastized humanity for not developing
comprehension and charity, wisdom and love, *prema* and *karma*. His
great disciple, Asoka, when he found his empire inhabited by men of
different races and religions, said that concord is necessary. The root
of tolerance is respect for all religions and for all cultures. When once
this intellectual realization comes there will be peace and tranquility.
Absence of this intellectual recognition is the root cause of all troubles.[15]

It would be unrealistic to expect total social cohesion and understanding to occur in north-east India in the coming decades. In years to come, the identity crisis of the Assamese people will dominate the conflicts in the region. The cultural identity of the indigenous people of Assam can be retained and further strengthened only with the assimilation of immigrant Muslims and those who have permanently migrated to Assam and adopted the Assamese way of life. Leadership will have to come from the Assamese middle class and the elites as well as organizations like the Assam Sahitya Sabha, Bodo Sahitya Sabha and several other cultural organizations representing smaller ethnic groups comprising the Assamese cultural stream. A solution will be less difficult if the leadership of these institutions is manned by people who are not chauvinists but men and women of vision and dedication. There are economic dimensions of the problem as well, as will be discussed below.

Economic Development

The 'identity crisis' of cultural groups and tribes in the region has a strong economic aspect. In fact, the main sustaining force behind the 'identity' syndrome emanates from the complex operation of economic forces in the region. The scene in north-east India is characterized by both general trends prevailing in the country and several special features unique to the region. A number of major tendencies at work in the north-east which are similar to the economic problems faced elsewhere in India. There is increasing pressure to remove inequalities, generate employment and accelerate the pace of development. Consumer articles are now in greater demand, and a new generation is becoming familiar with the application of science and technological advances. There are, however, certain problems peculiar to the region arising out of historical neglect, and the development achieved in decades elsewhere needs to be encapsulated here in a comparatively short period of time.

As already noted, the economy of north-east India is rural and particularly backward. Agriculture continues to carry over 75 per cent of the total work force and the urban population is below 10 per cent, or almost half the all-India average. It is a backward economy as both agriculture and industry are characterized by primitive technology in their crucial spheres of operation.[16] In the industrial field, there has been marginal to insignificant exploitation of the natural resources in the fields of hydro-power, coal, gas and forests. The growth in basic infrastructure facilities in terms of communications, power, credit and marketing in the region are far behind the national average. In each field of critical economic activity, the scientists and entrepreneurs of the region are hampered by lack of information, technology and a viable market.

At the organizational level, the crucial task of development is within the sphere of activity of three agencies—The Central Government, the North-Eastern Council and the local governments of the States. While the main thrust of the Central schemes is on the establishment of industries and extension of communication facilities, the North-Eastern Council aims to create an infrastructure involving more than one political unit. The development of the common man is more directly the responsibility of the State administration and its planning process. The State governments have, in pursuance of central directives and on their own, floated schemes of development from time to time. Important programmes like the Integrated Rural Development Programme (IRDP) and the National Rural Employment Programme (NREP) aim to redistribute rural income and accomplish a massive uplift of the rural poor. But all these well intentioned programmes, have yet to have a meaningful impact on the common people in north-east India. The programmes have not been linked to manpower planning either with the rural educated or unorganized uneducated rural poor. There has been no attempt to estimate the total quantum of unemployment in villages and onwards, the abilities of local able-bodied manpower, or to match these elements with the jobs in existence and many more than could be created with careful planning. Over the years, three features of national policy in north-east India have crystallized: first, a higher allocation of resources is made to the States and Union Territories of the region than elsewhere; second, the infrastructural development in the region has been accorded high priority with major changes in the fields of railways, roads, power-generation and telephone services in the next fifteen or twenty years becoming clearly visible; and third, the Central Government, the North-Eastern Council and the respective State Governments are moving in the direction of expanding industry and a network of industries connected with oil refineries, petro-chemicals, fertilizers, cement, pulp and paper; these have been planned and are being set-up in the region.

However, there are several factors that militate against the successful implementaton of the plans outlined. There is justifiable unanimity among economists and planners that the rate of economic growth in the region so far has been much too inadequate to make the process continuous and beneficial to all classes. The planning process has in certain areas even aggravated the differentiated economic development of the past decades. In the field of agriculture, Jhummia cultivators have been subjected to greater hardships for lack of familiarity with modern agricultural technology and the lack of irrigation in hilly terrains. In the plains, cultivators have more or less continued with the traditional practice of 'one-crop' cultivation of *sali*(wet) rice and seem to lack the skills and enterprise to raise a second crop. Irrigation facilities are inadequate and the use of fertilizer is the lowest in the country. Industry has remained backward, except in organized sectors like tea and oil, and the growth of urbanization has been tardy.

Although the poor are numerically large in the region, they are not organized to articulate their demands and put pressure on the State system. In a democracy the political parties might be expected to organize the poor in a bid to capture power, but this has not happened in the north-east The politicization of ethnic, caste and religious symbols has greatly blunted the self-awareness of economic classes in the region. In certain cases the rural poor are so dependent upon their rich landlords that they fear that confrontation will ultimately lead to a loss of livelihood, or worse.

The local political elites are no doubt becoming more concerned with unemployment, but there has generally been a lack of commitment and the necessary preparedness amongst them to facilitate the economic development of the people. In a survey conducted in 1970[17] on the attitudes of the members of the legislative assemblies of Assam, Nagaland, and Meghalaya, as many as 60.71 per cent of the respondents accorded political freedom first preference, while entrepreneurship was not accorded first preference by anyone and was the second preference of a mere 13.04 per cent of the respondents. On the other hand, the nascent middle class in the north-east, in conjunction with its brethren in north India and Calcutta, has grown rich by diverting and selling scarce raw materials to capitalists before they reach any part of the north-east. It is not uncommon to find that in the execution of even limited tasks only fifty per cent of total outlay is actually utilized as it should be, with the rest siphoned off and distributed among corrupt vested interests.

Efforts have no doubt been made to build private business organizations, but for a variety of reasons the lives of such organizatons have proved to be distressingly temporary, some not lasting beyond the life-spans of their founders. The Assam experience in the management of rural co-operatives in the light of the above is worth recapitulation.

A significant organizational innovation was made in Assam in August 1973, when 663 Gram Panchayat level co-operative societies were set up with the main objective of meeting all the needs of the rural population and to act as catalytic agents in rural areas. The major functons assigned to these societies were broadly: (a) to provide agricultural credit (short, medium and long-term) and inputs to farmers by raising funds through deposits or borrowing from members and non-members, including co-operative and commercial banks, financial institutions and the Government; (b) the distribution of essential commodities to the rural population; (c) to procure marketable surpluses of agricultural produce; (d) to provide agro-services, including processing facilities; and (e) to engage in various other activities, such as processing and storing rural products, improving livestock lift irrigation, road construction, digging wells, tanks, canals, etc.

The management of the new societies was entrusted to a Committee of fifteen, of which two belonged to the Government, one to the financing bank and one to the affiliated co-operative societies. The remaining twelve members were elected, of which not less than eight were to belong to the 'weaker sections' of the community. The secretary of the society was a full-time, paid worker and appointed with the approval of the Government and the financing bank. Eight banks were persuaded to adopt the 663 societies. Sarat Chandra Sinha, Assam's Chief Minister (1972–8) who fathered the scheme, was deeply interested in making these co-operatives economically viable and effective instruments for ushering in a new and equitable society in rural Assam. I had the opportunity of being closely associated with the societies in Kamrup district during 1973–5 as Deputy Commissioner. The scheme faced several initial problems and one of the most difficult tasks was persuading banking institutions to adopt these societies. Once this was achieved, several shortcomings came to notice: strengthening and activizing the co-operative department of the State government so as to enable it to supervise more effectively the functioning of the co-operative societies; and enabling the secretaries of the societies to devote greater time and attention to credit business in preference to other activities, particularly the distribution of edible items such as sugar and mustard oil.[18]

It was soon realized that the transformation of an underdeveloped society into a modern one is not merely the mechanical addition of a stock of physical capital, but that a revolution in the pattern of life and a cardinal change in the relative power and position of various groups of population is necessary. As soon as the co-operatives started creating a new power base from among the hitherto deprived sections of society, the established elites of the society began opposing the new arrangements. With the exit of Sarat Chandra Sinha from power, most of the societies became dysfunctional and financial irregularities became a normal feature. The experiment for orderly management of socio-economic change through village co-operatives failed.

There is also a psychological aspect to the development experience. The indigenous people have come to believe that their failure to meet the basic needs of life has been caused not by their inactivity, sloth or lack of entrepreneurship but by 'outsiders' who have robbed them of their economic opportunities, both in the agrarian sector as well as in government offices. There are two special features in the development experience of north-east India. First, a widely shared view, particularly in Assam, that no important development project was ever initiated in the region without clamour from the local people. This phenomenon is not peculiar to Assam or north-east India but in every state of India, particularly in the 1960s and 70s when people agitated for prestigious industrial or communications projects to be established in their areas. But in Assam and other parts of north-east India this has created the feeling that the central administration is not sympathetic to the demands of the people of the region. Neither the State government nor the Central Government has taken any meaningful measures to remove this widespread mis-understanding. Secondly, the words 'development', 'industrialization', and 'urbanization' are considered in several quarters in the region to be ways of favouring outsiders. This impression has persisted ever since the tea industry in the second half of the nineteenth century led to the influx of 'outsiders' into Assam. The steps taken towards industrialization in the region under successive Five-Year Plans brought more skilled and unskilled manpower into the region from outside and further strengthened this feeling.

In this situation, a new look at the strategy of development itself, with view to reaching the benefits of planned development to the common people in north-east India, is called for. An effective answer could be to move in the direction of guaranteeing employment to the rural people in terms of Article 41 of the Constitution, which provides that 'the State shall, within the limits of its economic capacity and development, make effective provision for securing the right to work ... and to public assistance in cases of unemployment', while continuing vigorously with the policy of infrastructural development. The full employment scheme would mean provision of productive work to every able-bodied person in the 18–60 age-group on a fixed remuneration, on a daily, weekly or monthly basis.

The scheme should be formulated at the micro-level, through the organized *gaon* panchayats. Planners, village level leaders and the bureaucracy acting in unison should carefully assess the number of jobs and overall work that could be created in an area comprising a *gaon* panchayat. An effort should be made to match the work with the skills and expectatons of each able-bodied person. The manpower rendered surplus by each *gaon* panchayat should be carried forward to the block, the subdivision and the district levels. Side-by-side with public works, the potentialities for self-employment should be assessed at each *gaon* panchayat and the resources needed to promote self-help provided to willing persons. The area of meaningful economic activity would relate to harnessing energy, controlling floods, reclaiming land, soil conservation, dairy development and animal husbandry, works on irrigation, the development of horticulture, plantations, forestry and the promotion of agriculture, handlooms and handicrafts.[19]

A question may naturally be asked why north-east India

should be singled out for a full employment scheme when the right to work is already a national goal. The north-east is still sparsely populated. It is in real economic difficulties thanks to centuries of neglect and, more importantly, it is strategically vital for national security: Arunachal Pradesh is contiguous to China, Meghalaya touches Bangladesh, Mizoram has borders with Burma and Bangladesh, Nagaland and Manipur are adjacent to Burma, and Assam and Tripura have borders with Bangladesh. It is widely felt that there is a substantial job-potential in the north-east in view of its abundant natural resources and the various schemes for infrastructural development already undertaken by the Central agencies in the region. Manpower, even ordinary unskilled labourers, were in the past brought in from outside to work in the region for a variety of reasons. If full-employment schemes are launched, it will be possible to provide this input locally.

I am painfully aware of the lack of confidence both in the local bureaucracy and political leadership in implementing the task of full employment in the region. The local 'bourgeoisie' and capitalist class, in conjunction with its allies outside would not want the state to undertake full-employment schemes, for this would weaken their hold in the region. Here, Kalecki's rationalization is relevant:

> The reasons for the opposition of 'the industrial leaders' to full employment achieved by government spending may be subdivided into these categories: (i) the dislike of government interference in the problem of employment as such; (ii) the dislike of the direction of government spending (public investment and subsidizing consumption); (iii) the dislike of the social and political changes resulting from the maintenance of full employment.

> There is an imperative requirement to overcome the lack of confidence and to resist capitalist manipulations. (*The Last Phase of Transformation of Capitalism*, p.39).

CHAPTER IX
Future Perspectives

Never in recorded history has there been such rapid change in north-east India as during the years after Independence. During this period, the customs of centuries, music and the arts, production and consumption patterns, have undergone radical transformations. There has been a swift monetization of the economy, a phenomenal expansion of the middle class, the intelligentsia, professionals and the bureaucracy. In the hill areas, the efficacy of institutions related to the communal ownership of property has declined. The spread of education has increased manifold the capability of the population to interact with economic, political, cultural and administrative organizations, and these organizations themselves are multiplying in number and widening their areas of operation. Since 1982 television has rapidly emerged as an important agent of change. Some of the changes have been violent rather than peaceful, exploitative rather than harmonizing. For some groups, the intense social change and culture-shock has been more than they can comprehend.

Today, every section of society demands the fruits of 'progress' leaving in its wake advocates of a return to easier conditions, an escapist approach to the management of change and the resolution of conflict. Meeting new wants and aspirations in itself casts a major burden on existing socio-political and administrative institutions, compounded by a multiplicity of forces operating in the name of culture, language, religion and ethnic ties. The experience gained elsewhere in the country is not always of help, because of the unique character of the peoples involved and the fact that the inhabitants of north-east India have not had more than six decades in which to imbibe and assimilate the ideas of modernization. There is thus need to view together (a) the aspirations of the people; (b) the forces of cultural separatism; (c) the capacity of the political system to cope with increasing and different tasks; and (d) identify the steps or new policies which will strengthen integrative forces in north-east India.

Economic Aspirations

Attitudes towards work, the accumulation of wealth and social ownership of the means of production have undergone rapid change even in remote areas of north-east India. The earlier immunity from change of various societies in the region was possible not because of any particular virtue or shortcoming in them, but because of the remoteness and the apparent poverty of their environments. As soon as the British found the land suitable for tea cultivation and oil production, the process of exploitation commenced. Demographic changes have occured most dramatically. Ownership of the means of production graduated from community ownership to private ownership, facilitating the transfer of land from indigenous cultivators to more enterprising migrants. The spread of education and the extension of health care facilities reduced the mortality rate and accelerated the pace of modernization, which, in turn, has brought in an awareness of new articles of consumption.

At present, a great wave of economic aspirations is sweeping the middle class of north-east India. The support to culture and language emanates from a desire for economic advancement. The Assamese want 'foreigners' to go because they primarily perceive in them a threat to their land and scarce jobs. The Meiteis, too, want to renounce Hindi Vaishnavism and get back to the tribal fold, for that would give them legal rights by way of reservations in jobs and certain advantages in tenancy rights. It may seem strange that the people of Meghalaya do not want the extension of railway lines into their territory, a widely accepted conduit to economic growth; but the Meghalayans fear that railways will lead to the migration into their territory of people who could harm their interests both in industry and agriculture. The Nagas' bid to acquire land from neighbouring districts in Assam in the name of their traditions and practices arises from an acute need to get agricultural land for their growing population; every political party of Nagaland has to keep this demand alive for its own political survival, irrespective of the logic behind such claims. Mizoram is struggling amidst its own self-contained culture, with dissident elements represented until recently by the insurgents and a general problem of adjustment with the security forces characterizing the entire social order. The motivating force, however, is economic betterment and protest against the influx of Chakmas from the Chittagong Hill Tracts of Bangladesh. The resentment against non-Mizos from other parts of India has to be viewed primarily in economic terms. The tribal revolt in Tripura against Bengali domination has also to be seen primarily in terms of land and economic interests.

Cultural Separatism

A country of India's size and population must appreciate regional cultures and their multi-dimensional influence over development as well as national integration. But over the years it has seen strong cultural separatism or exclusiveness in operation, and this has been sustained as well as furthered by frequent calls to ethno racial loyalties and linguistic pride to the detriment of the growth of a composite Indian culture. These demands are yet to be effectively substituted by allegiance to a State-system that is democratically constituted or by ideological exhortations about cultural diversity that are contained in the Constitution of India and are the legacy of the freedom struggle.

In recent years, following the tremendous ethnic resurgence in north-east India, references to the so-called Mongolian culture of the seven political units have increasingly been made. Why has there been such a resurgence of ethnic identity? The answer to this question is found not only in the history of the migration of various ethnic groups to the region and the forces that helped their integration or in keeping them apart, but also in the recent spurt in modernization and the increasing politicization of ethnic elements. The failure of the Congress and other political parties to provide an overall umbrella for different ethnic groups has indicated in clear terms the breakdown of political compromise in almost every political unit of the region. The role of foreign powers in the propagation of divisive ideas and rendering help to insurgent elements has been no mean factor in the promotion of a revivalistic temper. Besides, the emergence of the middle class in the north-east was late, and this class has failed to displace ethnic identity as a factor in social, economic and political relations.

Broadly, four sets of policies were adopted to restore ethnic conflicts. First, political boundaries were redrawn so as to give maximum opportunities to major ethnic groups in the political management of their affairs. This was in keeping with Nehru's philosophy of allowing the tribes to have full say in shaping their own genius in a democratic set-up. Secondly, certain districts, which could not be given statehood or Union Territory status, were allowed to have their districts councils with considerable devolution of financial and administrative authority. Thirdly, the plan allocations in respect of the north-eastern states were augmented and special consideration given to them in comparison to other states of the Indian Union. Finally, central ministries, like Railways, Communications, Transport, Civil Aviation and Tourism, have taken special developmental measures for the region. The allocation of funds to the North-Eastern Council has also been raised. All these measures, though sound, have in operation meant making a vast range of political adjustments to accommodate the primordial loyalities of the region.

We have noted earlier the magnitude and relevance of religious diversity in the region. In recent years, language, perhaps more than religion, has been an extremely strong force in the northeast. Linguistically, north-east India is both diverse and conflict-ridden. As many as 420 languages and dialects are spoken in the region; 168 in Arunachal Pradesh, 95 in Nagaland, 87 in Manipur, 112 in Tripura and 192 altogether in Assam, Meghalaya and Mizoram. (The regional breakdown exceeds the aggregate figure because some dialects are spoken in more than one political unit.) In a multi-lingual, multi-ethnic, and multi-religious developing society, language often acts as a criterion for ethnic identity and ethnic consciousness. Certain groups of people, like the Assamese of the Brahmaputra Valley, now view it as the most important criterion, and as a major factor in retaining political power. However, each state has sizeable linguistic minorities and, since Independence, the language controversies have caused considerable inter-community hostilities. The overzealousness of Assam's political leadership and the Assam Sahitya Sabha led to Assamese being made the official language of the entire state of Assam in 1962: this, in turn, accelerated the break-up of Assam. The bilingual status of Assam, Meghalaya and Tripura cannot be abruptly altered and any attempt to make one language the sole medium of education and administration will inevitably lead to conflicts. The leaders of Meghalaya, who fought against the

imposition of Assamese on them are now faced with their own lin-
guistic complexities, as the three major groups of the State, the
Garos, Jaintias and Khasis do not speak the same language.
While there is considerable affinity between Khasi and Jaintia,
Garo is totally different. Thus, the linguistic diversity of
Meghalaya is likely to continue.

Efficacy of Political System

The efficacy of the political system is of primary concern in north-
east India, but the system has been seriously threatened by
insurgency (a subject which needs a separate study). The post-
Independence insurgencies of the Nagas from 1959 onwards, of
the Mizos from 1966 and the Meiteis from 1978 have all periodically aimed at secession from India. The various hill tribes in
north-east India are courageous and adventurous, singularly free
and independent, and scornful of any control. Several tribes have
indulged in head-hunting practices and quick to seek revenge
when fearing that they are being harmed. These character-traits
have been exploited in defiance of the political norms by charismatic ethnic leaders like Phizo, Laldenga and Biseswar. The
region has international borders with Burma, China, Bhutan and
Bangladesh: the border with Burma is inhabited by people of the
same ethnic groups as the insurgents and thus quelling
insurgency in the north-east becomes more difficult. Besides, the
insurgents within the region have always drawn inspiration from
the insurrectionary movements in Burma, Malaysia and
Indonesia that began in the wake of the Japanese invasion during
World War II. The Chinese attitude towards insurgency in
north-east India has also been a well-known, persistent cause for
concern.

No tidy solutions of complex socio-economic and cultural problems are possible. While the major political re-organization of
1971–2 clearly established a unity of purpose towards progress,
security and cultural affinity in the north-east, subsequent
developments have made several political scientists, administrators and social workers increasingly feel that the vision of
building a state-system has once again become blurred. Various
suggestions have been made in this book for future action and
some of these need recapitulation.

Social Integration

Writing about 'nationalism' in India in 1917, Rabindranath Tagore observed: 'Our real problem in India is not political. It is social'. He went on to elucidate that India has 'tried to make an adjustment of races, to acknowledge the real differences between them where these exist, and yet seek for some basis of unity'. A 'basis' was, in fact, provided by the ideas and tolerance evident in the preachings of India's spiritual leaders like Buddha, Mahavir, Kabir, Chaitanya, Nanak, Tulsidas, Sankardev, Vivekananda and Gandhi. This helped India keep her society united and alive. In the post-Independence years, Nehru's policy of allowing tribal people to 'develop along the lines of their own genius' of avoiding the imposition of alien values proved beneficial. It was realized that an integration between the tribals and plains' people could be achieved only through cultural tolerance and an appreciation for tribal values. National integration does not require that tribal land be opened to the private economic pursuits of the plains' people and that the tribals be given jobs in these private enterprises. The tribal communities, both of the hills and the plains, are greatly attached to the land that they possess. While in the hill States and the hill districts of Assam, outsiders are not permitted to acquire heritable and transferable rights in land, the plains' tribals, particularly in Assam and in Tripura, have lost their lands to outsiders and been driven into the interior. The Central as well as the Assam Government have no doubt made great efforts to bring about such changes in the existing laws as to help restore the sanctity of tribal belts and blocks; they have also taken steps to constitute autonomous tribal councils so as to stop tribal land being alienated and attempted to restore such lands to tribals. Notwithstanding all these measures, a deeper study is necessary, a possible framework for which has been set out in Chapter 8. Once new policies are formulated, they will need to be implemented with greater sincerity and determination than in the past.

The 'inner-line' system in certain parts of north-east India has been an important factor in the perpetuation of the psychology of isolationism. But since the system has helped in curbing the alienation of land and the influx of outsiders into these areas, a demand for the application of an 'inner-line' system has been voiced in other States of the region as well. While an extension of the inner-line to new areas would be retrograde and impracticable, the existing inner-line system will nevertheless have to be retained in the foreseeable future in view of the support it receives from the indigenous people of the region.

It has been brought out that a gradual decline in the role of voluntary organizations in north-east India is an important reason for the growth of isolationism and a weakening of the process of socialization in the region. It may be wise for the North-Eastern Council to initiate consultations with the various social and cultural organizations operating in the region and to provide a forum for co-ordinated action. The information available with the Social Welfare Department of the Central and State Governments about these organizations, their capabilities and past performance could perhaps form the basis for consultations and lead to the formulation of meaningful programmes of action.

Economic Integration

The rapid changes in the demographic profile of north-east India during the twentieth century surpass those in all other parts of the country. Our analysis has shown that there is an imperative need to formulate a demographic policy which would stop migration from Bangladesh and Nepal into this region, and also provide a degree of security and contentment to the indigenous people vis-a-vis the migrants. We have, however, found that there can be no population policy for Assam or Tripura alone, or even for northeast India as a whole. The States of Bihar, West Bengal and Sikkim are also involved. In fact, a demographic policy has to be the product of understanding between different political units in eastern India and the Central Government. In order to be realistic the policy must adequately reflect the concerns of the local people, but the immediate requirement is to completely stop the movement of population across international boundaries. The issue of identity cards to Indian nationals domiciled in north-east India is recommended as part of a demographic policy. The cards would help identify foreigners, in granting employment in rural schemes and other avenues such as admission to medical and engineering colleges; the sale, purchase and settlement of land; the award of contracts and business; and employment in offices and factories.

The cost of the operation would be more than offset by the likelihood of peace and progress in the region.

In a region of rapid change, insurgency and cultural conflicts, the need to involve the common people and to let them have an economic stake in development is an obvious prescription. Towards this end, it is suggested that north-east India should be singled out for a full-employment scheme, which would be the single most effective method of strengthening nation-building objectives in the region. An inevitable consequence of this scheme would be that, in a region so far characterized by administrative under-development, organizational and administrative units of welfare administration should also be decentralized and dispersed to villages, blocks and subdivisions. In formulating employment schemes and implementing them, interaction between grass-root level representatives of the people and a decentralized bureaucracy is essential. While there is sufficient work for the able-bodied, financial assistance would have to come from the Centre, in view of the poor resource position in all the political units comprising north-east India.

Political Integration

Our analysis has shown that, though political re-organization in north-east India was resorted to at frequent intervals in the hope that such a measure would help solve economic and social issues and bring the region to the level of more developed parts of the country, it has been an inadequate answer to the problem. Yet, even today, there are many believers in this approach. Our experience has shown that territorial re-organization alone is no solution for economic or social problems. The re-organization of north-east India in 1971-2 has no doubt given this region a fairly 'neat' political look, with a regional planning and security organization in the North-Eastern Council; but the temptation to re-organize the region further continue and gain fresh impetus at times of crises. Presently, there are suggestions to bifurcate Cachar from Assam and make it a Union Territory, to carve out a separate Udayachal State for the Bodo-Kacharis in the Brahmaputra Valley, to de-link the hill districts of Assam and tag them on either to Cachar or to Meghalaya, to accord a separate territory to the Meiteis in Manipur, etc. If past experience is any guide, these measures would not ensure either accelerated economic development or greater social harmony, as virtually every district or subdivision in the region has the inherent contradictions of a polyglot society in ample measure. The proposals pertaining to upgradation of the Union Territories of Mizoram and Arunachal Pradesh to full statehood have been wisely accepted. Likewise any further strengthening of the North-Eastern Council would be useful. Similarly, the creation of a separate ministry for north-east India in the Central Government, or an institutional framework for interaction between the North-Eastern Council and the committee of union ministers aimed at the economic development of north-eastern region is strongly recommended.

The crucial role of political parties, regional as well as national, in the management of any democratic polity cannot be overemphasized. However, a national political party is preferable to a regional one in north-east India, as the former can play a greater role as co-ordinator and integrator than a regional party. It is also advisable to create a regional unit of each national party co-terminus with the jurisdiction of the North-Eastern Council so as to encourage party theoreticians and active workers to reflect upon the problems of the region as a whole. Such an input would help in the growth of political groups for the entire region, cutting across the boundaries of a state.

In north-east India, different political units have different elites and a common elite group for the region is yet to emerge. The emergence of such an elite, which could play the role of a catalyst in the integration of the society of north-east India would be greatly facilitated if the state system, including the North-Eastern Council and various national political parties, consciously orient their efforts to foster meetings and dialogue among industrialists, businessmen, lawyers, doctors and social workers at formal and non-formal levels. In highlighting the role of an elite, I am aware that, in the past, progress has been the concern largely of and for elites, but the concept of progress now covers an entire society. Elitism is admittedly a negation of an ideal democratic system; but in developmental efforts and the maintenance of democracy itself in the north-east, constructive elitism is an imperative requirement.

Before 1947, Calcutta was the main centre of trade, education and politics for Bengal and all the political units comprising north-eastern India. Although Assam formed a part of East Bengal under the Curzon Plan during 1905–12, Dacca never replaced Calcutta as the centre for education and ideas of modernization for the people of north-east India. Calcutta dominated the Assamese mind. After Independence, Delhi rapidly became the principal centre of politics as well as education, but, being distant from the north-east, Delhi could not become an effective substitute for Calcutta. Unfortunately, the north-east lacks a cosmopolitan centre which can draw people to it and stimulate a cross-fertilization of cultures. Industry in the region is scattered; being largely in minerals and forestry, perhaps it has to remain close to the source of raw materials. Similarly, educational institutions of higher and technical learning have grown up in isolation in each political unit. The role of urbanization and industrialization in encouraging greater socialization among the different groups is crucial, and in the north-east this could be best secured by the development of Gauhati and Shillong as complementary cities.

The establishment of an upper house in each legislature of north-east India would help utilize the educated and experienced amongst the indigenous people who are not willing to join the election fray for assembly seats. The setting-up of upper houses is thus recommended to broaden the political system of the region.

Administrative Integration

Institution-building has not been very successful so far in north-east India. Political leaders in the newly formed States and Union Territories have no doubt attempted to create new subdivisions and up-grade old subdivisions as districts, etc, in an effort to strengthen the system; but adequate provision has not been appropriately made for administrative and financial resources, or sufficient care exercised to make the new units effective instruments of development. Various reforms suggested by the central government, like the establishment of district industrial centres or the creation of nodal agencies to clear applications to establish industrial units and so on were all formally accepted by the states of the region, but given little substance.

Similarly, at the regional level, if the experiences of the last decade is any guide, it is necessary to fully use the North-Eastern

Council. Some of the steps in this direction could be: (1) that the Council be given a permanent Chairman who is also to be a common Governor for all the north-eastern states; (2) that the Council, besides giving priority to the development of infrastructure, plays a greater role in manpower development and planning, and helps ensure that local skills and talent are fully used—a measure needed to remove the widely prevalent fear that the exploitation of natural resources does not benefit as it always brings in people from outside the region. The very formulation of a long-term plan in this direction would help considerably in dispelling the fears of the people of the region; (3) the establishment of a regional institute in Shillong to study ethnic problems and insurgency. The institute also should collate and evaluate information on matters which have a bearing on the promotion of economic development and the maintenance of social harmony in the region, and should closely interact with the North-Eastern Council; (4) that the Chairman of the North-Eastern Council and the proposed common Governor of the north-eastern states be increasingly involved in strategic and internal security matters involving more than one state; the location of a separate North-Eastern Command of the army could help in this matter.

Although at present, the north-east has two Governors and two Lieutenant-Governors, a return to the previous practice of having a common Governor would help in the development of a common personality for the north-eastern states. Many of the ceremonial duties, which make heavy demands on a common Governor's time and energy, could surely be handled by the chief ministers of the various states. This would enable the common Governor to concentrate on policy matters and function effectively as Chairman of the North-Eastern Council.

Conclusion

The national leaders had envisaged that after Independence the north-east, the colourful corridor between the two great civilizations of India and China, would grow and forge new links between these two countries and also become 'an important link between the East and the West' through East Asia. The compulsions of international politics and the Sino-Indian conflict for 1962 have perhaps foreclosed these visions for decades to come What then is the future?

The least optimistic scenario turns on the possibility of a recurrence of insurgency and a breakdown of the democratic process. The propounders of this view point to the periodic outbreaks of ethnic or linguistic violence as portents of doom. This view, however, ignores the immense power and strength of the cultural inheritance which has held Indian society together over the centuries. The pace of economic development has been below expectations; it has nevertheless been significant and strengthened these foundations. The occasional eruption is, in essence, a painful adjustment to change. Few in the 1950s or 1960s thought that Nagaland would attain the level of peace that it has enjoyed from the late 1970s; or more recently, that the Brahmaputra Valley would survive the crisis of the kind witnessed after 1979. The future of the region as an inviolate part of the country is clear and explicit as a feeling of identity with the Indian nation grows.

The major effort now required, however, is to meet the needs of the poor and socially neglected, particularly those who have migrated to the region over the past one hundred years. Both the institutions and social psychology of the area have to adjust. Unfortunately, the state-system, which could have played a role in bringing about the transformation independently of the control of the region's dominant class, failed to do so. The state-system was crippled by an ad-hocism oriented to fire-fighting natural calamities or severe social stress, with a consequent loss of perspective. It did not free itself from dependence on the local upper-middle class and bourgeoisie, to the cost of its relations with the deprived. The continuing unorganized state of the poorer classes in the region does not suggest that matters will be different on this count in the near future. On the other hand, the increasing politicization of ethnic, religious and linguistic groups have generated powerful pressures that political parties have exploited in order to remain in power, even at the cost of society. The break-up of the Indian National Congress for the first time in Assam in 1978 thwarted the progress of secularization and gave a fillip to the politicization of primordial loyalties.

At the present reckoning, the crucial issue continues to be the need to strike a balance between the conflicting claims of different ethnic and linguistic groups, between the indigenous peoples and migrants. Much depends on the vision of the leadership of each political unit and the enlargement of economic opportunities in the region. Regrettably, there has been a sharp decline in the quality of the region's leadership since the days of the stalwarts of the freedom struggle. Yet the demands on them are no less severe than before, even if different. The managers of change, who have at their command modern information systems and media, will be respectfully heard and followed only if seen to be truly concerned with the problems of the basic social categories of the populace — the villager, peasants, artisans and labourers. The existing social pressures and absence of feudal norms in the region, could lead to the emergence of an interactive leadership from today's morass. This would help ease the stress and strain of social and economic development, particularly amongst groups who may feel that they are being left behind.

An increasingly large number of far-reaching events is taking place in north-east India and it is necessary to distinguish between those which carry fundamental messages and those which are transitory in nature. For instance, the voice of students in 1979 on the 'aliens issue' in the Brahmaputra Valley was not properly understood or appreciated. Many of the initial administrative and political failures in dealing with it could be attributed to this lack of appreciation. Collective decision-making is the essence of political leadership and essential for the advancement of long-term social and economic goals, but this has been lacking in the north-east.

Several encouraging developments have occurred recently in north-east India, despite ethnic conflicts and violence. Assam now has a fully representative and democratic Government, following the agreement reached between the Government of India, the All-Assam Students' Federation and the All-Assam Gana Sangram Parishad to resolve the problem of foreigners in Assam. A similar agreement has been reached in Mizoram. Laldenga the rebel leader became the Chief Minister of Mizoram after the Mizo National Front under his leadership secured an absolute majority in the Assembly election in February, 1987. A number of erstwhile insurgent leaders have chosen to contest elections and some, notably Biseswar of Manipur, are members of legislative assemblies. India is generally much more interested in happenings in north-east India than ever before. The country has shown a genuine willingness to accord favoured treatment to the people of this region, who have undergone hardships through centuries of economic neglect, the migration of population from different parts of the subcontinent and inadequate administrative institutions. Above all, the operation of the democratic process, national and regional planning institutions, the banking system, political parties, developments in communications, the introduction of television and an increasing media coverage of events in the region, have all dispelled the earlier isolation of the region and brought about a familiarity and understanding between its people and the country at large. There is no tangible threat to national integration in north-east India, despite the undoubted existence of elements within the region and outside the country that seek to endanger it. However, given a history of limited socialization in the region, ethnic conflicts, and rapid modernization after 1917, the north-east seems likely to continue being volatile for some years to come.

Epilogue

On 15 August 1985, Rajiv Gandhi, Prime Minister of India, announced from the ramparts of the Red Fort, New Delhi, that the Government of India has signed an agreement with the All-Assam Students Union (AASU) and the All-Assam Gana Sangram Parishad (AAGSP) to solve the problem of foreigners in Assam. This announcement was warmly greeted in most parts of India, and students in the Brahmaputra Valley in particular, paraded the streets dancing with joy and happiness. Nevertheless, Bengali Muslims and Hindus and a few other groups were unhappy with details of the Agreement.

The settlement was characterized by three broad features. First, all the foreigners who had come to Assam on or after 25 March 1971, were to be detected and expelled from the country, in accordance with law. In the preparation of electoral rolls, foreigners who had come to Assam between 1 January 1966 and 24 March 1971 were to be denied voting rights and their names deleted from the electoral rolls. Second, appropriate constitutional, legislative and administrative safeguards are to be provided to protect, preserve and promote the cultural, social, linguistic identity and heritage of the Assamese people. Third, the Government renewed its commitment to the speedy all-round economic development of Assam. Special emphasis will be placed on education, and science and technology, through the establishment of national institutions in the region.

The movement on the 'foreign nationals' issue was reminiscent of Assam's political response to certain proposals of the Cabinet Mission Plan of 1946. The Mission, which consisted of Lord Pethick-Lawrence, the Secretary of State for India, Stafford Cripps, the President of the Board of Trade, and A. V. Alexander, the First Lord of Admiralty, arrived in India on 23 March 1946 'with the intention of using their utmost endeavours' to help India 'attain her freedom as speedily and fully as possible' and to arrange the framing of a constitution. On 16 May 1946, after detailed discussions with various parties, groups and individuals, it made an announcement which provided, amongst other features, that 'provinces should be free to form Groups with executives and legislatives, and each Group could determine the provincial subjects to be taken in common'. With regard to the Constitution-making body, the Mission proposed a representation of population on the basis of General, Muslim, and Sikh; and the States were divided into three Sections, 'A', 'B', and 'C'. Assam was grouped with Bengal in Section 'C' which provided 60 seats for Bengal (27 General and 33 Muslim) and 10 seats for Assam (7 General and 3 Muslim). As soon as this was announced, there was a sharp and unprecedented reaction in Assam against the grouping clause. Assamese caste-Hindu leadership was galvanized overnight and viewed the Mission's decision to deny Assam provincial status as tantamount to effacing its culture and identity. Gopinath Bardoloi forcefully articulated the strong fear of domination by Bengali Muslims over the Assamese and the then leadership of the AASU placed its services at the disposal of the State Congress in opposing the grouping plan through a nation-wide agitation. Mahatma Gandhi fully supported Assam's opposition to the 'grouping' plan. The 'grouping' was ultimately abandoned, but it was followed by Partition and the transfer of the major part of Sylhet from Assam to Pakistan. In several ways, the 1946 political movement was consciously re-enacted under the student leadership of Prafulla Mahanta and Bhrigu Phukan in the early 1980s; but this time it was not conducted in conjunction with the local Congress leadership. It was no coincidence that the student leaders of the early 1980s carried Gandhi's portrait at the head of every rally and made him their leader three decades after his death.

The partition of India changed the whole outlook of Assam Congress politics, for, the detachment of the major portion of Sylhet lessened the Assamese fear of Muslim colonization and domination. Ironically, after Independence Assam's Congress politicians banked heavily on Bengali Muslims as a reserve vote bank and as allies of the Assamese in their conflict with Bengali Hindus. This enabled Bengali Muslims to consolidate their control over vast tracts of barren and riverine lands and led to the migration of their kith and kin from East Pakistan into Assam. Migration also occurred from other parts of the Indian Union and Nepal. The situation continued to deteriorate from the 1950s to the 1970s. The revision of electoral rolls in 1978–9 brought into focus the fact, that a large number of foreigners were willing to be registered as voters. The then Chief Election Commissioner of India noted that the population likely to be recorded in the 1991 census would be more than 100 per cent that of 1961. He cautioned: 'a stage would be reached when the State may have to reckon with the foreign nationals who may in all probability constitute a sizeable percentage, if not the majority population in the State'. This announcement had an explosive effect and the agitation against 'foreign' nationals in Assam began. The agitation affected every aspect of human life in the Brahmaputra Valley. The Janata Party, had already split at the national level and in Assam its local variant, the Asom Janata which was then the ruling party, became the first casualty of the agitation and went into oblivion. President's Rule was imposed in Assam for the first time in December 1979, but it was unable to stem the linguistic, ethnic and political struggles that had gained momentum under the leadership of students. The 1983 elections, which many fondly hoped to be the answer, turned out to be the bloodiest elections in the history of India. The Congress came to power, and notwithstanding severe limitations to its representative character, it gave Assam an administration that ensured greater order and peace than the State had experienced during 1980–3. Politicization on ethnic lines had, however, gone unchecked and social cohesiveness suffered grievous injuries.

In total contrast, the 1985 elections were peaceful and orderly, notwithstanding the fact that ethnic feelings operated very strongly. The six-year agitation in Assam over the 'foreign nationals' issue had politicized Assamese caste Hindus and consolidated them into one group. In turn, other communities also sought to unite on ethnic lines. The electoral registration process, in particular, politicized every eligible Bengali Muslim voter by forcing him to move from one office to another in search of electoral or land documents at considerable expense and loss of wages. In the Baghbar constituency of Barpeta district, in a bid to cleanse the electoral rolls of suspected foreigners, students filed objections against over 90 per cent of the names on the draft electoral rolls — a majority of which had featured in the 1971 rolls which were considered by the Election Commission to be the basis for the voters lists in the 1985 elections. When the final electoral rolls were prepared, nearly a million names, mostly of Bengali Muslims, were declared ineligible on grounds of nationality.

The December 1985 elections resulted in an outstanding victory for the Asom Gana Parishad (AGP), which secured 64 seats in the Assam Legislative Assembly out of a total of 126. Prafulla Mahanta, a 32 year-old bachelor and still a student, became the leader of the new party and Chief Minister of the State. Thus, the groups of students who had been agitating since 1979 were overnight converted into a political party and then, equally dramatically, voted to power. The biggest challenge facing the youthful Cabinet is turning an inexperienced party skilled in running an agitation, into a cohesive government.

The actual act of governing always seems less picturesque and impressive than conducting a successful movement. The demands of day-to-day governance compel the leadership to be totally involved with seemingly prosaic and mundane issues which are intricate and stubbornly problem-ridden. Few political movements have achieved their purposes, and the euphoria of victory has usually been short-lived, with its elan still shorter. I have witnessed the jubiliation in 1971–2 in Shillong when the APHLC succeeded in carving out Meghalaya from Assam and captured the reins of government, and the still greater exultation in Delhi in 1977 when the Janata Party replaced the Congress, only to break-up within three years. Since the electoral base of the ruling AGP, Assams' caste Hindus, had agitated against an imminent threat to its cultural, political and economic identity, it was feared that, once in power, it would run amok and twist itself and the administration into becoming instruments of tyranny against other ethnic groups, particularly the Bengali Muslims and Bengali Hindus. A democratic government that comes to power on the shoulders of a popular uprising often begins by settling old scores with the previous regime and, in the process, makes itself ineffectual as an instrument of development and stability. That the AGP leadership has shown sobriety, generosity and fairness in the first few months of being in office is a welcome signal and arouses hopes that Assam might cast off its history of ethnic tensions and violence. Against this backdrop, the moot question facing the AGP is its sense of history. Will it work for reconciliation among ethnic, linguistic and religious groups and rise above the compulsions of its own electoral base? Will it work to strengthen

and enlarge the heritage of secularism and brotherhood of Sankardev and Mahatma Gandhi?

The recent history of Assam appears curiously predictable in
retrospect. However, even when the events were unfolding it was
evident that, since the basic objective of the agitation on the
foreign nationals' issue was political, students would have to
willy-nilly join politics formally. Similarly, as soon as the Asom
Gana Parishad (AGP) was born at Golaghat on 5 October 1985,
it was logical to conclude that hard-core Bengali Muslims and
others would temporarily leave the Congress and form a political
group of their own. The launching of the United Minority Front
(UMF) on 10 November, 1985 at Hojai, a sub-division town in
Nowgong district, was a response based on linguistic considerations to the political challenge posed by the formation of the AGP.
The AGP elite is drawn from Assam's landowners, professionals
and civil servants who have close ties with the traditional
Assamese way of life. It was this class which came to power after
a long struggle during India's freedom movement, that fought
against the Cabinet Mission Plan and held power from the 1950s
to 1970s. The new rulers of Assam belong to the same economic
strata, but there is a fundamental difference in the political
philosophy between the old and new groups in that the latter is a
regional party, whereas the former belonged to the mainstream of
the Indian National Congress. Prafulla Mahanta's description of
his party as a 'regional party with a national orientation' does not
take away the ethnic and caste bases of his party. While
regionalism is not necessarily bad politics, should the ruling elite
pursue a policy of narow regionalism or parochialism on ethnic
and caste considerations it will hurt itself and, in the process, also
injure national integrity. The regional party in Assam may well
merge with the Indian National Congress, as occured with the
Naga National Council of Nagaland in the 1960s and the APHLC
of Meghalaya in the 1970s.

The desire of Assam's caste Hindus for a hold over the levers of
economic and political power is not a special feature of this community. In the recent past the caste Hindus, who have actively
participated in national politics from 1920 onwards captured
political power in 1946 and have generally been running the
affairs of Assam since then. They view the Brahmaputra Valley as
their main base and the Assamese language as being fundamental

to their subnationality perception. The adjustment that started with the Bengali Muslims in the beginning of the twentieth century was on condition that the migrants would accept the Assamese language — which they did; in the agricultural sector, Bengali Muslims were to concede pre-eminence to Assamese caste Hindus and landowners or absentee landlords; and in politics they were to vote for Assamese caste Hindus, a practice which more or less prevailed up to 1978. A similar understanding developed with the tea garden workers. They too, accepted the Assamese language and voted for the caste Hindu Congressmen. The essence of the problem relates to Bengali Hindus, who have their own developed language, and literary and cultural traditions. They did not concede pre-eminence to the Assamese caste Hindu, as others did.

What is the future outlook? An affinity between Bengali Hindus and Bengali Muslims, who speak the same language, could perhaps develop in the light of events after 1979. But religion is likely to thwart this possibility. Besides, the cultural renaissance in West Bengal from the time of Raja Ram Mohan Roy to Rabindranath Tagore period gave the Hindu Bengali a cultural personality that is not fully shared by Bengali-speaking Muslims. Commenting in September 1985 on the future of the Assamese caste Hindu and Bengali Muslim relationship, a knowledgeable Bengali Muslim quoted a proverb at me in Barpeta to the effect that a rupture between two communities is like the break-up of a wooden log and beyond repair. This feeling was shared by several other Bengali Muslim leaders in Assam. I detected then that both the communities feared each other and, at the same time, wanted to shed their differences. At economic and professional levels there were no ostensible breaks, and in schools and colleges, students from the two communities met, but, as in the past, did not mix freely. The middle men, particularly full-time politicians, were playing havoc and igniting their worst fears, spreading hatred within their own community against the other. Another aspect of this fear was that each community wanted the support of someone else.

In social relations, as in politics, inter-community dialogue is essential for progress. The dialogue has to begin at the level of the elite. In Assam the elite has been fragmented by ethnic divisions. In a letter of 29 January 1986 to me, a teacher from Barpeta has posed the predicament of the future relationship between Assamese caste Hindus and Bengali Muslims in the following words: 'You know that a new party was born in Assam just before the election to oppose the Assam accord. This party, known as United Minority Front, I think, has the blessings of Muslim fundamentalists and may make Assam as their first testing ground, which might spread to other States in the near future. Do you think that we should try to win over these immigrant Muslims and bring them back to our fold, only to see them betray us in the next election?'

The Bengali Muslims in Assam have, in fact, so nurtured their children that the future of the latter lies solely in Assam and not in Bangladesh, the country of their origin. Although interaction with other ethnic groups is taking place in agriculture and other professional activities, marriages between Assamese and migrant Bengali Muslims are rare, even in districts with a sizeable presence of Bengali Muslims, like Barpeta, Nowgong, Mangaldoi and Nalbari. A new equation between the indigenous Assamese youth and migrant Bengali Muslim youth will emerge in the coming decade and is bound to be more equitable than that prevailing in the recent past. There was no violence between Bengali Hindus and Assamese Hindus before Independence. The new social and political leadership in Assam will have to build bridges between the various ethnic groups of the state not only in words but in more meaningful ways — by offering employment to Bengali Muslims, tribals and tea-garden labourers in revenue and police jobs so that at day-to-day contact points every ethnic group in the state is reassured that the administrative apparatus is broad-based and functions with comparative impartiality.

The Assamese have made it very clear that they are totally opposed to any further influx of 'foreign' nationals into Assam and want the deportation of as many 'foreign' nationals as feasible. But Assam's border districts of Cachar, Karimganj and Goalpara are largely Bengali speaking and the sensitivities of the people of these districts must be considered in framing a population policy. Meghalaya, Tripura, West Bengal, Bihar and Sikkim are also concerned parties in the formulation of a population policy for the region. Regarding Bangladesh, the main plank of a population policy for north-east India seems to be the installation of barbed wire fencing between India and Bangladesh. India has a total boundary of 4046 kms with Bangladesh, with Assam accounting for 270 kms (of which 103 kms are formed by water), West Bengal 2188 kms (355 kms water), Tripura 861 kms (83 kms water), Meghalaya 421 kms (all land), and Mizoram 306 kms (46 kms water). Thus, any population policy or plans for sealing the border must take into consideration not only the border of Assam with Bangladesh, but also the borders of all the concerned states with Bangladesh.

The Bangladesh factor has both social and economic dimensions. The country's density of population is the highest in the world, 1511 per square mile and its annual shortage of foodgrains is 2-3 million tonnes. In 1977 nearly 41 per cent of Bangladesh's total population was landless and this percentage has since increased. In 1951 the Hindu population in Bangladesh (then East Pakistan) was 22 per cent of the total population, but thanks to migration and conversion it has now declined to 14 per cent. The Hindu population in Bangladesh is equally divided between the higher castes and scheduled castes and Bangladesh observers openly point out that, should serious problems arise between Hindus and Muslims, the low-caste Hindus would accept conversion, while the higher castes would migrate to India.

A population policy for north-east India has to be formulated keeping in view the totality of its situation. That demands taking into account not only the sensitivities of the states sharing a boundary with Bangladesh, but also makes it incumbent upon India to consider how Bangladesh's population will react should there be a serious famine, or a break-up of the country's polity, or a communal conflagration. So long as there are comparatively greater economic attractions in north-east India than in Bangladesh, immigration into India will continue. India must enhance its controls on the border, but it should be noted that even the United States, with all its vast resources, has not been able to control the influx of Latin Americans through the relatively simple Mexican border — a sobering thought for those who feel that borders can be effectively sealed-off. Those who have migrated from Bangladesh are unlikely to leave north-east India, but the denial of political rights to the migrants is unlikely to provide a long-term solution. The denial will, at the same time, create fresh tension with the children of the present migrants as, being born in India, they will automatically be Indian nationals and unlikely to accept the domination of the Assamese if the process of hatred is not replaced by conciliation. If the migration from Bangladesh is to be stemmed, it will be in India's interest to help the population of Bangladesh as much as possible within the geographical boundaries of that country — and this may prove in the long run to be more effective than anything else.

The influx into Assam has consequences in other areas, too. Even as efforts are under way to work out a difficult peace in terms of the Assam 'accord', the All-Meghalaya Students Union (AMSU), in keeping with the demands of students in Assam, has argued that the Centre should also accept 1971 as the cut-off year for Meghalaya, as it has for Assam. These demands have found expression in the deportation of several hundred Nepalese-speaking people from Meghalaya to West Bengal. This, in turn, has provoked the Gurkha National Liberation Front (GNLF) to demand a separate political personality for Nepalis by carving out Darjeeling from West Bengal. The impact of this movement in Sikkim, Bhutan and Nepal is likely to complicate matters further.

For nearly six years the 'aliens' issue has dominated conversation in every government office, university, school and bazar in Assam. It takes a long time for ethnic groups to shed unhappy memories, but, if in the meanwhile there is a blatantly partisan use of the state machinery to further the economic, linguistic or political interests of a group to the detriment of others, the ethnic loyalties and slogans for protection of cultural identity will again be raised and create serious problems in the maintenance of order within Assam. Looking into the future, the foreigners issue in Assam will be regarded by subsequent generations not as the opening of a new chapter in socialization between ethnic groups in the Brahmaputra Valley, but as a mere footnote to the conflict between the question of Assam's interests and the narrower one of exclusive rights for Assamese caste-Hindus. I have no doubt that, as we enter the twenty-first century, the narrow issue of exclusive rights for a particular community will yield place in a more meaningful way to a wider one of the common interests of all those living in Assam.

What is the way of life which the Assamese people are seeking to preserve? To an Assamese, his way of living is inseparably connected with the Brahmaputra Valley, his language, his village, religious institutions, and still more, the caste-system. The

Brahmaputra Valley constitutes a distinct geographical unit within which nearly 18 million people of different origins and religions live. The indigenous ethnic groups and castes, however, form a cultural, linguistic and political system. In their consciousness, an attachment for the Valley is older than history. It is a part of their folk-lore, religious beliefs and literature. The Brahmaputra has a dominating presence, but the economic impact of the fertile soil of the Valley and its natural endowments have helped consolidate bonds of affinity for generations of Assamese with the Valley. The fact that several migrant families are also developing a similar attachment with the Valley, or indeed, are even entitled to do so, is resented by the indigenous Assamese who view this as a threat to their way of living.

The States Reorganization Commission, which accepted the principle of linguistic states temporarily checked the tempo of cultural and linguistic movements in the country. With hindsight it is now being appreciated that the principle of linguistic states set in motion more conflict than it resolved. Assam was the most baffling state since the linguistic minorities constituted as much as 45 per cent of its population in the 1950s. The suggestion of the Commission was equally unique: it recommended that other units of the region, i.e., Arunachal Pradesh, Manipur and Tripura should also become part of Assam. History, however, moved in the opposite direction and, instead of a composite Assam in the north-east, we have today seven political units. The main question in Assam is whether Assamese will continue to be the principal language of communication among the people, as well as of culture, literature and administration. Will Assam's Assamese character be like Tamil Nadu's intrinsic Tamil nature or Bengal's Bengali character? Will the political consequence of demographic change mean that Assam might have a Chief Minister whom the indigenous Assamese consider to be non-Assamese? These questions are linked with the role of Assamese language, thus making language a highly emotive and political issue.

The continuing problem of language in Assam has so far defied solutions, notwithstanding the fact that under the Assam Official Language Act, 1960, Assamese was to be used for official work in the districts, barring the two hill districts of Karbi-Anglong and North Cachar, where English was to continue, and Cachar (now divided into Cachar and Karimganj districts), where Bengali would be used. The question of language as a medium of instruction in schools and colleges has been posing serious problems. On 28 February 1986, the AGP-led administration in Assam issued a circular making Assamese a compulsory third language in schools from Class VIII onwards: this has triggered off massive agitations in the Barak Valley reminiscent of the agitations concerning the medium of instruction in 1972. Like their predecessors in office, the framers of this new circular have failed to realize, that, making a composite Assamese personality into a durable component of Indian nationhood cannot be rushed by formalizing the state's position on the Assamese language. The attempts of the Assamese leadership since Independence to make Assam a unilingual state have only led to law and order problems and eventual fragmentation, not to linguistic cohesiveness. Considering the genesis of the problem, psychological feelings of the linguistic minorities, whether living in the hills or in the Barak Valley, have to be taken into account. Given the polyglot population, Assam cannot be turned unilingual overnight by legislative injunctions or administrative circulars. But the primacy of maintaining the territorial integrity of the present Assam is in the interest of every ethnic, linguistic and religious community in Assam, and the real need is to strengthen the forces of economic development, social equity and orderly change. The history of bitterness on the language issue should not determine the future of economic progress of the people, particularly the poor, inhabiting Assam.

While both villages and towns constitute political units, these are not necessarily social units in Assam. While the socialization process in urban areas is characterized by much mixing between caste, ethnic and even professional groups, in the rural areas the situation varies greatly. A large number of Assamese villages are predominantly inhabited by one or other indigenous ethnic or caste group. There are also villages exclusively belonging to Bengali Muslims, Bengali Hindus and tea-garden labourers, and, of course, there are mixed villages as well; but the level of socialization within villages inhabited by exclusive ethnic or caste groups is higher and make these villages both political and social facts. There is also a high level of intermixing in villages inhabited by members of indigenous Assamese ethnic groups like Kalitas, Brahmins, Kayasthas, Keots and others. The commonality of religion (including daily attendance in *Namghars*) and language have facilitated socialization, even though marriages take place only within the respective ethnic and caste group.

In four typical villages (Kollapara, Kochpara, Harpara and Rajapani Chanda) of Kamrup district in lower Assam where I conducted a survey with the help of students of Cotton College, Gauhati, it was found that in all the villages except Kollapara, high schools were vibrant institutions that helped not only in the modernization of society but also in the socialization process (in Kollapara, there is only one lower primary school). All the educational institutions were set up after Independence, except in Harpara village. The landless labour in each village constituted 50 per cent of the total population and the road-linkage between the village and the town usually got disrupted during the monsoon. On my visits to several Bengali Muslim villages, mostly located near river islands, the lever of socialization between the villages was found to be very high, but with the outside world very low. The villages on the outskirts of a town tell a different story. In most of them land alienation has taken place on a large scale. Although the new settlers live within the geographical precincts of the village, they look more towards neighbouring urban centres and pursue a separate social existence. The phenomenon has been aptly described by a perceptive surveyor of Panbari village in Sibsagar district in upper Assam as follows:

> A number of rich men in the town, including Marwaris, have invested in extensive tracts of land in Panbari which are kept against future appreciation as the town expands; in the meantime, they are cultivated by hired labour or used for bamboo. In the east of Panbari is a colony of Sikhs adjacent to a Sikh engineering works. Although these houses are only a few hundred yards from an Assamese hamlet, no Assamese in the village has entered a Sikh house. In the south-east of Panbari is a colony of tea-garden labour which has spilled over from Narkari Tea Estate. Here again, there is no social intercourse between the Assamese and the tea-garden workers: if an Assamese were to have a liaison with a tea-garden girl or eat in a tea-garden house, he would be ostracized. Different communities in Assam, living juxtaposed to one another, rarely attempt to assimilate.[1]

The history of Assam highlights some unique processes by which tribes became castes. Historically, the Vaishnavite movement in Assam not only recognized the existence of the caste order but also helped consolidate various castes and in the formation of caste-Hindus as a group. The process of conversion to a caste had started much before the Bhakti movement, but it never attained rigidity and, until the beginning of the nineteenth century the caste structure had a degree of openness. One of the original castes in Assam, not found anywhere in India, is the Kalita. Migrant Kayasthas from north Bihar and Bengal have entered this caste. Edward Gait explains this development as follows:

> The reason seems to be that in early days the number of Hindu settlers and adventurers was small, and they confined their attention to the king and his chief nobles, from whom alone they had anything to gain. They would convert them, admit the nobles to Kshatriya rank and invent for the king a noble descent, using as will be seen, the same materials over and over again, and then enjoy as their reward, lucrative posts at court and lands granted to them by their proselytes. They would not interfere with the tribal religious rites, as to do so would call forth the active animosity of the native priests; nor would they trouble about the beliefs of the common people, who would continue to hold to their old religious notions. If the dynasty lasted long enough, the influence of Hindu ideas would gradually filter down to them and they would follow the example of their betters, as has now actually happened in the case of the Ahoms. But before this could come to pass, the dynasty would ordinarily be overthrown; the downfallen survivors of the old aristocracy would become merged in some Hindu caste, such as the Kalita, and Hinduism would sink into insignificance until, in course of time, its priests should succeed in inducing the new rulers to accept their ministrations.[2]

Similarly, while the politicization of the caste-system began quite early, it took concrete shape only during the struggle for Independence. in recent years, the movement in the Brahmaputra Valley has politicized the Assamese caste Hindus uniformly and has indeed made them into the base which brought the AGP to power.

The Hindus in Assam have two remarkable institutions, a village *Namghar* and the *Satra*, which have facilitated socialization. These institutions are a direct product of the Vaishnavite reformation movement initiated by Sankardev. Every evening, the villagers assemble in their *Namghar* for prayer and to hear a religious discourse. A *Satra* consists of a guru and his disciples and also gives a prominent place to prayer. A *Satra* has a much larger area of influence than a *Namghar* and has also linkages with Hindu shrines in other parts of the country. Every organized village in

Assam has a *Namghar*, but there are not more than a dozen *Satras* of eminence. While the *Namghars* are still popular and lively institutions of socialization, the *Satra* system declined with the break in its traditional relationship with the state. During Ahom rule, the *Satras* were rich and powerful organizations; the support of the state for them suddenly disappeared with the advent of British rule, in which period state support was made available to the newly set up churches in the region. After Independence, the *Satras* continued to fend for themselves in a secular India. A reform movement had nevertheless begun under the leadership of Haldhar Bhuyan and Ramkanta Atoi, who organized the Shri Sankardev Sangha to serve the cause of education, medical and health care and other forms of social service on the lines of the Ramakrishna Mission. The Sangha worked for the abolition of caste distinctions and preached unity among all people living in Assam, including tribals and Muslims. In 1966, as a District Officer in North Lakhimpur, I had the opportunity to interact with leaders of this organization in setting up highly successful eye-relief camps and, later, in providing assistance and succour to flood victims. The *Namghar, Satra* and the Sangha have effectively served as vehicles for the propagation of the idea of Assamese culture and in facilitating a high level of socialization among the Hindus of the Brahmaputra Valley.

Loyalties emerge out of a social matrix and take time to form, grow and change. The idea of mass political loyalty and the concept of the state as the ultimate and most comprehensive object of loyalty are really no older than the eighteenth century. As far as north-east India is concerned, these ideas permeated to the elite and middle class only in the twentieth century. In a political system that has in several areas started consolidating itself only after 1947, the weakness of loyalty to a nation-state is not surprising. Ethnic and caste bonds, religious affiliations and linguistic affinities continue to receive loyalty from their members. Even in states like Bihar and Gujarat, main centres of the independence movement, the loyalties to caste affiliations frequently seem to be stronger than those to the state.

Notwithstanding the assurances of both liberals and Marxists that, with modernization and industrialization, the old loyalties and conflicts become things of the past, with internal competition and class conflict replacing the traditional confrontations, nothing of this kind really happens. Politicians of all parties have often deviated from secular goals for they are aware of the power of ethnic and religious appeals. Many politicians have used these for their own ends, encouraging the revival of primordial values. Modernization has, in fact, fuelled all manner of conflicts based on ethnicity, religion, language, etc., as in Assam and, more recently, in Punjab and Sri Lanka. Similarly, the institution of marriage has been adopted to serve ethnic ends. In Punjab, despite the well established practice of inter-marriage between Hindus and Sikhs and the Hindus' respect for gurdwaras, sectarian conflict is a strong feature of social and political behaviour. In the Brahmaputra Valley, the Ahoms came single in the thirteenth century and married local women. But in a society characterized by caste, inter-community marriages soon became a thing of the past. After some generations of free marriages, Ahom society soon settled down to a caste psychology, and Ahoms now marry only amongst themselves. The real answer to exclusiveness lies in a combination of measures: the true secularization of democratic organizations and the state, acceleration of the pace of economic development and modernizaton, and inter-community marriages. These could help free Assam's and India's polity from the grip of primordial loyalties.

As society faces change, problems and conflicts will continue to arise. Despite several challenges, the ideals of democracy are widely accepted and have been sustained through difficult periods. The vigour of its practice and the growing faith of people all over India in democratic processes of governance, is an encouraging sign. A new society should emerge from the intense conflicts and accelerated transformations taking place. Keshav Mahanta, an Assamese poet, has captured the nuances of the problem of change when he sings:

Why are you startled
At the growling of the pitcher
Lying on the dry ground?
Listen, be all ears if you can
It is the wind humming—
The new wind humming over there.

Notes

CHAPTER I
Setting and Argument

1. The development of industries occurred particularly after 1962.
2. See Chapter 1 of Dimbeswar Neog, *Introduction to Assam*, Vora and Co., Bombay, 1947.
3. The Kamrup Kingdom was founded by Pusyavarman in the fourth century A.D. and reached his peak in strength and glory in the reign of Bhaskaravarman in the seventh century. A Hinduized Indo-Mongoloid empire was created in Assam in the seventh century.
4. The Ahoms belonged to the Tai race of south—west China and came to Assam from Upper Burma.
5. 'The civil dissensions still rage in Assam to the destruction and ruin of that once opulent Kingdom' observed Hugh Baillie, Goalpara, 9 November 1789.
6. Between 1826–98, the British annexed all the hill areas bordering the plains of the Brahmaputra and the Surma Valleys and established formal relations with the Maharajas of Manipur and Tripura.
7. C. Becker, *History of the Catholic Missions in North-East India*, V.M. Institute, Shillong, 1980, p.67.
8. Speech by Jawaharlal Nehru at the opening session of the Scheduled Tribes and Scheduled Areas Conference at New Delhi, 7 June 1952 (available with Nehru Memorial Museum and Library, New Delhi).
9. Nagaland was carved out of Assam and made into a State of the Indian Union on 1 December, 1963.

CHAPTER II
Inheritance: Ethnicity, Religions and Polity Management

1. Bridget and Raymond, *The Rise of Civilisation in India and Pakistan*, Cambridge University Press, 1983, pp. 351–2.
2. K. L. Barua, *Early History of Kamrupa*, Lawyers' Book Stall, 1966, pp. i-ii.
3. *Buranjis* were records of events prepared under the orders of the Ahom kings and were treated as secret documents.
4. *The Cambridge Economic History of India*, Vol. I, Cambridge University Press, 1982, p. 490.
5. B. K. Nehru in his Foreword to B. M. Pugh, *The Story of a Tribal: An Autobiography*, Orient Longman Ltd., 1976.

6. The religious profile of the people of north-east India as at 1971 is shown in the table below (in percentages):

Region	Hindus	Muslims	Christians	Other major religions	Local tribal faith	Total population (in lakhs)
Assam	71.0	24.0	4.5	S 0.1 B 0.3	neg.	146.25
Manipur	59.0	6.6	26.0	S 0.10 B 0.05	8.1	10.73
Meghalaya	18.5	2.6	47.0	S 0.12 B 0.19	31.6	10.12
Nagaland	11.4	0.6	66.8	S 0.13 B 0.04	20.9	5.16
Tripura	89.6	6.7	1.0	S 0.02 B 2.72	neg.	15.56
Arunachal	22.0	0.2	0.8	S 0.27 B 13.13	60.6	4.68
Mizoram	6.4	0.6	86.1	B 3.81	0.1	3.32
All-India	82.7	11.2	2.6	S 1.90 B 0.71	0.4	5481.60

S = Sikh, B = Buddhist, neg. = negligible

7. S. K. Chaterji, *The Place of Assam in the History and Civilisation of India*, Gauhati University Press, 1970, p. 16.
8. Shri Harsha had personal contacts with Bhaskaravarman. The Nidhanpura and Dubi copper plate inscriptions of the Kamrup kings, as well as Banbhatta's *Harsacharita* have references to Kamrup and Bhaskaravarman.
9. *The Cultural Heritage of India*, Vol. I, Ramakrishna Mission Institute of Culture, 1958, pp. 76–90.
10. The Hinduization of the Meitei tribes in Manipur has been comprehensively dealt with by S. N. Parratt in *The Religion of Manipur: Beliefs, Rituals and Historical Development*, Firma K. L. Mukhopadyaya, 1980. Three significant books on Manipur by British officers are Johnstone, *My Experience in Manipur and the Naga Hill (1896)*; Mc Culloch, *Account of the Valley of Munnipore* (1980); and Shakespeare, *The Lushai Kuki Clans* (1912).
11. K. N. Saikia, 'Assam-Muslim Relations and their Cultural Significance', unpublished Ph. D. Thesis, Gauhati University, 1968.
12. N. R. Ray, (ed.), *Sources of the History of India*, Vol. III, Institute of Historical Studies, Calcutta, 1980, pp. 183–4.
13. Pugh, B. M., *The Story of a Tribal: An Autobiography*, Orient Longman Limited, New Delhi, 1976, p. 145.
14. Fuller, *Studies of Indian Life and Sentiment*, John Murray, 1910, pp. 175–6.
15. A famous Assamese song runs as follows:
    'Bangal, bangal letera bangal
    bangala nidihi thai
    ratite uthi gharat sindhi di
    bangal palaye jay'.

The alien, the alien, the dirty alien,
Do not give him a place,
He gets up at midnight and breaks into the house,
In the darkness does he escape.

16. Dutta, 'Emotional and Rational Aspects of Assamese Nationalism', *Assam Tribune,* Gauhati, 26 December, 1982.

CHAPTER III
The Middle Class, the Elite and Regional Consciousness

1. Medieval Assamese society basically had three broad classes: (i) the privileged aristocracy, (ii) the peasantry, and (iii) slaves, serfs and bondsmen. The privileged aristocracy were of two categories: temporal and spiritual. The temporal class included the kings, tribal chiefs and nobles. They had hereditary states on which slaves, bondsmen and tenants carried on cultivation. The spiritual aristocracy consisted of priests and *satradhikars;* they held revenue-free land grants—the *dharmottar* lands of *satras, brahmottar* lands of Brahmins and *devottar* lands of temple-gods(who were recognized as legal persons by the British). The peasantry was composed of the large majority of farmers and also included fishermen and artisans. They were required to render physical service to the state, unlike the privileged, or to pay a tax in lieu of this in kind or cash. The last class served their respective masters and were free from the operation of the *khel* system. An enterprising member of this class could, however, join the highest class. (See *Cambridge Economic History of India,* Vol. I, pp. 478–505.)

2. A. J. M. Mills, *Report on Assam,* Gian Publications, pp. 31–60, 1980 reprint. Mills submitted this report to the Govt. of Bengal on 24 July 1853. Phukan's memorandum to Mills, which forms a part of the *Report,* is a major document that highlights the aspirations of the nascent Assamese middle class.

3. Myron Weiner, *Sons of the Soil: Migration and Ethnic Conflict in India,* Oxford University Press, Delhi, 1978, pp. 75–143.

4. In Meghalaya, people like Jeebon Roy and Don Roy were the first to graduate from agriculture to lime-quarry owners in the Khasi Hills Similarly, the educated family of Nichols Roy in Shillong identified with or belonged to the services, political interests or business, are now the owners of the United Fruit Company, Shillong. Migrants who went to Shillong, say from Bihar or Rajasthan, did not suddenly join the middle class. Thanks to restrictions on the transfer of land, S. K. Singh, who fled from his village in Arrah, Bihar, to Shillong had to start his life in a lowly job, by dint of hard labour and enterprise he rose to be a shopkeeper and transport owner in Laitumkhrah, Shillong. However, J.M. Bawry of Rajasthan, who had connections in Calcutta, joined the middle class in

Shillong thanks to his capital, skill and ownership of modern means of production.

5. Reid, *Years of Change in Bengal and Assam*, Ernest Benn Limited, 1966, pp. 101–12.
6. For detailed analysis of employment policies see chapter 6 in *India's Preferential Policies* by Myron Weiner and M.F. Katzenstein, University of Chicago Press, 1981, pp. 90–119.
7. *Encyclopaedia of the Social Sciences*, Vol. 13, pp. 208–18.

CHAPTER IV
The Political System

1. The emergence of political organizations in the Brahmaputra Valley preceded those in the hills. The rising Assamese middle class formed the Assam Association in 1882, which merged with the Indian National Congress in 1920. Politicization began in the Hills with the Jaintia Durbar in 1900, the Khasi National Durbar in 1923, the Khasi States Federation in 1934, the Naga Club in 1918, the Naga Hills District Council in 1945, and the Mizo Union in 1946.
2. The political process received a set-back with the 1986 revolt in Mizoram and an insurgency situation in Manipur that began in 1978.
3. The statistics pertaining to the election results have been obtained from the Election Commission of India, New Delhi.
4. All national political parties are not necessarily free from regional or parochial bias, and a believer in caste or communalism in political affairs does not automatically become secular if he joins a national political party. Similarly, all regional groups or parties in the north-east are not opposed to integration within the region or between the region and the rest of India. However, for an empirical study of electoral behaviour the grouping suggested in this paper provides a practical approach.
5. *Assam Tribune*, Gauhati, 3 Sept. 1983.
6. Personal papers of L.P. Singh, former Governor of the North-Eastern States.
7. The experience of regional parties in other parts of the country does not suggest that they would be better instruments of change and social management than the national parties.

CHAPTER V
Attractions of Political Reorganization in Assam

1. File No.P.4(1)–1937, AICC Files, Nehru Memorial Museum and Library, New Delhi.

2. When I mentioned this fact to an Assamese scholar, she first showed disbelief and then mentioned the predominance of the Assamese language in the Brahmaputra Valley and the threat to its position from migrants who speak Bengali, Hindi, etc.

3. Rao, Venkata, V., 'North East India: Problems and Prospects', unpublished paper, India International Centre, New Delhi, 1984, p. 8.

4. Dass, Sasanta Krishna, 'Assam's Bengali Unit', *The Statesman*, Delhi, 9 May, 1983.

5. Das, B.T., 'Separation of Cachar: A Point of View', *The Assam Tribune*, Gauhati, 23 May, 1983

6. Kakati, Satis C., 'Assam's Bengali Unit', *The Statesman*, Delhi, 10 May, 1983.

7. Nikhil Chakravarty, in the 2 April 1983 issue of *Mainstream* has argued against the further political reorganization of Assam: 'The plea for the vivisection of Assam to form a plain tribal entity and for the separation of Cachar, is really a cry of despair, an admission of impossibility of peaceful coexistence which is the organic link that binds the entire Indian Union with its many splendoured diversity. If this vivisection is attempted, it will re-enact the tragedy of the 1947 partition with its bloody trail of killings and displacement of millions. Tomorrow, if Cachar is separated from Assam, who will guarantee the safety and well-being of thousands upon thousands of Bengalis living in the Brahmaputra Valley? And why should they for no folly of their own be forced to quit their hearth and home? . . . One shudders to think of its chain reaction all over India. The disease will spread from one corner of our vast country to another, bringing in its trail the most devastating wave of destabilization which may threaten the very foundations of our Republic'.

8. The interests of cultivators belonging to the tea gardens, Santhals, Nepalis and members of the Scheduled Castes were protected by a separate notification in December 1947 in pursuance of Chap. 10 of the Assam Land and Revenue Regulation.

9. The list of OBCs in Assam is as follows: (1) Ahom, (2) Baria, (3) Barui, (4) Barjibi, (5) Baroi, (6) Chutia, (7) Choudhang (8) Gank of Cachar, (9) Ghosh, Gopa, Gowala, (10) Kupadhar, Kushiari, Rarh, (11) Moran and Matak, (12) Mukri, (13) Napit, (14) Mahisya and Das, (15) Rajbanshi or Koch, (16) Saloi, (17) Sudra Das or Das, (18) Sut, (19) Yogi (Nath), (20) Teli, (21) Marja, (22) Kumar, Rudra Paul or Cachar, (23) Manipuri including Brahmins and Manipur Muslims, (24) Scheduled Castes converted to Christianity, (25) Sikh Harijans or Sikh Scheduled Castes, (26) Tentripal, Tanti, Tantri'(27) Maimals (Muslim fishermen), (28) Tea garden labourers or tribes, (29) Ex-tea garden labourers or tribes, (30) Nepali (Thapa, Lama, Gurung, Magar, Lohar, Dami, Gaine, Rai, Chetri, Limbu and Sarki). The following communities were notified as more backward among the other backward classes: (1) Moran and Matak, (2) Tea garden labourers and tribes, (3) ex-tea garden labourers and tribes, (4) Rajbanshi or Koch, (5) Choudhang, (6) Maria,(7) Chutia.

CHAPTER VI
Administrative Philosophy and Institutional Framework

1. S.K. Bhuyan, *Anglo-Assamese Relations*, Dept. of Historical and Antiquarian Studies, Gauhati, 1949, p. 34.
2. The British annexed the hill regions of north-east India after initial hesitation. Immediately after the annexation of Assam, David Scott established the headquarters of the administration at Cherrapunjee, but in 1874 Shillong became the headquarters. With the creation of Meghalaya in 1972, the capital was brought to the plains of the Brahmaputra Valley and temporarily housed at Dispur, a village adjacent to Gauhati. A permanent capital is essential for Assam's administrative efficiency as well as the maintenance of secrecy; its new location at Pragjyotishpur near Gauhati was announced in 1984.
3. The special responsibilities of the Governor were further strengthened under the Govt. of India Act, 1919 where it was explicitly mentioned that no act of the provincial legislature would apply to the Hill tracts save as, or with such modifications and exceptions as the Governor thought fit. This provision was given clearer shape under the 1935 Act. All the Hill areas and frontier tracts were placed in one of the following three categories: (1) Tribal areas — along the frontier of India — to be administered by the Governor of Assam in his discretion as Agent of the Governor-General under the administrative control of the External Affairs Department; (2) Excluded areas — Mizo district, Naga hills district, North Cachar Hills, Frontier Tracts of Balipara, Sadiya, Tirap and Lakhimpur — to be directly administered by the Governor of Assam in his discretion; and (3) Partially Excluded areas — Khasi and Jaintia Hills district (excluding Shillong), Garo Hills district and the Mikir Hills — when the Governor of Assam acted in his individual judgement. Under Section 92(1) of the 1935 Act, no act either of the central or provincial legislature would apply to these Excluded and Partially Excluded areas unless extended to the areas with or without modifications by the Governor. During a debate in the House of Commons in May 1935 regarding the administration of the tribal areas the need to protect the tribal people was emphasized. This protective role was entrusted to the Governor, a feature that was retained in free India's Constitution which gave the Governor of Assam the responsibility of administering NEFA.
4. Report of the Indian Statutory Commission, 1930 (commonly known as the Simon Commission), Vol. II, Part III, Chap. 2.
5. On the evolution and working of the Inner Line, see P. C. Chakravarti *The Evolution of India's Northern Borders*, Asia Publishing House, 1971, pp. 23–91, and H. K. Barpujari, *The Problem of the Hill Tribes in the North-East Frontier, 1873–1962*, Vol. III, Spectrum Publications, 1981, pp. 1–27.
6. Nicholas Mansergh (ed.), *Constitutional Relations between Britain and India, 1942–7*, Vol. IV, HMSO, 1973, pp. 1125–31.
   Nicholas Mansergh (ed.), *Constitutional Relations between Britain and India,*

1942–7, Vol. VII, HMSO, 1977, pp. 30–5.

8. Quoted in V. Venkata Rao, *A Century of Tribal Politics in North-East India (1874–1974)*, S. Chand, 1976, pp. 151–3.

9. Andrew Clow, *The Future Government of the Assam Tribal Peoples*, Assam Govt. Press, 1945, pp. 46–7.

10. S. Gopal(ed.) *Selected Works of Jawaharlal Nehru*, Vol. 14, Orient Longman, 1981, pp. 277–8.

11. The report of the committee has been reproduced in B. Shiva Rao(ed.) *The Framing of India's Constitution*, Vol. III, Indian Institute of Public Administration, 1967, pp. 685–713.

12. Ibid, pp. 770–3.

13. Since the start of the present century a large number of migrants have entered Assam, mostly from East Bengal (now Bangladesh) and spread into areas occupied by the plains' tribal people, who retreated into the interior. Administrative measures were taken to protect them from land-hungry outsiders by drawing imaginary lines dividing the areas occupied by the tribals from those occupied by migrants. This was known as the Line System; however, this did not work satisfactorily. Later colonization schemes and development schemes were taken up but they, too, failed. In 1947, provisions for the protection of the plains' tribals rights in land were made under the newly formulated Assam Land and Revenue Regulation. These provisions sought to prevent non-tribals from acquiring land in separately constituted tribal belts and blocks and also required the state government when disposing of waste land in these areas to consider the bonafide needs of those who (1) permanently resided within these areas; (2) temporarily resided, but were likely to become permanent; and (3) lived elsewhere in the district. That these provisions have also proved inadequate in protecting the tribals' rights to land is another story of inefficiency and wilful violation by officials, of deception by high castes and a lack of will on the part of the political executive.

14. The distinctive feature of the Sixth Schedule is the constitution of district and regional councils vested with the powers of 'administration of an autonomous district'. The District Council has such executive powers as are essential for the developmental administration of a district. As a legislative body, it has the power to make laws relating to the appointment or removal of chiefs or headmen, the use and allotment of land, regulation of *jhuming*, management of forests (except reserved forests), etc. It has minor judicial powers as well. In all these tasks it has under its administrative control a large number of officials lent by the state government.

15. Verrier Elwin, *A Philosophy for NEFA*, North-East Frontier Agency, 2nd ed., 1959. See the Foreword by Jawaharlal Nehru.

16. There has been no study of the wider question of the effectiveness of these district councils, their impact on political culture and their efficacy as instruments for the promotion of economic development and social change; the Asoka Mehta Committee, which inquired into Panchayati Raj in 1978 did not study district councils. The grant of separate statehood to major tribes has diluted the importance of district councils in Meghalaya and Mizoram. The Government of Meghalaya set up a com-

mission to inquire into the scope and functioning of 'autonomous district administration' but its findings are awaited.

17. *Report of the Commission of the Hill Areas of Assam, 1965–66*, Govt. of India. The Commission was headed by H.V. Pataskar and established under a resolution dated 16 March 1965.

18. On 13 January 1967, the Govt of India announced the federal plan after discussions with the APHLC leadership.

19. This was another reorganization proposal floated by the Govt. of India.

20. The plan is named after Asoka Mehta who headed a committee constituted by the Govt. of India in July 1967, but it was later boycotted by the APHLC.

21. The approach of B.P. Chaliha, Assam's Chief Minister and Nehru's confidant, has been best summed up by Verrier Elwin: 'when I once asked B.P. Chaliha, the great-hearted Chief Minister of Assam, what magic he had used for the solution of the human and political problems in the Autonomous Districts of the State, he replied "A little understanding, a genuine respect, a lot of affection". This is the real magic that works wonders in human hearts'. See Elwin, *A Philosophy for NEFA*, p. 283.

22. Lok Sabha debate, 22 Dec. 1971: speech by Dinesh Chandra Goswami.

23. Inaugural speech of Indira Gandhi on 7 Nov. 1972 at Shillong. In this speech she said that the Council 'is not a super government. It does not abridge the power of the State and Union Territories in any manner whatsoever. It is not an extension of the Union Government. It is an advisory and not a supervisory body. It does not alter the relationship of the member units with the Central Government. The Central Government will not use the Council to interfere with the affairs and functioning of the various Governments of this region'. See *Focus on the North-East Region*, North-Eastern Council, published 22 Dec. 1980.

24. Lok Sabha debate, 11 May 1970: speech by Y.B. Chavan, Home Minister of India.

25. Lok Sabha debate, 11 May 1970: speech by Asoka Mehta.

26. Section 4 of the North-Eastern Council Act, which lays down the functions of the Council, also provides for its security role. Section 4(4) categorically prescribes: 'The Council shall review from time to time the measure taken by the States represented in the Council for the maintenance of security and public order therein and recommend to the Government of the States concerned further measures necessary in this regard'.

27. P.K. Goswami, Chief Justice, Gauhati High Court, in his speech of 5 April, 1973. See *Silver Jubilee Commemoration Volume* (1974) of the Gauhati High Court, pp. 11–16.

28. Assam was under the Governor-General of India from 1826 to 1854, the Lieutenant-Governor of Bengal from 1854 to 1874, a Chief Commissioner from 1874 to 1905, the Lieutenant-Governor of East Bengal and Assam from 1905 to 1912, a Chief Commissioner from 1912 to 1921 and has been under a Governor from 1921 onwards. During the British period, the Governor of Assam had jurisdiction over the entire region comprising north-east India.

29. Journalists and politicians have dramatized the physical movement of the common Governor in their writings and speeches by calling it an extraordinary spectacle. Harji Malik's dispatch in the New Delhi edition of *Indian Express* dated 27 May 1980 is a case in point.

30. Prakash Mehrotra, a politician, became Governor of Assam and Meghalaya; and S.M.H. Burney, a civilian, of Manipur, Nagaland and Tripura, in succession to the last common Governor of the north-eastern states, L.P. Singh.

CHAPTER VII
Policy Perspectives: Points of View

1. Lok Sabha debate 15 Dec. 1971: speech by D.C. Goswami.
2. See Radhakrishna, 'Gandhian Social Workers in Border Areas' in Ram Rahul (ed.), *Social Work in the Himalaya*, University of Delhi, 1969, pp. 59–64.
3. Verrier Elwin, *The Tribal World of Verrier Elwin*, Oxford University Press, 1964, pp. 287–303.
4. Christoph von Furer-Haimendorf, 'The Position of Tribal Population in Modern India', in Philip Mason (ed.), *India and Ceylon: Unity and Diversity*, Oxford University Press, 1967, pp. 182–222.
5. Christoph von Furer-Haimendorf, *Tribes of India*, Oxford University Press, 1982, p. 322.
6. Nari Rustomji, *Imperilled Frontiers, India's North-Eastern Borderlands*, Oxford University Press, 1983, p. 147.
7. Ibid, p. 26.
8. Nari Rustomji 'Frontier Blunders', the *Statesman*, New Delhi, 25 and 26 October, 1982.
9. B.K. Roy Burman, 'Problems of Nation-Building in North-East India', *Mainstream*, 14 June 1980, New Delhi. pp. 7–9.
10. H.K. Barpujari, *The Problem of the Hill Tribes: North-East Frontier*, Vol. III, Spectrum Publications, 1981, p. 349.
11. H.K. Barpujari, 'The Nagas, Mizos and People of Arunachal Pradesh', unpublished paper, India International Center, New Delhi, 1984.
12. V. Venkata Rao, *A Century of Tribal Politics in North-East India, 1874–1974*, S. Chand, 1976, p. 546.
13. V. Venkata Rao and Niru Hazarika, *A Century of Government and Politics in North-East India, 1874–1980*, Vol. I, S. Chand, 1983, p. 30.
14. B.K. Nehru, 'North-Eastern India', *Illustrated Weekly of India*, 21 November 1976, Bombay, pp. 19–23.
15. Mohammad Masum, *Unemployment and Underemployment in Agriculture—A case study of Bangladesh*, 1982.
16. *Assam Tribune*, Gauhati, 2 May 1983.

CHAPTER VIII

Demography, Culture, Identity Crisis
and Economic Development:
An Overview

1. *Census of India Report, 1981.*
2. S. K. Bhuyan, *Anglo-Assamese Relations 1771–1826*, Gauhati, 1949, p. 57.
3. Bangladesh is amongst the most densely populated areas in the world with 1511 people per square mile and a population growth rate ranging from 2 to 3 per cent per annum. An economist has calculated that the proportion of the rural population living below the poverty line increased from 40 per cent in 1963 to 62 per cent in 1975. This trend has not been reversed.
4. There is considerable distrust between the majority Muslim community and minority or Hindus in Bangladesh. A continuous migration of Hindus from Bangladesh into north-east India and West Bengal has taken place. According to the 1951 census, Hindus constituted 22 per cent of the population; the 1961 census showed the figure as 18.4 per cent, but by 1974 it was down to 13.73 per cent. This phenomenon was caused both by the conversion of scheduled caste Hindus to Islam, and the migration of upper caste Hindus to India. A major communal riot in Bangladesh might accentuate both the conversion and migration processes. See Talukdar Maniruzzaman, 'The Future of Bangladesh' in *The States of South Asia, Problems of National Integration (Essays in honour of W.H. Morris-Jones)*, edited by A. J. Wilson and D. Dalton, Vikas, New Delhi, 1982, pp. 265–94.
5. *Basic Statistics of the North Eastern Region, 1980*, N.E.C. Secretariat, Shillong, pp. 29–32.
6. Nari Rustomji, *Imperilled Frontiers, India's North-Eastern Borderlands*, Oxford University Press, 1983, p. 50.
7. By 1973-4, in 37 tribal belts and blocks of Assam about 2,000 hectares of periodic *patta* land had changed hands from tribals to ineligible non-tribals. About 1,000 hectares of government land was encroached upon by non-tribals in thse areas. (See *Tribes of the Assam Plains*, Govt. of Assam, Gauhati, 1980, p. 11.)
8. In Kamrup district, the two villages of Jatiya and Dispur in the South Kamrup Tribal Belt adjacent to Gauhati were heavily encroached upon by the non-tribals. By an executive order dated 30 July 1969 the state government excluded these two villages from the tribal belt. Later, Assam's temporary capital was located at Dispur in 1973.
9. B. K. Nehru, 'North-Eastern India', *The Illustrated Weekly of India*, 21 November 1976, Bombay, pp. 19–23.
10. Quoted in E.A. Gait, *The History of Assam*, Thacker Spink & Co., Calcutta, 1933, p. 153.
11. Scholars have yet to study the contrast in the development of these erstwhile tribes under Islam in Bangladesh and under Hinduism in West

Bengal: both speak the same language and are inheritors of the same great tradition, and this different evolution needs to be examined.

12. *Census of India Report, 1951.*
13. *Census of India Report, 1981.*
14. The projections have been made on the basis of the 1971 census.
15. V. Venkata Rao, 'North-East India: Problems and Prospects', unpublished paper, 1983, India International Centre, New Delhi.
16. Out of a total area of about 23 million hectares, only 2.9 million hectares (9.08 per cent) are under permanent cultivation and another 2.7 million hectares (9 per cent) are used for shifting cultivation; out of 2.7 million hectares available for shifting cultivation only 0.45 hectares is under cropping at any moment. Fertilizer consumption is very low, and although irrigation potential is enormous, agricultural operations continue to be dependent upon the monsoon. Thus (1) the average net area per cultivator of the region is 0.63 hectares against the all-India average of 1.80 hectares; and (2) the per capita per day availability of foodgrains was 369 grams compared to 439 grams for all-India. (Based on P. K. Wadia, 'Control of Shifting Cultivation in the North-Eastern Region' in T. Mathew (ed.), *Tribal Economy of the North Eastern Region,* Spectrum Publications, Gauhati, 1983, pp. 62–4; and *Basic Statistics of the North Eastern Region, 1980,* NEC Secretariat, Shillong.)
17. Dilip Goswami, 'Elites and Economic Development', *North Eastern Research Bulletin,* Dibrugarh Univesity, Summer 1974, pp. 93–101.
18. Reserve Bank of India, *Bulletin,* Feb. 1977, Bombay, pp. 181–6.
19. In its *World Development Report 1982,* the World Bank has singled out the Employment Guarantee Scheme (EGS) of Maharashtra. Under this, every rural adult in Maharashtra is guaranteed rural employment close to his home within 15 days of his registration. If no employment is immediately available, the person is given an allowance until he gets a job. Unemployed village heads are usually provided useful work in public work projects undertaken by the government. The EGS was responsible for the 21 per cent decline in unemployment in Maharashtra during 1973–8, when the population increased overall by 17 per cent. The scheme has been evaluated as a success both in ending unemployment and in capital formation through the development of productive infrastructural and other projects.

Epilogue

1. Andre Cantlie, *The Assamese,* Curzon Press, 1984, p. 2.
2. E.A. Gait, *The History of Assam,* Thacker Spink & Co., 1933, p.9.

Assam Accord 15 August 1985
MEMORANDUM OF SETTLEMENT

Government have all along been most anxious to find a satisfactory solution to the problem of foreigners in Assam. The All Assam Students Union (AASU) and the All Assam Gana Sangram Parishad (AAGSP) have also expressed their keenness to find such a solution.

2. The AASU through their Memorandum dated 2nd February, 1980 presented to the late Prime Minister Smt. Indira Gandhi, conveyed their profound sense of apprehensions regarding the continuing influx of foreign nationals into Assam and the fear about adverse effects upon the political, social, cultural and economic life of the State.

3. Being fully alive to the genuine apprehensions of the people of Assam, the then Prime Minister initiated the dialogue with the AASU/AAGSP. Subsequently, talks were held at the Prime Minister's and Home Minister's levels during the period 1980–83. Several rounds of informal talks were held during 1984. Formal discussions were resumed in March 1985.

4. Keeping all aspects of the problem including constitutional and legal provisions, international agreements, national commitments and humanitarian considerations, it has been decided to proceed as follows:—

Foreigners' Issue

5.1. For purposes of detection and deletion of foreigners, 1.1.1986 shall be the base date and year.

5.2. All persons who came to Assam prior to 1.1.1966, including those amongst them whose names appeared on the electoral rolls used in 1967 elections, shall be regularised.

5.3. Foreigners who came to Assam after 1.1.1966 (inclusive) and upto 24th March, 1971 shall be detected in accordance with the provisions of the Foreigners Act 1946 and the Foreigners (Tribunals) Order 1964.

5.4. Names of foreigners so detected will be deleted from the electoral rolls in force. Such persons will be required to register themselves before the Registration Officers of the respective districts in accordance with the provisions of the Registration of Foreigners Act, 1939 and the Registration of Foreigners Rules, 1939.

5.5. For this purpose, Govt. of India will undertake suitable strengthening of the governmental machinery.

5.6. On the expiry of a period of ten years following the date of detection, the names of all such persons which have been deleted from the electoral rolls shall be restored.

5.7. All persons who were expelled earlier, but have since re-entered illegally into Assam, shall be expelled.

5.8. Foreigners who came to Assam on or after March 25, 1971 shall continue to be detected, deleted and expelled in accordance with law. Immediate and practical steps shall be taken to expel such foreigners.

5.9. The Government will give due consideration to certain difficulties expressed by the AASU/AAGSP regarding the implementation of the Illegal Migrants (Determination by Tribunals) Act, 1983.

Safeguards and Economic Development

6. Constitutional, legislative and administrative safeguards, as may be appropriate, shall be provided to protect, preserve and promote the cultural, social, linguistic identity and heritage of the Assamese People.

7. The Government take this opportunity to renew their commitment for the speedy all round economic development of Assam, so as to improve the standard of living of the people. Special emphasis will be placed on education and science and technology through establishment of national institutions.

Other Issues

8.1. The Government will arrange for the issue of citizenship certificates in future only by the authorities of the Central Government.

8.2. Specific complaints that may be made by the AASU/AAGSP about irregular issuance of Indian Citizenship Certificates (ICC) will be looked into.

9.1. The international border shall be made secure against future infiltration by erection of physical barriers like walls, barbed wire fencing and other obstacles at appropriate places. Patrolling by security forces on land and riverine routes all along the international border shall be adequately intensified. In order to further strengthen the security arrangements, to prevent effectively future infiltration, an adequate number of check posts shall be set up.

9.2. Besides the arrangements mentioned above and keeping in view security considerations, a road all along the international border shall be constructed so as to facilitate patrolling by security forces. Land between border and the road would be kept free of human habitation, wherever possible. Riverine patrolling along the international border would be intensified. All effective measures would be adopted to prevent infiltrators crossing or attempting to cross the international border.

10. It will be ensured that relevant laws for prevention of encroachment of government lands and lands in tribal belts and blocks are strictly enforced and unauthorised encroachers evicted as laid down under such laws.

11. It will be ensured that the relevant law restricting acquisition of immovable property by foreigners in Assam is strictly enforced.

12. It will be ensured that Birth and Death Registers are duly maintained.

Restoration of Normalcy

13. The All Assam Students Union (AASU) and the All Assam Gana Sangram Parishad (AAGSP) call off the agitation, assure full co-operation and dedicate themselves towards the development of the country.

14. The Central and the State Government have agreed to:—

(a) review with sympathy and withdraw cases of disciplinary action taken against employees in the context of the agitation and to ensure that there is no victimization;

(b) frame a scheme for ex-gratia payment to next of kin of those who were killed in the course of the agitation;

(c) give sympathetic consideration to proposal for relaxation of upper age limit for employment in public services in Assam, having regard to exceptional situation that prevailed in holding of academic and competitive examinations, etc. in the context of agitation in Assam;

(d) undertake review of detention cases, if any, as well as cases against persons charged with criminal offences in connection with the agitation, except those charged with commission of heinous offences;

(e) consider withdrawal of the prohibitory orders/notifications in force, if any.

15. The Ministry of Home Affairs will be the nodal Ministry for the implementation of the above.

Sd/-   Sd/-
(P.K. Mahanta)   (R.D. Pradhan)
President   Home Secretary
All Assam Students Union. .   Government of India

Sd/-
(B.K. Phukan)
General Secretary
All Assam Students Union.

Sd/-   Sd/-
(Biraj Sharma)   (Smt. P.P. Trivedi)
Convenor   Chief Secretary
All Assam Gana Sangram Parishad.   Government of Assam

In the presence of
Sd/-
(Rajiv Gandhi)
Prime Minister

Date: 15th August 1985.
Place: New Delhi.

Mizoram Accord 30 June 1986
MEMORANDUM OF SETTLEMENT

Preamble

1. Government of India have all along been making earnest efforts to bring about an end to the disturbed conditions in Mizoram and to restore peace and harmony.

2. Towards this end, initiative was taken by the late Prime Minister, Smt. Indira Gandhi. On the acceptance by Shri Laldenga on behalf of the Mizo National Front (MNF) of the two conditions, namely, cessation of violence by MNF and holding of talks within the framework of the Constitution of India, a series of discussions were held with Shri Laldenga. Settlement on various issues reached during the course of the talks is incorporated in the following paragraphs.

Restoration of Normalcy

3.1. With a view to restoring peace and normalcy in Mizoram the MNF·party, on their part, undertakes within the agreed time-frame, to take all necessary steps to end all underground activities, to bring out all underground personnel of the MNF with their arms, ammunition and equipment to ensure their return to civil life, to abjure violence and generally to help in the process of restoration of normalcy. The modalities of bringing out all underground personnel and the deposit of arms, ammunition and equipment will be as worked out. The implementation of the foregoing will be under the supervision of the Central Government.

3.2. The MNF party will take immediate steps to amend its Articles of Association so as to make them conform to the provisions of law.

3.3. The Central Government will take steps for the resettlement and rehabilitation of underground MNF personnel coming overground after considering the schemes proposed in this regard by the Government of Mizoram.

3.4. The MNF undertakes not to extend any support to Tripura/Tribal National Volunteers (TNV) People's Liberation Army of Manipur (PLA) and any other such groups, by way of training, supply of arms or providing protection or in any other manner.

Legal, Administrative and Other Steps

4.1. With a view to satisfying the desires and aspirations of all sections of the people of Mizoram, the Government will initiate measures to confer Statehood on the Union Territory of Mizoram, subject to the other stipulations contained in this Memorandum of Settlement.

4.2. To give effect to the above, the necessary legislative and administrative measures will be undertaken, including those for the enactment of Bills for the amendment of the Constitution and other laws for the conferment of Statehood as aforesaid, to come into effect on a date to be notified by the Central Government.

4.3. The amendments aforesaid shall provide, among other things for the following:—

    (I) The territory of Mizoram shall consist of the territory specified in Section 6 of the North Eastern Areas (Reorganisation) Act, 1971.

    (II) Notwithstanding anything contained in the Constitution, no Act of Parliament in respect of:—

        (a) religious or social practices of the Mizos,

        (b) Mizo customary law or procedure,

        (c) administration of Civil and Criminal justice involving decisions according to Mizo customary law,

        (d) ownership and transfer of land,

        shall apply to the State of Mizoram unless the Legislative Assembly of Mizoram by a resolution so decides.

        Provided that nothing in this clause shall apply to any Central Act in force in Mizoram immediately before the appointed day.

    (III) Article 170, Clause (1) shall, in relation to the Legislative Assembly of Mizoram, have effect as if for the word 'sixty', the word 'forty' has been substituted.

5. Soon after the Bill for conferment of Statehood becomes law, and when the President is satisfied that normalcy has returned and that conditions conducive to the holding of free and fair elections exist, the process of holding elections to the Legislative Assembly will be initiated.

6. (a) The Centre will transfer resources to the new Government keeping in view the change in status from a Union Territory to

a State and this will include resources to cover the revenue gap for the year.

(b) Central assistance for Plan will be fixed taking note of any residuary gap in resources so as to sustain the approved Plan outlay and the pattern of assistance will be as in the case of special category States.

7. Border trade in locally produced or grown agricultural commodities could be allowed under a scheme to be formulated by the Central Government, subject to international arrangements with neighbouring countries.

8. The Inner Line Regulations, as now in force in Mizoram, will not be amended or repealed without consulting the State Government.

Other Matters

9. The rights and privileges of the minorities in Mizoram as envisaged in the Constitution, shall continue to be preserved and protected and their social and economic advancement shall be ensured.

10. Steps will be taken by the Government of Mizoram at the earliest to review and codify the existing customs, practices, laws or other usages relating to the matters specified in clauses (a) to (d) or para 4.3 (II) of the Memorandum, keeping in view that an individual Mizo may prefer to be governed by Acts of Parliament dealing with such matters and which are of general application.

11. The question of the unification of Mizo inhabited areas of other States to form one administrative unit was raised by the MNF delegation. It was pointed out to them, on behalf of the Government of India, that Article 3 of the Constitution of India prescribes the procedure in this regard but that the Government cannot make any commitment in this respect.

12. It was also pointed out on behalf of the Government that as soon as Mizoram becomes a State,

(i) the provisions of Part XVII of the Constitution will apply and the State will be at liberty to adopt any one or more of the languages in use in the State as the language to be used for all or any of the official purposes of the State;

(ii) it is open to the State to move for the establishment of a separate University in the State in accordance with the prescribed procedure;

(iii) in the light of the Prime Minister's statement at the Joint Conference of the Chief Justices, Chief Ministers and Law

Ministers held at New Delhi on 31st August, 1985, Mizoram
will be entitled to have a High Court of its own, if it so
wishes.

13. (a) It was noted that there is already a scheme in force for payment of ex-gratia amount to heirs/dependants of persons
who were killed during disturbances in 1966 and thereafter in
the Union Territory of Mizoram. Arrangements will be
made to expeditiously disburse payment to those eligible persons who had already applied but who had not been made
such payments so far.

(b) It was noted that consequent on verification done by a joint
team of officers, the Government of India had already made
arrangements for payment of compensation in respect of
damage to crops; buildings destroyed/damaged during the
action in Mizoram; and rental charges of buildings and lands
occupied by the Security Forces. There may, however, be
some claims which were preferred and verified by the above
team but have not yet been settled. These pending claims will
be settled expeditiously. Arrangements will also be made for
payment of pending claims of rental charges for lands/build-
ings occupied by the Security Forces.

Sd/-   Sd/-
(Laldenga)   (R.D. Pradhan)
on behalf of   Home Secretary
Mizo National Front   Government of India
Dt. 30.6.86   Dt. 30.6.86

Sd/-
(Lalkhama)
Chief Secretary
Government of Mizoram
Dt. 30.6.86

Date: 30th June, 1986.
Place: New Delhi.

Select Bibliography

BOOKS

Aditya, Rabindranath, *From the Corridors of Memory*, Karimganj, 1970.

Alam, K., *The Development Experience in Assam*, Dutta Baruah & Co., Gauhati, 1983.

Allen, B.C. and others, *Gazetteer of Bengal and North-East India*, Mittal Publications, Delhi, 1979 reprint.

Barpujari, H.K., *Assam in the Days of the Company (1826–42)*, Spectrum Publications, Gauhati, 1980.

————, *Problem of the Hill Tribes, North-East Frontier (1822–42)*, Vol. I, Lawyers Book Stall, Gauhati, 1970.

————, *Problem of the Hill Tribes, North-East Frontier (1843–72)* Vol. II, United Publishers, Gauhati, 1976.

————, *Problem of the Hill Tribes, North-East Frontier (1873–1962)*, Vol. III, Spectrum Publications, Gauhati, 1981.

Barua, K.L., *Early History of Kamrupa*, Lawyers Book Stall, Gauhati, 1966.

Becker, C., *History of the Catholic Missions in North-East India*, V.M. Institute, Shillong, 1980.

Bhuyan, S.K., *Anglo-Assamese Relations*, Dept. of Historical and Antiquarian Studies, Assam, Gauhati, 1949.

Cambridge Economic History of India, Vols I and II, Cambridge University Press, Cambridge, 1982–83.

Chakravati, P.C., *The Evolution of India's Northern Borders*, Asia Publishing House, New Delhi, 1971.

Chand, Tara, *History of the Freedom Movement in India*, Vol. I, Publications Division, New Delhi, 1961.

Chaterji, S.K., *The Place of Assam in the History and Civilisation of India*, Gauhati University, 1970.

Clow, Andrew, *The Future Government of the Assam Tribal Peoples*, Assam Govt. Press, Shillong, 1945.

Cotton, Sir Henry, *Indian and Home Memories*, London, 1911.

Crozier, Michel, *The Bureaucratic Phenomenon*, Tavistock Publications, U.S.A., 1964.

Das, A.K., *Assam's Agony*, Lancers Publishers, New Delhi, 1982.

Datta, Ray B., (ed.), *The Emergence and Role of the Middle Class in North-East India*, Uppal, New Delhi, 1983.

De Bary, W.T., (ed.), *Sources of Indian Tradition*, Columbia University Press, New York, 1958.

Dubey, S.M., (ed.), *North-East India, A Sociological Study*, Concept, New Delhi, 1977.

Elwin, Verrier, *A Philosophy for NEFA*, North-East Frontier Agency, Shillong, 1959.

———, *The Tribal World of Verrier Elwin*, Oxford University Press, Bombay, 1964.

Fuller, Bampfylde, *Studies of Indian Life and Sentiment*, John Murray, London, 1910.

Furer-Haimendorf, Christoph von, *Return to the Naked Nagas*, Vikas, New Delhi, 1976.

———, *Tribes of India*, Oxford University Press, New Delhi, 1982.

Gait, E.A., *A History of Assam*, Thacker Spink & Co., Calcutta, 1905.

Goswami, P.C., *The Economic Development of Assam*, Asia Publishing House, Bombay, 1963.

Government of Assam, *The Land of Seven Sisters*, Gauhati, 1976.

———, *Tribes of the Assam Plains*, Gauhati, 1980.

———, *Political History of Assam*, Vol. I (1826–1917), Gauhati, 1977.

———, *Political History of Assam*, Vol. II (1920–1939), Gauhati, 1978.

———, *Political History of Assam*, Vol. III (1940–1947), Gauhati, 1980.

Guha, Amalendu, *Planter-Raj to Swaraj*, ICHR, New Delhi, 1977.

Haksar, P.N., *Reflections on Our Times*, Lancers Publishers, New Delhi, 1982.

Hansaria, B.L., *Sixth Schedule to the Constitution of India, A Study*, Ashok Publishing House, Gauhati, 1983.

Johnstone, Sir James, *My Experiences in Manipur and the Naga Hills*, Marston, Sampson Low, London, 1886.

Kothari, Rajni, *Politics in India*, Little Brown & Co., Boston, 1970.

Lall, J.S., (ed.), *The Himalaya*, Oxford University Press, Delhi, 1981.

Lyall, A.S., *Asiatic Studies*, 2 vols. Cosmo Publications, Delhi, 1976.

Mackenzie, A.A. *History of the Relations of the Government with the Hill Tribes of the North-East Frontier of Bengal*, Calcutta, 1884.

Mansergh, Nicholas (ed.), *The Transfer of Power* (1942–7), Vols. I-XII, *Constitutional Relations between Britain and India*, HMSO, London, 1970–83.

Masum, Mohammad, *Unemployment and Underemployment in Agriculture, A Case Study of Bangladesh*, Delhi, 1982.

Mead, Margaret (ed.), *Cultural Patterns and Technical Change*, UNESCO, Paris, 1954.

Mills, A.J.M., *Report on the Province of Assam*, Calcutta, 1854 (reprinted by Gian Publications, Delhi, 1980.)

Nath, R.M., *The Background of Assamese Culture*, Dutta Baruah & Co., Gauhati, 1948.

Nehru, Jawaharlal, *The Discovery of India*, Oxford University Press, New Delhi, 1981.

Neog, Maheswar, *Annals of Assam Sahitya Sabha (1917–1975)*, Jorhat, 1976.

Nibedon, Nirmal, *The Ethnic Explosion, North-East India*, Lancers Publishers, New Delhi, 1981.

Prasad, Rajendra, *India Divided*, Bombay, 1946.

Pugh. B.M , *The Story of a Tribal: An Autobiography*, Orient Longman, New Delhi, 1976.

Ram, Rahul, *The Himalaya as a Frontier*, Vikas, New Delhi, 1978.

Rao, V. Venkata and Hazarika Niru, *A Century of Government and Politics in North-East India (1874–1980)*, Vol. I, S. Chand, New Delhi, 1983.

Rao, V. Venkata, *A Century of Tribal Politics in North-East India (1874–1974)*, S. Chand, New Delhi, 1976.

Reid, Robert, *Years of Change in Bengal and Assam*, Ernest Benn Ltd., London, 1966.

_____, *History of the Frontier Areas Bordering on Assam (1883–1941)*, Eastern Publication House, Delhi, 1983.

Rustomji, Nari, *Imperilled Frontiers, India's North-Eastern' Borderlands* Oxford University Press, Delhi, 1983.

Sen, Anupam, *The State, Industrialisation and Class Formations in India*, Routledge and Kegan Paul, London, 1982.

Silver Jubilee Commemoration Volume of the Gauhati High Court, Gauhati High Court, 1974.

Singh, Chandrika, *Political Evolution of Nagaland*, Lancers Publication, New Delhi, 1981.

Singh, K.S., (ed.), *Tribal Movements in India*, Vol. I, Manohar, New Delhi, 1982.

Srinivas, M.N., *Social Change in Modern India*, Orient Longman, New Delhi, 1982.

Statistics of North-Eastern Region, North-Eastern Council Secretariat, Shillong, 1980.

Vasu, N.N., *Social History of Kamrup*, Vols. I–III, Calcutta, 1922.

Weiner, Myron, and Katzenstein, M.F., *India's Preferential Politics*, University of Chicago Press, 1981.

Weiner, Myron., *Sons of the Soil, Migration and the Ethnic Conflict in India*, Oxford University Press, Delhi, 1978.

Wilson, A.J. and Dalton, D (ed.), *The States of South Asia, Problems of National Integration*, Vikas, New Delhi, 1982.

ARTICLES

Barpujari, H.K., 'The Nagas, Mizos and People of Arunachal Pradesh, Historical Perspectives and Cultural Aspirations', India International Centre, New Delhi, 1983 (unpublished paper).

Battacharyya, Birendra Kumar, 'Assam Revolts Against Foreign Nationals', *Janata*, 2 December 1979, Bombay.

Bourah, K., 'Foreigners in Assam and the Assamese Middle Class', *Social Scientist*, Vol. 8, No. 11, June 1980, New Delhi.

Chaube, S.K. and others, 'Regional Development and the National Question in North-East India', *Social Scientist*, Vol. 4, No.1, August 1980, New Delhi.

Das, Susanta Kumar, 'Immigration and Demographic Transformation of Assam' (1891–1981), *Economic and Political Weekly*, 10 May 1980, Bombay.

Desai, S.P., 'My Thirty-Five Years in Assam', in K.L. Punjabi(ed.), *The Civil Servant in India*, Bombay, 1965.

Dewan, Birendranath, 'What has been Wrong with North-East', *Democratic World*, 13 July 1980, Delhi.

Dharma Vira, 'National Integration and the Assam Agitation', *Man and Development*, Chandigarh, June 1980.

Gohain, Hiren, 'Origins of the Assamese Middle Class', *Social Scientist*, Vol. 2, August 1973, New Delhi.

Goswami, Dilip, 'Elites and Economic Development', *The North-Eastern Research Bulletin*, Vol. V, 1974, Dibrugarh University, Dibrugarh.

Guha, Amalendu, 'Impact of Bengal Renaissance on Assam (1825–1875)', *Indian Economic and Social History Review*, Vol. 9, September 1972, New Delhi.

————, 'Little Nationalism Turned Chauvinist: Assam's Anti-Foreigner Upsurge (1979–80)', *Economic and Political Weekly*, Special Number, October 1980, Bombay.

————, 'Indian National Question, A Conceptional Frame', *Economic and Political Weekly*, Special Number, 1982, Bombay.

————, 'Medieval Economy of Assam (1200–1750)', in *Cambridge Economic History of India*, Vol. I, London, 1982.

Khound, T.P., 'Role of the NEC in the Economic Development of North-East India', *The North Eastern Research Bulletin*, Vol. VII, 1976, Dibrugarh University.

Kutty, N. Madhavan, 'Social Parameters of Assam', *Link*, 22 August 1982, Delhi.

Misra, Tillottoma, 'Assam, A Colonial Hinterland', *Economic and Political Weekly*, 9 August 1980, Bombay.

Nehru, B.K., 'North-Eastern India', *Illustrated Weekly of India*, Bombay, 21 November 1976.

Patwardhan, Achyut, 'The Crisis in the North-East', *Janata*, 20 July 1980.

Prabhakar, M.S., 'The Bengal Bogey', *Economic and Political Weekly*, 16 December 1972, Bombay.

Rao, V. Venkata, 'North-East India, Problems and Prospects', India International Centre, New Delhi, 1983 (unpublished paper).

Roy Burman, B.K., 'Problems of Nation-Building in North-East India', *Mainstream*, Delhi, 14 June 1980.

_____, North-East India, 'An Overview', *Mainstream*, Delhi, 6 December 1980.

Sen Gupta, Bhabani, 'South Asia, The Ethnic Cauldron', *India Today*, 31 August 1983, New Delhi.

Sharma, Mohan Lal, 'Elite Conflicts, Regionalism and the Comparative Crisis: A Study of the Autonomy Movements in North-East India', in Ramakant (ed.), *Regionalism in South Asia*, Aalekh Publishers, ·Jaipur, 1983.

Srinivas, M.N., 'A note on Sanskritisation and Westernisation', *Journal of Asian Studies*, University of Michigan, Vol. 15, 1955–56, U.S.A.

Srinivas, M.N. and Sanwal, R.D., 'Some Aspects of Political Development in the North-Eastern Hill Areas of India', *The North-Eastern Research Bulletin*, Dibrugarh University, Vol. 1, 1970.

Vittachi, V.T., 'The Poor Can't Eat Theories', *Newsweek*, 19 September 1983, New York.

REPORTS AND DISSERTATIONS

AICC File No.P.4(1)–1937 (available at the Nehru Memorial Museum and Library, New Delhi).

Baruah Srinath, 'A Critical Analysis of the Planned Economic Development of India, with special reference to Assam (1951–1974), An Economic Approach', Ph.D. thesis, Gauhati University, 1978 (unpublished).

Census of India Reports (1901–1981), parts pertaining to North-East India, New Delhi.

Das, Lakshahira, 'Development of Secondary Education in Assam from 1874–1947) and its impact on Social Development', Ph.D. thesis, Gauhati University, 1972(unpublished).

Devi, Renu, 'Progress of Education in Assam (1882–1937)', Ph.D. thesis, Gauhati University, 1972(unpublished).

Dutta, Promatha Nath, 'Impact of the West on the Khasi and Syn-tengs: A survey of Political, Economic and Social Change (1765–1874)', Ph.D. thesis, Gauhati University, 1980 (unpublished).

Kuzhipalil George, 'The Impact of the Catholic Missions on Educa tion, Literature and the Social Life of North-East India (1890–1980)' Ph.D. thesis, Gauhati University, 1982 (unpublished).

Lok Sabha Debates dated 5 May 1970, 15 and 22 Dec. 1971.

Nag, Chitra Ranjan, 'The Impact of Christianity on the life of Mizos', Ph.D. thesis, Gauhati University, 1973(unpublished).

Nagar, Rama Sankar, 'Development of Education in Manipur from 1891 to 1970', Ph.D. thesis, Gauhati University, 1978 (unpub-lished).

Nehru, Jawaharlal, Speech at the opening session of the Scheduled Tribes and Scheduled Areas Conference, New Delhi, 7 June 1952 (available with the Nehru Memorial Museum and Library, New Delhi).

'The Problems of the Transfer and Alienation of Tribal Land in Assam', Tribal Research Institute of Assam, Gauhati, 1974(un-published; available with Assam Government).

Reports of the Commission of the Hill Areas of Assam, 1965–66 Gov-ernment of India, Ministry of Home Affairs, New Delhi, 1967.

Report of the Committee on Welfare of Scheduled Castes and Scheduled Tribes Relating to Land and Revenue, Assam Legislative Assembly, Dispur, 1979.

Reports of the Election Commission of India (1972–84 pertaining to North-East India), New Delhi (published and unpublished).

Report of the Sub-Committee of the Advisory Council for Welfare of Scheduled Tribes(Plains), 1976, Gauhati.

Saikia, K.N., 'Assam-Muslim Relations and their Cultural Signifi-cance', Ph.D. thesis, Gauhati University, 1968 (unpublished).

Sharma, Bharati, 'Impact of Culture on the Pattern of Personality in two Indian Tribes (Khasi and Naga)', Ph.D. thesis, Gauhati Uni-versity, 1978 (unpublished).

Subject Index

Name Index